ALSO BY RON SUSKIND

The Price of Loyalty:
George W. Bush, the White House, and the Education of Paul O'Neill

A Hope in the Unseen:
An American Odyssey from the Inner City to the Ivy League

RON SUSKIND

SIMON & SCHUSTER   New York • London • Toronto • Sydney

The ONE PERCENT DOCTRINE

Deep Inside America's Pursuit of Its Enemies Since 9/11

SIMON & SCHUSTER
Rockefeller Center
1230 Avenue of the Americas
New York, NY 10020

For information about special discounts for bulk purchases,
please contact Simon & Schuster Special Sales at
1-800-456-6798 or business@simonandschuster.com

Designed by Dana Sloan

Manufactured in the United States of America

10 9 8 7 6 5 4 3 2 1

Library of Congress Cataloging-in-Publication Data is available.

ISBN-13: 978-0-7432-7109-7
ISBN-10:   0-7432-7109-2

To Jack Downey, a hero and a friend, for his courageous optimism.

Whenever the people are well-informed, they can be trusted with their own government.

—THOMAS JEFFERSON

CONTENTS

The ONE
PERCENT
DOCTRINE

PREFACE

The "what ifs" can kill you.

Something missed. A failure of will. A turn in one direction when the other way was the right path.

Over time, people tend to get past them. *We did what we could,* they say, and move on.

But, in terms of the tragedy of 9/11, a particular regret lingers for those who might have made a difference.

The alarming August 6, 2001, memo from the CIA to the President—"Bin Laden Determined to Strike in US"—has been widely noted in the past few years.

But, also in August, CIA analysts flew to Crawford to personally brief the President—to intrude on his vacation with face-to-face alerts.

The analytical arm of CIA was in a kind of panic mode at this point. Other intelligence services, including those from the Arab world, were sounding an alarm. The arrows were all in the red. They didn't know place or time of an attack, but something was coming. The President needed to know.

Verbal briefings of George W. Bush are acts of almost inestimable import in the affairs of the nation—more so than is the case for other recent presidents. He's not much of a reader, this President, and never has been, despite White House efforts to trumpet which serious books he is reading at various times. He's not a President who sees much value in hearing from a wide array of voices—he has made that clear. His circle of truly trusted advisers is small—smaller as President, in many ways, than it was when he was governor. But he's a very good listener and an extremely visual listener. He sizes people up swiftly and aptly, watches them carefully, and trusts his eyes. It is a gift, this nonverbal acuity, that he relies on in managing the almost overwhelming duties of the presidency: countless decisions each day, each one important; a daunting array of issues to grasp; an endless stream of politicized experts and expert politicos, all speaking in earnest tones. What does George W. Bush do? *He makes it personal.* He may not have had a great deal of experience, especially in foreign affairs, before arriving in the job, but—because of his trust in these interpretive abilities—he doesn't view that as a deficit. The expert, sitting before him, has done the hard work, the heavy lifting, and the President tries to gauge how "certain" they are of what they say, even if the issues may be unfamiliar to him. Do they seem nervous or unsure? Are they fudging? Why do they think what they do . . . and what do they think of *him?* That last part is very important.

The trap, of course, is that while these tactile, visceral markers can be crucial—especially in terms of handling the posturing of top officials—they sometimes are not. The thing to focus on, at certain moments, is *what* someone says, not who is saying it, or *how* they're saying it.

And, at an eyeball-to-eyeball intelligence briefing during this urgent summer, George W. Bush seems to have made the wrong choice.

He looked hard at the panicked CIA briefer.

"All right," he said. "You've covered your ass, now."

George Tenet and his team had evacuated their offices at CIA headquarters by midmorning on September 11, 2001, but they didn't get far.

Across a concrete square were vacant offices in the CIA's print shop—a nondescript two-story building on the Langley, Virginia, campus that generates, daily, the output of a dozen Kinkos, including regular, numerous briefing books over the past year on al Qaeda, or *the base.* That's where they fled to—the place that printed the reports.

Tenet, his deputy John McLaughlin, and a few others crowded into a conference room, a windowless, white square room, and frantically began to work a bank of phones, trying to get updates, status reports, anything. It was early, midday. Facts that would soon be common knowledge—familiar even to schoolchildren—were coming into focus. *Where* was clear, as was *when* and *how*—visible to anyone with a television. *Why*—if it was, indeed, the Islamic extremists they suspected—was the unanswered question since the World Trade Center bombing in 1993. The steady growth of jihadist terror had produced a rising hum inside the CIA and, eventually, in other parts of the government. Yet the causes, a clear strategic understanding of what drove the enemy and what they wanted, remained cloudy.

This day brought newfound clarity. At 1:10 p.m., an analyst burst into the room holding printouts. There were manifests from the four flights, just sent to him from an official at the Federal Aviation Administration—an agency that had spent the nightmare morning locating and grounding hundreds of planes that were airborne at the moment of the first attack. Sending passenger lists to CIA for review was among the day's first acts of recollection.

"Two names," the analyst said, flattening a page on the table. "These two we know." Everyone crowded around, looking at the printout for American Airlines Flight 77, which had left the Pentagon in flames. Staring back were the names of Khalid al-Mihdhar and Nawaf al-Hazmi, men who had appeared on various internal lists as members of al Qaeda. Everyone stared at the names. *Who . . .* was now visible in history's unforgiving light.

"There it is," said Tenet, quietly, a man meeting a recurring nightmare in daylight. "Confirmation. Oh, Jesus." And then silence. Could have been ten seconds. Could have been a minute.

Two hours later, Air Force One landed at Offut Air Force Base in Nebraska. A shaken George W. Bush assembled principal advisers for a video conference, the first high-level meeting since the attacks. Tenet reported the discovery of known al Qaeda operatives on the manifest of American Airlines Flight 77, including al-Mihdhar, who, noticed by CIA a year before in Malaysia, had a valid U.S. visa, and seemed to have slipped into the country unnoticed by both CIA and FBI. Bush murmured something terse and scolding about miscommunication between the agency and the bureau, but it was flattened by the crush of incoming evidence: *al Qaeda*. The culprit.

Starting points are ever elusive—when does anything really start in the ever-repeating human journey?—but this is as close as we will probably get. The facts were indisputable. And a war, some sort of war, was bound to begin.

What happened on September 11 was almost matched in importance by what would happen on September 12.

That was the day America began to gather itself for a response. The reply to tragedy would, ultimately, shape the nation's character.

Familiar faces guiding the ship of state quickly became vessels of an acute yearning—a public prayer that the President, his advisers, and the men and women atop government would be capable and courageous and sufficient to the moment. This book is surely about them, carrying new, clarified renditions of what they did, why they did it; what they've learned, what they haven't.

But it is also about a community of Americans who, up to now, have remained largely unseen, the ardent and expert who care not one whit for matters of presentation, for how best to manage the attentions of an anxious American public, or the U.S. Congress, or a wary global community.

These men and women—these *invisibles*—are actually fighting the fight. They have to worry *only* about the battle against shadowy global armies bent on destruction, and about winning it. After grand pronouncements are made describing a new kind of war and the vanquishing of evil, they are the ones who must then fashion a plan, and figure out where to turn and what to do when there is no map, no compass, and a darkened horizon. They report back about how things are really going, and then watch, often in disbelief, as the public is apprised of progress and the latest developments. In an age when assertion tends to overwhelm evidence, when claim so easily trumps fact, they know precisely where the breakpoints lie. That makes them valuable and dangerous; that makes their silence a priority to those who must answer to the vox populi, or, eventually, to posterity.

There are optical illusions at work here. The *notables*—Bush and Cheney, Rice and Tenet—are ever conspicuous, magnified, commanding our attention. They take credit and, if unavoidable, blame for things they often had little to do with; they tell us that everything will be fine, or that we should be very afraid, or both. They exude confidence, a key to modern-day success, even while they're privately solicitous of those upon whom their fortunes truly rest: the twenty-something with a flair for Arabic, trolling Web sites day and night; the agent who figures out how the money flows from the vitriolic to the truly violent; the spy who identifies a source ready to talk, and then protects that golden goose at all costs; the paratrooper wearing night-vision goggles who kicks down the door of an apartment in Karachi.

For those at the top, the defining posture is relentless impatience: impatience to justify action and rhetoric and to assuage the guilt that haunts anyone who was in a position of power before 9/11, and might have done something differently. For the sleep-starved professionals just beneath the line of sight—as invisible, in many ways, as their murderous opponents—the basic emotion is suppressed panic; and a willed conviction, despite contrary evidence, that every problem has a solution.

To understand America's actual response to 9/11, you have to talk to both groups, and hear them talk to each other, an often tense dialogue between those who sweat the details and improvise action plans, the doers; and those—from the President on down—who check on progress, present the results, and are repositories of public faith. The crucial task, for both sides, is to come up with answers, under pressure that is almost beyond measure.

Grab some shoes and walk in them.

From on high, it's a dance of fitful indirection, furrowed brows, and passive verbs. Of getting reports on one potential threat after another, knowing most of them are specious, but not understanding exactly why that is indisputably so, or what you might be missing, and then calling another meeting to try to better target your questions. And, along the way, deciding what people—busy Americans on the partisan landscape or some congressional oversight committee—should know, in an era when political savants contend that speaking truth in public is a dangerous practice. And then, it's time for the next briefing, the next conference table and spiderweb chart filled with hard-to-parse Arab names and gossamer connections. In a quieter time, Bill Clinton could grouse to Alan Greenspan that his presidential fortunes—and those of the country's economy—would be determined by judgments from the bond market. Now, they may be determined by whether some mall security guard in Palo Alto notices that the guy in Neiman Marcus is wearing an overcoat in the summer and smells like gardenias and is carrying a funny suitcase; and it will be further determined—the nation's fate, that is—by whether that guard calls the FBI, and whether someone answers, and whether the call is transferred to somebody else who knows what all that means, *in time.*

But, wait, does the FBI even know that the CIA is all but sure that a hundred or so suitcase nuclear weapons, produced way back when by the Soviets, are unaccounted for? And that bin Laden, along with the Chechen rebels and a bunch of terrorist groups you've never heard of, have been actively trying to get their hands on that kind of a weapon for years? Should they know? Does it *help* if FBI knows?—or, for that matter, the busy pedestrian, who can be easily frozen by fear into not buying, or doing, or dreaming big, and if people stop any of those things, en masse, the gears of prosperity and uplift will start to slow,

God forbid. Then again, fear, no doubt has *its place,* trumping other emotions, focusing a distracted rabble and getting them orderly and seeing clearly what their earnest leaders are up against. Appreciation, especially without too many probing questions, is a lovely thing. So, at day's end, maybe we'll release a little information, just a tiny part of this bracing story or that, to let everyone know that they should be afraid, of course, but not so very much because we—the duly elected and our trusted appointees—*are in control of the situation.*

And while this is decided, across the conference table sit a group of unheralded warriors who are trying to pick up your subtly self-interested line of reasoning. You suspect that they're sizing you up, all the while, and you're probably right that it's not all that favorably, but they're sympathetic to your modern-day dilemma, as you are to theirs, especially because theirs may be the tougher job—the one upon which everything really rests.

From their shoes, you can actually feel the soft turf of a shifting landscape. Changes with each step. Walk a while, and you begin to know enough to sense what you don't know, or can't be sure of, as well as the few helpful things that have been discovered and verified about how the world's terror networks now operate, and how they are evolving. You know that the enemy is everywhere and nowhere, crouched, patient and clever, watching how you move so they can move in the opposite direction, the surprising direction, undetected. You whipsaw between grudging respect for their methodology and murderous rage—if you only get your hands on the courier, the cell leader, the top lieutenant, then they'd know suffering. And tell all. If only. And then you could sleep, at least that night, because you'd know where to aim the armed aerial drone or the muscled-up unit with the night-vision goggles—so much firepower, built up and ready; so few clues about where to point it. Or so few *good* clues, *solid* clues. Plenty of noise, God knows, leads galore, piled to the ceiling, and you spend half your life chasing nothing, garbage. Everything starts to look suspicious: whole groups of people with their strange tongues and habits and deeply held certainties prompt alarm, because the ways they move from anger to rage to violence are not so very clear, and if one out of a hundred, a thousand, makes that jump you're talking an army—a vast, invisible army—un-uniformed and moving freely through a marketplace where anything can be found and tried—unbelievably destructive stuff—all click and buy, with downloadable manuals. And you haven't seen your wife, or husband, or kids, or whoever you care about in weeks, or months; and while you thrash this way and that, everyone you meet, including your bosses, asks "Are we safe, are we safe yet?"— even people who should know better—while you miss everything: the baby showers, the school plays, the weddings and funerals. And you look for handles, a framework from the familiar, to make sense of the solemn insanity of this life, deep inside the so-called "war on terror," and you realize you're neck-deep in a global game of Marco Polo, in an ocean-size pool—but all of it deadly serious, winner take all. It's terrible in that pool. Especially when it's deathly quiet—the way it is in the months after 9/11—and no one is answering when you yell "Marco," and you only feel the occasional *whoosh* as your opponent silently passes, and you snap around while images of burning buildings and exploding planes dance behind your closed eyelids.

Tucked within the colliding perspectives, there were, from the very start, a few things that were shared. The notables and the invisibles together embraced a profound sense of urgency. All parties took a vow of sorts on September 12. As public servants, they solemnly swore to do whatever they could to confront and defeat al Qaeda and its global network of terrorists and supporters. They vowed to work each day and every night. They'd press themselves toward clear-eyed and innovative thinking. They'd stop at nothing.

Just as soon as they figured out where to start.

The preferred analogy inside government for these early days is *the Apollo 13 challenge,* a reliable standard, as well, of management schools and motivational speakers. It refers to a particular moment in 1970 when an air filter on a disabled NASA craft, 200,000 miles from Earth, needed to be built with whatever the astronauts had on hand. An engineering team in Houston gathered a sampling of all the loose items aboard the distant spacecraft—duct tape, hoses, medical equipment—dumped them on a table, and got to work. They needed a remedy, a way to attach a square filter into a round fitting, in a few hours, or the crew would be asphyxiated. The solution also had to be elegant; it was no good if the crew couldn't manage the construction. Driving the proceedings is a mantra that has become ubiquitous since Ron Howard's movie about the mission was released in 1995: "Failure is not an option."

All this applies nicely to the "war on terror." Decisions made in the wake of the catastrophe carried the same improvisational and emotional force. That latter part is easy to forget: the desire to help, in any way possible, was the first, pure impulse. Agencies of the world's most powerful nation were impelled to employ whatever they had available to match an unforeseen mission, a new charge; to find, each of them, a worthwhile avenue for their institutional might. Sometimes this worked. Often it did not. Paths were set early, in crisis. Failure—or even the admission of small defeats or confusion—was not an option. The Pentagon had a standing army. CIA, and its eavesdropping affiliates from the National Security Agency (NSA) on down, had intelligence—the night vision to pierce the darkness. Justice had the rule of law, and FBI an army of domestic agents. Treasury had access to global financial data . . . and so forth, building by building, across the frightened capital. Where each path led, in large measure, would define the coming four-plus years, where we, as a nation, are now. And where we are bound.

All throughout, however, humming beneath the smooth surface of press releases and official-speak, has been a rising din of "cognitive dissonance"—that evocative term for how collisions of competing ideas create *dissonance,* a discomfiting noise that compels the mind to modify existing beliefs or invent new ones as it searches for quiet. It is that process that so often drives forward motion in the cacophony of modern life.

The vast federal government, under stress, does not work quite so efficiently as a single mind. It has protective urges, competing agendas, rules for who does what and who represents actions to the citizenry, the sovereign, the bosses; it accomplishes a great deal, yes, but is defined often by its dysfunctions. And that means it lies and dissembles, hides what it can, and sometimes acts out of self-preservation, because without your trust it is nothing but office space.

This has long been the case—a matter of life force trapped inside bureaucracies that everyone from Max Weber to Stephen R. Covey has fretted over—and maybe that's just something to be accepted, a point of resignation. Maybe, people don't really want to know about the internal disputes and roiling uncertainty, the *dissonance*. Or maybe they don't want to take on the turmoil and clarity that inhabit those on history's fault line—both the notables, who watch each active verb, and their fierce, frank invisible partners, whom you will now meet in the coming pages—as, side by side, they chase shadows on the cave wall of an enemy who is newly armed with destructive capability and sectarian certainty, and patience, and clever resolve, and, maybe, tactical advantage.

In sleepier times, you could just go about your life and shrug, and say that there are mortgages to pay and children to school, sitcoms to watch, and that, from the start, two centuries ago, even some founding fathers felt the noisy rabble, beyond the ramparts, couldn't "handle the truth."

But these are not ordinary times. Knowledge, in fact, is power, enough to burn off fear. And you at least ought to know what the hell's been going on.

It's what Americans do.

CHAPTER ONE

FALSE POSITIVES

At noon on September 13, a passing agent ducked his head into Dennis Lormel's office. He said that someone had called from the Omaha FBI office. A company named First Data Corporation, with a huge processing facility out there, wanted to help in any way it could. A red-eyed Lormel looked up from his desk. "Oh, that's big," he said, breaking into a weary smile. "That could be very, very big."

The son of a New York City cop, Lormel had spent two decades working the financial angle of some of the bureau's biggest cases, from corrupt congressmen in the Abscam scandal, to allegations of Billy Carter being bribed by Libyans, to the Bank of Credit and Commerce International, or BCCI, the mother of all international bank frauds.

First Data is one of the world's largest processors of credit card transactions, a company with $6.5 billion in revenues and a global reach. Lormel knew there would be scores of names to check, starting with the nineteen hijackers, and that each name would produce several hits—false positives—that would then have to be checked against the place and time specifics of spending histories. There would be civil liberties issues—legally, each credit card search demanded a warrant. There might not be time for that; another attack might be on the way.

But Lormel also knew something most of the agents running sleepless around FBI headquarters two days after 9/11 didn't know: First Data was *not only* the world's leading credit card processor—an extraordinary ally at this moment. "Inside that company," he told the young agent, "is a gem."

Western Union.

The old telegraph company was the engine of a technological revolution many generations removed from the present. Its heyday was in the 1850s, when it began stringing wire cables across the Northeast, then the first transcontinental cable in 1861. Five years later, those cables carried trading on the New York Stock Exchange to cities up and down the East Coast on "tickers." It was hailed as a miracle.

The world moved on. But many of the twenty-two nations in the Arab world still have a foot planted in this past. Western Union, with nearly $2.7 billion in revenue, remains a destination for a wide slice of the Arab world's 300 million residents. In some less favored parts of the globe, the only way to wire funds is the old-fashioned way. You bring your money to the Western Union office. You hand it over. They count it. And soon, transmission is made to another of the company's offices, a hot flash of cold cash.

The so-called "war on terror" is about unlikely twists, strange alliances, about things you least expect. The unexpected is, in fact, what catches a swiftly adaptable enemy—namely, a global village of Islamic terrorists—by surprise. Lormel is a financial crimes wizard, who talks like a longshoreman, knows how to play rough, and has a fine-tuned capacity to think like his prey—a perfect character for a moment that demands innovation. The previous night, he'd arrived home for dinner after wandering in a daydream through a frantic FBI headquarters for much of the day. He told his wife, Molly, "I figured a lot of stuff out . . . we need a massive integrated approach to this—the whole government working together—and we can wrap them up, all of them, the bastards. There's a lot we can do now on the financial side that we could never do before. If, for once, we can just get everyone organized."

Now, sitting in his office, Lormel told the young agent to go get him a number for First Data, and he chewed over an idea: "We need to turn this company into a deadly weapon."

On the seventh floor of CIA headquarters, at midnight on September 13, George Tenet, an exhausted forty-eight, slumped into his office. He hadn't slept more than a few hours since the attacks, and it was starting to show. Jami Miscik, Tenet's deputy associate director of intelligence, stuck her head in the doorway.

"Ready to crash?"

"Maybe soon," he said. "But not for long."

Miscik, a slender brunette in her fifties, had affection for Tenet, who'd made her his executive assistant back when he was the deputy director in 1996, and, as director, promoted her to the number two job in the Directorate of Intelligence, or DI—home of CIA's army of analysts. They'd been through a lot together. Nothing, though, like what was to come.

She loves George. They all seem to on the seventh floor at CIA, a rarity in a place where the walls are primed with secrecy and the distrust it breeds. Among recent DCIs (Directors of Central Intelligence) he's an anomaly, with a kind of clumsy, shirt-untucked openness, and a behavioral tic whereby he has trouble criticizing anyone, even when they deserve it. Most of the trouble he gets into is because he aims to please, even when he's screaming at you.

She eased in and sat on the arm of a cushioned chair across from his desk, a conditional posture, so she could slip out if he was too tired, or if a call came from somebody more important, anxious to talk. The upper reaches of government were—at this moment—jammed with anxious somebodies.

Miscik, who joined the agency in 1983 as an economic analyst, now watched over thousands of analysts who read the human intelligence, or *humint,* collected by field agents, clandestine agents, and foreign sources of human intelligence, and the signals intelligence, or *sigint,* from the vast U.S. network of eavesdropping. Their goal is to make sense of it in so-called "operational time"—which translates into *when needed,* or, in the current parlance, in time to save lives. On that, they had failed. Things had been missed. Miscik knew that. It didn't matter that her task—or theirs, at the DI—was a task that flirted with abstract limits: knowing everything you need to know, when you need to know it.

"We need to figure out new ways that we can take this story apart and put it back together again," she said. "See what else might there be . . . what we may be missing."

Tenet grabbed his pad. "All right," he said. "Where do we start?"

"With a few of the most creative people we can find to head up a unit of people who've *never* worked on terrorism," she said. "See what they see as they look at what we're facing, see if they see anything different."

"Fresh eyes," Tenet said, rubbing his own. "We could use some of those." They discussed names, until Miscik slipped out, saying she'd have a list compiled by morning.

Tenet turned toward the window, and leaned back in his chair. Just above the line of trees that obscures the CIA campus, the lights of Washington—an altered city, reconstructing its worldview—were barely visible in the distance. An endless day was now ending. Not that it hadn't gone well. It had, better than he could have hoped. That morning, one of Tenet's key deputies—the tough, theatrical Cofer Black, head of the agency's Counter-Terrorist Center—had given an astonishing performance in the White House Situation Room. After nine months of daily presidential briefings, Tenet knew Black would be the right man to stir George W. Bush's blood. And he was. The President was getting his bearings. Now that it was clear who was behind the attacks, he was anxious to think clearly about the U.S. response. Pacing the floor in the Situation Room, under the quizzical gazes of National Security Council (NSC) principals and an anxious President, Black had laid out a plan that Tenet and other senior agency officials had swiftly constructed: a campaign led by CIA, supported by U.S. Special Forces, that would soon invade Afghanistan, employ local tribal leaders and hard-bitten fighters, and decapitate al Qaeda in its Afghan refuge. There would be a cost, Black said—U.S. soldiers and CIA operatives would die—but the enemy would "have flies walking across their eyeballs."

The President—in full action mode—nodded, alert and hard-eyed. Later, he'd call this a "turning point in my thinking," the framing of a plan to invade Afghanistan. In the afternoon, at another NSC meeting, Bush had given a preliminary nod as well to ideas Tenet had for granting the CIA added powers. Powers, as Tenet told him, "to take off the shackles" and really go after the enemy. To rise to this occasion, the agency would need more money, more trained bodies, more latitude. They'd need a global strategy. Bush agreed. Already, just two days after the attacks, he wanted more—more details, more ideas, more of everything.

All of which made George Tenet fairly sure he wouldn't be fired.

It was thoroughly logical to have wondered, of course. Presidents, all leaders, need someone to blame at moments like this. When a country is caught by surprise, the person designated with knowing enough to prevent surprises—a vizier, an archduke, a particular general, an intelligence chief—will generally take the fall.

"Of course, you knew we all could be fired," said John McLaughlin, Tenet's deputy, looking back. "No one had a whole lot of time to think about that. It was mostly, 'Go, go, go. We know what to do. Let's pull a plan together. If someone wants to fire us, fine! We'll just give him a plan on our way out the door.' "

To understand what would occur over the coming four years, it is crucial to understand this mix of insecurity and gratitude—this survivor's guilt, survivor's surprise, survivor's appreciation—and how it played out, especially in terms of George Tenet.

It is the key to a central relationship in the "war on terror"—the dance between the two Georges. They were a natural pair from the start—gregarious men, blunt, physical, cut-the-crap types—but from very different worlds. Tenet, the son of working-class Greek immigrants, a New Yorker, was a self-made man, a Democrat, who'd come up through Congress—as a staff director on the Senate Intelligence Committee, then over to the NSC, then to CIA's number two position in the mid-nineties, having impressed Clinton—and always felt he needed to prove himself, to earn his way. Bush, on almost all those points, hailed from a smug loyal opposition, having stamped advantages of birth with his own mark and risen to the nation's highest perch, matching his father. When Tenet was kept on after the 2000 election, there were whispers of surprise from within the White House. The old man had a role, knowledgeable insiders said, telling his son that Tenet was a good man and that CIA should remain beyond politics, a point made by keeping Tenet aboard. In theory, fine, but let's see how it works out, they said. See how he fits with Bush and Cheney. Tenet heard them, and each day—at each official ceremony and early-morning briefing—he sought to prove his worth. Every top official serves "at the pleasure of the President." For Tenet, an outsider in the inner circle, the phrase was served, cold, at each day's breakfast.

And that was all before the tragic events. Had Bush fired the CIA director in the wake of 9/11, Tenet would have been cast into an abyss of almost unfathomable censure, the kind that crushes lives. The unseen attack matched with someone to blame. Judgment. Eternal vilification.

When Republican congressmen attacked Tenet in the days after 9/11, Bush swiftly came to his aid. "We cannot be second-guessing our team," the President told a group of angry congressmen aboard Air Force One on September 27, "and I'm not going to. The nation's at war. We need to encourage Congress to frankly leave the man alone. Tenet's doing a good job. And if he's not, blame me, not him."

At that point, George Tenet would do anything his President asked. *Anything.* And George W. Bush knew it.

On Friday, September 14, when the President of the United States wanted a grant of special powers from Congress, his team arrived on Capitol Hill well prepared.

It so happened that administration lawyers had for months been incubating theories about how to expand presidential power. The ideas were originally seeded by the Vice President, a believer, since his harrowing days in the death throes of the Nixon administration, that executive power had been dangerously diminished.

In both the House and Senate, White House negotiators pressed for the broadest possible legislative language, including authorization to engage in wide-ranging activities on U.S. territory.

The language of the proposed resolution authorized the President "to use all necessary and appropriate force against those nations, organizations, or persons he determines planned, authorized, committed, or aided the terrorist attacks that occurred on Sept. 11, 2001, or harbored such organizations or persons, in order to prevent any future acts of international terrorism against the United States by such nations, organizations or persons." A sweeping mandate. Minutes before the vote, the White House officials had pressed for even more—after "use all necessary and appropriate force," they wanted to insert "in the United States," to, essentially, grant war powers to anything a president deigned to do within the United States. Senators shot that down. That would be without precedent. A resolution passed in the Senate by a vote of 98 to 0 and in the House by a vote of 420 to 1.

Two days later, on Sunday morning, September 16, Vice President Dick Cheney settled into a secure cabin overlooking Camp David, the presidential retreat in the Maryland mountains, to explain how the President would use this extraordinary grant. Cheney, with more executive branch experience than any vice president in modern times, knew this was his moment. The President had spoken briefly in televised addresses, and then on Friday afternoon from the rubble of the World Trade Center with a bullhorn. Now, it was Cheney's turn to speak about execution, how to get the job done, his métier. The lights came up, and it was clear that Tim Russert of NBC's *Meet the Press* would ask few questions today. Viewers wanted to hear the Vice President speak. In a moment, Cheney settled into his stentorian rhythm, the grumbling, *got-this-covered, call-you-if-I-need-you* thrump of crew-cut speech. In fighting al Qaeda, he said, the government needed to "work through, sort of, the dark side." Crises prompt candor. The country was in trauma. Cheney was, against his nature, opening the playbook on national television. "A lot of what needs to be done here will have to be done quietly, without any discussion, using sources and methods that are available to our intelligence agencies, if we're going to be successful. That's the world these folks operate in. And so it's going to be vital for us to use any means at our disposal, basically, to achieve our objective."

Experts on Osama bin Laden often advise, "Listen to what he says. It's all there. He says what he means." In this one case, that was also true of the Vice President. So much is in that one statement, so much more, in its way, than the bold, blood-quickening calls to bring "infinite justice" to our enemies abroad—and, yes, maybe hiding among us—evildoers who would soon taste the fury of might sharpened by right. Not that those calls to arms weren't effective. They were; just maybe not suited for the challenge America now faced. The real action, Cheney said, would not happen with armies assembled and banners waving. It would happen in the shadows.

At a special cabinet meeting on Monday morning, September 17, the President handed out assignments. After a weekend of deliberation with his top officials at Camp David, it was time for action. The mission was to oust al Qaeda from its Afghanistan refuge and, if necessary, destroy the country's ruling Taliban regime. The response, in this case, would bridge old and new, engaging intelligence officers, airpower, and a light military footprint. "The CIA is in first," Bush told the seventeen top officials of the U.S. government gathered around the cabinet table that morning, each of whom—the Secretaries of State, Treasury, Energy, Defense, Justice—would leave with a task list. The CIA teams would immediately begin by engaging with the Afghan tribes—supporting, directing, bribing—and prepare the terrain for the arrival of U.S. Special Forces. Targeted bombings would most likely commence soon, it was hoped by early October. A limited number of U.S. troops—a few thousand—would then arrive, guided by a map largely drawn by CIA agents who had experience in the region and, now, the full faith of the President.

Washington, day by day, had already become the bustling capital of a twilight struggle—the so-called "war on terror," a term that was settling unevenly into the global vernacular. Close facsimiles had been floated for a week or so after the attacks and before President Bush used it, just so, in his landmark speech of September 20, 2001, declaring before a joint session of Congress that "Our 'war on terror' begins with al Qaeda, but it does not end there. It will not end until every terrorist group of global reach had been found, stopped and defeated."

The term's meaning drifted fitfully, being defined mostly by what it was not—a kind of definition by default. White House spokesman Ari Fleischer parried with reporters at a press conference on the key issue: use of the word "war."

"You don't declare war against an individual, surely?" puzzled one.

"How can you declare war against a nation when you don't know the nation involved?" the reporter asked.

"I don't know whether we should use the word 'war,' " French president Jacques Chirac said, standing next to George W. Bush at a press conference shortly after 9/11, when the two countries stood united. "But what I can say is that now we are faced with a conflict of a completely new nature."

Several immediate responses would, indeed, be of a "new nature." One, that the CIA—an intelligence agency—would be the central actor, a kind of loosely assembled army, with many tasks. Too many. Though the agency had failed in its prime mission—specific advance warning of the 9/11 attacks—more than any other arm of the U.S. government it was ready for the aftermath. While other parts of the government looked at what institutional capabilities they might now employ to protect and defend America, CIA was already several years into "the plan," a strategic analysis of how to fight al Qaeda that the agency had started in 1999—a full year after Tenet said to his staff that "we'd spare no expense in funds or bodies" in fighting this threat from transnational terrorist groups.

Strong words. But, as months slipped into years, not much to show for the bluster. While, surely, funds had been tight, and proposed budget increases had been turned down by both Clinton and Bush, only a modest share of overall CIA resources had been put toward the counterterrorism effort. There were too many weaknesses in too many areas at the agency, which had lost nearly a quarter of its budget in the 1990s as part of the "peace dividend." The clandestine service had been gutted. Humint assets in the Arab world were almost nonexistent. Tenet's strategy to counter the growing terrorist threat had been to rebuild the entire agency—a strategy devoid of priorities. All boats, the thinking went, would be lifted together, and the CIA was on its way to doing that, step by step, with plans, so many plans.

Some of those plans would now be implemented overnight. After the cabinet meeting on the morning of September 17, Bush had signed a classified "Presidential Finding" that authorized an astonishing expansion of CIA authority, especially in the area of covert operations. The agency could use lethal measures against terrorists, largely without civilian oversight. It would also manage what was essentially a covert foreign policy—a channel between CIA and foreign intelligence services that, theory had it, would always be open. The authorization of added powers was necessary to carry off the "Worldwide Attack Matrix"—a CIA plan presented to Bush in the preceding days that detailed operations against terrorists in eighty countries.

On September 18, Bush signed a secret executive order allocating immediately between $800 million and $900 million to CIA. Much of that money would go to the building of CTICs, or Counter-Terrorist Intelligence Centers, inside countries that heretofore were not seen as close, or, in any event, capable friends. In this war, we would need to make new friends.

CIA had mostly been an agency that collected information and passed it up the chain—its primary role, certainly, since the mid-seventies, when revelation of Watergate-era excesses in covert activities prompted commissions, constraints, and the formation of congressional oversight committees. Now necessity created reinvention. Even as demands on the precision of intelligence multiplied, CIA would expand swiftly into an agency of covert, and often deadly, action. The game was one of kill or be killed, finding individuals or small groups tucked in diverse cultures—some sympathetic to jihadists, some not, some incredulous. It was a man-on-man war.

The day the Presidential Finding was signed—September 18—discussions at Langley were fueled by adrenaline and testosterone. Cofer Black could claim a long history with al Qaeda, having first dueled with bin Laden in 1994 in Khartoum, Sudan, when each man had a team that spied on the other, a game that escalated, at one point, to car chases and bin Laden's assassination attempt on Black. Now there would be new boundaries. Black, after his motivational briefings of Bush and NSC, used the language of medieval conflict—of finding al Qaeda members and putting their "heads on sticks"—that soon caught on around the government, mustering aggression. Inside CIA and the White House, there was talk of bringing back the heads of bin Laden and Zawahiri "in a box." The CIA's freshly approved Worldwide Attack Matrix mentioned capture and interrogation of suspects only in passing, including a brief notation that captives were expected to be put through the U.S. justice system. "The mission is straightforward," Black told a colleague in Langley. "We locate the enemy wherever they are across the planet. We find them and we kill them."

Eight miles southeast in Arlington, at the world's largest office building, those specifically trained to kill—the U.S. military—would mostly watch from the sidelines.

America's standing army, with more firepower than had ever before been conjured by human ingenuity, would be in a supporting role. As the CIA became doers, the traditional doers at the Pentagon got ready for a small, targeted engagement in Afghanistan, with an expected deployment of a maximum 10,000 or so troops, a fraction of the total force, and waited for further instructions.

This was a particularly bitter pill for the civilian leadership of the Pentagon: Defense Secretary Donald Rumsfeld, his deputy Paul Wolfowitz, Under Secretary for Policy Douglas Feith, and their senior nonstaff adviser, Richard Perle—an assistant secretary of defense under Ronald Reagan and now chairman of the President's Defense Advisory Board. All had been pressing through the Clinton years and the first nine months of this administration for two things: transformation of the military into a leaner, high-tech, twenty-first-century fighting force; and the overthrow of Saddam Hussein.

They all also shared a well-seasoned antipathy for the CIA. The cited grievances were vast, a catalog of CIA failures and foolish pride dating back twenty years. It had missed the rise of Islamic fundamentalism and the Ayatollah Khomeni in Iran. It had missed the fall of the Soviet Union. It had missed Iraq's 1991 invasion of Kuwait. As to 9/11, the critics' case for CIA incompetence was clouded by the repeated warnings from Tenet and top deputies about the al Qaeda threat, starting with their first briefing to the incoming President. Neither Bush nor the more experienced Cheney had reacted with a plan of action. Bin Laden was a problem without a ready solution, a combination that often spells inertia for the vast U.S. government. The primary focus, instead—as national security adviser Condoleezza Rice framed it in January 2001 at the first NSC meeting of the Bush presidency—was on "how Iraq is destabilizing the region," and the overthrow of Saddam Hussein. Throughout the spring and summer of 2001, dozens of reports were generated inside the Defense and State Departments about a possible invasion of Iraq, as the CIA increasingly warned about the threat from al Qaeda.

Al Qaeda and Iraq were separate entities, with divergent goals, but on September 19, Bush made his first official stab at convergence. He had not been satisfied with an ad hoc exchange on September 12 near the doorway of the Situation Room with Richard Clarke, the NSC's national coordinator for security and senior adviser on counterterrorism. Bush had asked Clarke about Saddam's link to the attack. Clarke had said definitively there'd be no connection found—this was clearly al Qaeda, and al Qaeda and Saddam were natural enemies. Now, in a briefing with George Tenet on September 19, he and the Vice President made a more formal run at the issue. "I want to know about links between Saddam and al Qaeda," Bush said to Tenet. "The Vice President knows some things that might be helpful." He then turned to Cheney, who was participating in the meeting through a video link to a secure location.

Intelligence collection, like much of foreign policy, had been placed in the Vice President's portfolio from the first days of the administration. The breadth of Cheney's charge increased after 9/11. His office had nearly a dozen national security staffers and advisers. One of them, Cheney told Tenet, had picked up a report that one of the hijackers, Mohammed Atta, had met in Prague, in the Czech Republic, with a senior Iraqi intelligence agent five months before the attacks. The DCI was surprised. "We'll get right on it, Mr. Vice President."

An hour later, Tenet was back at CIA headquarters, where several top deputies gathered in his office. He told Jim Pavitt, head of the Directorate of Operations, about the request. "It's a direct request from Cheney and Bush," Tenet said, as Pavitt looked on skeptically. "Let's get right on it." Pavitt "tasked out" the assignment immediately—calls were made that day to the CIA's station chief in Prague.

On the morning of September 21, the CIA director, with a file under his arm and a top staffer from the Directorate of Intelligence at his side, arrived at the White House for that morning's intelligence briefings. "What have you got for me today, George?" Bush said, his usual opener. Tenet got right to it. "Our Prague office is skeptical about the report. It just doesn't add up." He noted, as well, other evidence, including credit card records and phone records collected by FBI and CIA that seemed to place Atta in northern Virginia all during the period in question—in an apartment, in fact, a few miles from the agency's headquarters.

Cheney, staring out from the video screen, shook his head in doubt.

Two weeks later, in early October, the Vice President's cluster of national security staffers was officially matched and mirrored by one inside the office of the Secretary of Defense. The Pentagon unit, called the Policy Counterterrorism Evaluation Group, run by Douglas Feith, the under secretary for policy, was designed to provide intelligence on demand to both Rumsfeld and the office of the Vice President. Each office, with its national security staffers, would support the other, and carry forward a shared purpose: to not have to solely *consume*—in bureaucratese—CIA intelligence. We'll grow our own, thanks.

The two hungry men at the table—the Vice President and the Secretary of Defense—had a long history of working side by side. Joining the Nixon administration in 1969, Donald Rumsfeld—in his mid-thirties and already an ex-congressman—showed skills as an executive branch warlord whom even Richard Nixon viewed with cautious regard. Rumsfeld had quickly turned an importunate assignment—heading the Office of Economic Opportunity, a Johnson-era holdover—into a power base, and drafted as his assistant a newly arrived White House staffer, a Wyoming-raised student of government with a quick mind and almost enough credits for a PhD. That was Dick Cheney.

As to their skills at planning and execution, an instructive moment occurs in 1975, when Rumsfeld was Gerald Ford's chief of staff and Cheney his deputy, with a charge to oversee intelligence matters. The two men orchestrated what was then called the "Halloween Massacre," a complex series of maneuvers that made Rumsfeld Defense Secretary and Cheney chief of staff, while stripping Secretary of State Henry Kissinger of his dual role as national security adviser, and marginalizing Vice President Nelson Rockefeller as insufficiently conservative in foreign affairs to appease the party's strong conservative wing—a wing Rumsfeld and Cheney convinced Ford they spoke for.

Rockefeller soon withdrew his name for consideration as Ford's running mate in the '76 elections.

The duo's actions were driven by the capital's familiar clasp of ambitions and ideas—the latter, in this case, that Kissinger's policy of Détente was soft on the Soviets. That position also placed both at odds with the CIA of the era. Instead of producing reports that showed a surge in Soviet military strength, the agency offered complex, hedged analysis, filled with caveats about the limits of Soviet power (which later turned out to be correct) and the overall difficulty of assessing our adversary's true capabilities. Thus, the last in the series of Halloween events was the ouster of CIA director William Colby, and a plan to cut CIA's influence in the policy process. They then replaced Colby with a man Rumsfeld viewed as a competitor—one who might be best sent into exile at a diminished CIA. That would be our emissary to China, George H. W. Bush.

This was thirty years ago. For Cheney and Rumsfeld, George W. Bush started as a footnote—the child of their contemporary. In these complex engagements of powerful men, it is important not to overlook basic human interaction, conventions that people know, surely, from their own lives. To wit: the son of a friend or colleague is always, in large part, a son, seen, for better or for worse, in reference to the parent. For Cheney, George W. Bush is the son of a man he admired, despite his belief that the former President missed history's call by not destroying Saddam Hussein. For Rumsfeld, he was the son of a man he never felt was an equal in intellect or enterprise, proven also by the fact that he missed history's call by not destroying Saddam Hussein. Now place this pair in their respective senior positions in the administration of that son, George W. Bush: a President without foreign policy experience of any kind, who, conveniently, has long struggled to emerge from his father's shadow. It's simple math. Such alignments—more than the play of competing memos or forgotten debates—often turn the wheel of history. Which is why, a hundred years from now, scholars will most probably look at this array of actors and say, clearly, that Saddam Hussein's days were numbered. It was, after all, about the only matter on which all three agreed, and felt passionately. In this view of personality guiding destiny—of people gravitating toward what they happen to share and, when in power, getting what they want—it is, in retrospect, no great surprise that the first National Security Council meeting in January of 2001 dealt with the overthrow of Saddam Hussein. And so did the second. It was a matter of *how,* not *whether.*

After 9/11, as America's standing army and its civilian leaders desperately and quite naturally looked for a way to contribute, it would become largely a matter of integration. By November, Bush would take Rumsfeld aside and tell him to construct a detailed plan for the military invasion of Iraq. It is all but a certainty that Cheney had already told Rumsfeld that the request was coming. Bush asked Rumsfeld to tell no one in the upper reaches of government, and to make the request to senior officers seem routine. If that second request was offered without a strategic prebriefing from Cheney, it would be surprising. This is one of the things Cheney has done countless times over thirty years: work behind the scenes, ever so deftly, to orchestrate what will seem like impromptu events. They're not. They are the bureaucratic equivalent of the media event. So, as America officially moved to a detailed action plan for the overthrow of Hussein, only three men would be in the know: Bush, Cheney, and Rumsfeld. The rationale for keeping it quiet is obvious. A thorny question remained: How could the ousting of Saddam Hussein be woven into something now called the "war on terror?" Up ahead would be more definitions by default.

Intelligence matters. That's a primary lesson of 9/11.

The entire government, groping across uncharted terrain, desperate, was starved for it. Neither convenient targets within the vast landscape of Afghanistan nor the precise nature and capabilities of our terrorist enemy were in clear focus.

Not long after U.S. aircraft began bombing Afghanistan on October 7—and American ground forces assembled throughout the Gulf to prepare their assault—a startling disclosure was presented to the United States by a Western intelligence service. What took shape were outlines of a nightmare.

The setting was a campfire in Kandahar on a warm night in mid-August, three weeks before 9/11. Men were dining and drinking tea. In the firelight were Osama bin Laden and his only peer, Ayman al-Zawahiri, the Egyptian surgeon who had, in 1998, brought his Egyptian Islamic Jihad organization—with its array of educated tacticians—together with bin Laden's jihadist network to form al Qaeda. These two men—soon to be household names, cult heroes to a billion people, pariahs to another billion—were, at this point, known for the most part to terrorism experts and adherents of obscure Islamist Web sites.

Across the campfire from bin Laden and al-Zawahiri were two men—believed to be Sultan Bashiruddin Mahmood and his associate Abdul Majid. Mahmood had been a key patriarch of Pakistan's three-decade mission, ultimately successful, to build a nuclear bomb. While the driving force behind these efforts was the headstrong, unmanageable Abdul Qadeer (A. Q.) Khan, who had stolen Western designs for the production of enriched uranium in the 1970s and brought them to explosive fruition in the 1980s, Mahmood's role as chairman of the country's atomic energy commission and an expert in methods to enrich uranium granted him a designation of national honor. With that honor came a platform that he had used in the late nineties to advocate the idea that nuclear weapons should be spread to other Islamic countries. He had become increasingly radicalized, believing that such a destructive grant would trigger an "end of days" scenario and the beatific triumph of Islam. In 1999, such pronouncements prompted his ouster from the country's officialdom; he was reassigned to a lesser job and then, in humiliation, resigned.

For him to resurface in this way, with bin Laden and Zawahiri, was daunting.

There was a great deal to do, and fast. The names of the conferees were solid. But who was Mahmood attached to at this point? What were his movements? What were bin Laden and Zawahiri's intentions in meeting with Pakistani nuclear scientists? And could we tell the Pakistanis what we'd found, or what we suspected? There was no area about which the Pakistanis were more secretive than their coveted nuclear program—the centerpiece of almost inestimable national pride. Tenet and McLaughlin decided to keep it all closely held—contacts, at the start, largely through the "intelligence channel."

Tenet and Pavitt contacted Bob Grenier, chief of the CIA's Islamabad station, an office that was growing—with the unfolding engagement nearby in Afghanistan—into one of the largest in the CIA network.

In secret cables and follow-up calls, Grenier was told everything that was known. The question: How much could he tell Pakistan's secret intelligence service, ISI, an organization with a reputation for ruthlessness and duplicity that had been instrumental in setting up the Taliban regime?

The first pressing espionage challenge of the post-9/11 era had surfaced—a shadowy path from Islamabad to Kandahar that could lead to bin Laden and a nuclear weapon. But before we could budge, the United States had to decide who, in that part of the world, we could really trust.

"Come in, Brent."

"Nice to see you, Dick."

In October, the two men sat across from each other in a place that couldn't be more familiar: the White House, where they'd spent their most satisfying years, often side by side, as men of consequence.

They had been present at each other's creation as trusted counselors—men who, though unelected, would wield sextant and map aboard the American ship of state. And, like old friends everywhere, they were the last to see each other age, or change, or establish new roles.

The world, of course, had changed on 9/11—just a month before—and today was the first real chance to discuss what was altered and what abided. This was a longtime specialty of both men. Judicious appraisals, parsed and contextualized; an ability to connect goals and strategies, and then know what must be done.

Or, more specifically, advise presidents about what must be done. Scowcroft, as national security adviser, had done this for the first President Bush, as he had for Gerald Ford. Under Richard Nixon, he was the deputy national security adviser to that era's most potent global architect, Henry Kissinger, his first major patron and mentor.

Having sat in these chairs for thirty years, Scowcroft had been afforded an almost unmatched perch to view the world as it is—and an understanding of how the roiling planet responded to American principles and exercise of power.

He had been central to a variety of experiments—such as opening relations with China, Détente, response to the fall of the Soviet Union, and the 1991 Gulf War to eject Saddam Hussein from Kuwait. A newly elected George W. Bush made Scowcroft—then approaching eighty, his capacities undiminished—head of the Foreign Intelligence Advisory Board, a bipartisan, sixteen-member council that was established by Dwight Eisenhower in 1956 to provide presidents with "an independent source of advice on the effectiveness with which the intelligence community is meeting the nation's intelligence needs."

George W. Bush didn't rely on the board. That was fine—it was his choice as President—but Scowcroft was not unrealistic to have expected more. He had been a mentor and guide to Colin Powell, the current Secretary of State, and had all but discovered national security adviser Condoleezza Rice—spotting her in 1989 when she was a Stanford professor with a specialty in Soviet power and European affairs. Stephen Hadley, Rice's deputy national security adviser, was also a Scowcroft protégé and had spent the nineties as a principal at Scowcroft Advisors, the general's foreign policy consulting firm.

Most notably, Brent had been the forty-first President's most trusted counselor. The Gulf War, the elder Bush's finest moment and his lasting legacy, was quietly compelled by Scowcroft's firm stance and exhortation that Hussein's invasion of Kuwait was a violation of

international law that collided with core U.S. interests. Just as
Kissinger sharpened Nixon's global ambitions, Scowcroft hardened
his boss's internationalist impulses with analytical rigor. He also
brought continuity, having helped shape the "realist" school of foreign
policy thinking—a view that America's ambitions, and its often soaring idealism, need to be tempered with pragmatism as to the limits and
appropriate uses of power. Then, there's one more thing: Brent and
the elder Bush, two straight-spined, polite men—reluctant to dig in
but unmovable when they do—are as affectionate as men of their generation tend to be. Scowcroft has a condominium near the Bush compound in Kennebunkport. He and the former President talk every
couple of days.

Which meant he already knew what few people outside the Bush
family itself understood: that the two Presidents were not particularly
close, and did not have the sort of substantive discussions one might
expect of two men now firmly connected by both blood and history.
This was an awkward fact. Scowcroft knew it might explain why he
hadn't been called upon more in the first ten months of this presidency. Still, he liked the younger Bush. The new President would
need seasoned advice, like any president, only more so. Scowcroft
waited. He did whatever he was asked, with his usual thoroughness.

In this case, it had been to assess the U.S. intelligence capability and
write a report for the President.

Scowcroft dove into this task with a young man's energy. He had
spent several decades as consumer of intelligence "products"—de-
vouring enough reporting from CIA and dispatches from NSA to
paper the Roosevelt Room. There was almost no one more expert on
the subject.

The report he'd produced by the late summer of 2001 said, in
essence, that U.S. intelligence was constructed to meet the needs of an
era now gone. The CIA was created in 1947—with a director who putatively would lead foreign intelligence efforts and report directly to
the President. That was about the same time that the Office of the Secretary of Defense (OSD) was created—a civilian office that would

sit atop the military and also report to the President. Both roles were somewhat ill-defined and ripe for growth. The various parts of the military—Army, Navy, Air Force—were independent nation-states, ruled by their own uniformed leadership, on top of which the civilian OSD precariously rested. Yet during the emerging cold war, the forty-five-year struggle with the Soviet empire, with wars in Korea and Vietnam, and with the creation of competing spheres of influence and security, the OSD answered for every institutional question. It grew and consolidated power on a vast scale, claiming authority over a budget that grew to be larger than the economy of all but a dozen or so countries in the world.

The CIA—Scowcroft wrote in his report—was focused primarily on a singular opponent, the Soviet Union, with its agents and analysts becoming expert in the game of move and countermove with their Communist doppelgänger. Meanwhile, the Department of Defense (DoD)—with a similar Soviet focus and a size that had soon dwarfed CIA—moved forcefully, as well, into intelligence collection. The National Security Agency, with an estimated annual budget of nearly $6 billion through the 1990s—nearly twice that of CIA—falls within the authority of the Defense Department. The same is true for most of the remaining dozen intelligence collection arms of the government. DoD, by 2000, would control about 80 percent of the nation's intelligence budget.

Scrowcroft's main assertion in his report was that the collapse of the Soviet Union meant that much of the nation's intelligence efforts—and its vast resources—were misapplied. He outlined the intelligence demands posed by a disparate array of regional competitors, terrorists, ideological movements, and opponents who, unlike the former Soviets, were generally not bent on destroying America—nor, in any case, capable of it.

On that August day, Cheney and Scowcroft had met in the Vice President's office to discuss the report's recommendations, which included "moving boxes," where the director of Central Intelligence would function as the nation's intelligence leader and claim the lion's share of the budgetary authority now housed under the Secretary of Defense. The Vice President mostly listened, and seemed to agree. It was a cordial meeting.

After 9/11, Scowcroft was asked to revise his report, based on the attacks. With the revised report now finished, and digested by Cheney, Scowcroft was back in the Vice President's office.

He and Cheney settled in, and talked a bit about 9/11. Scowcroft asked how the President was faring, and Condi, and how the Vice President was holding up under the pressure of the past month. It was odd for Scowcroft not to be called at a moment like this. Cheney said he was fine, the President, too; he appreciated Brent's concern.

The attacks, of course, were just the sort of threat—hard to monitor, hard to assess—that they'd discussed in the late summer. The twenty-page report was not much changed, Brent said.

"My God, it emerged from Afghanistan," Scowcroft said, "just about the most backward, forgotten country on the planet. It shows how little we know about where the threats are coming from."

Knowing what we need to know, when we need to know it, Scowcroft said to Cheney, would mean rethinking the nature of intelligence. The intelligence function was now parceled out among a wide array of agencies, and intelligence services of the military branches. "We need a massive intelligence research *library,*" Scowcroft said, using an old-school term that has been replaced by buzzwords like "aggregation" and "integration." Everything would be housed in this research library, in one place; people with proper security clearance could sign in, and there could be various clearances for particular areas, and the whole thing would be overseen by CIA and a newly empowered DCI. After all, CIA is still the lead agency, the collecting pool, where the hard analysis gets done.

Cheney nodded. The array and diversity of new targets for intelligence collection and analysis was, indeed, daunting, he said. There wasn't, as with the Soviets in 1947, one long learning curve to run up; there were fifty of them. Al Qaeda was a conglomeration of several terrorist organizations—in Egypt and Saudi Arabia, predominantly—but there were similar groups in a dozen countries. Newly entrepreneurial states were building newly destructive weapons and testing boundaries. They were serving as incubators for nationalist movements—the natural counterpoint to sweeping globalism. How to keep all this straight and in clear, actionable focus? Consolidation, and integration of all intelligence efforts. "It's our only chance," Scowcroft said, "or we'll be surprised again and again."

Then, Scowcroft brought it full circle. "This means we'll have to move the boxes," parlance for a wide-ranging reorganization.

Cheney disagreed. "Moving the boxes won't solve it," he said. "It never does."

"Not immediately," Scowcroft countered, but over time the institutional mandates and dictates start to shift and people "start to think in new ways." We have to move now, but think long term, he said. "The Soviets are already gone ten years. We've been attacked. We're long overdue."

And around they went, in essential agreement about what needed to be done—a massive breaking down of walls between agencies, a teardown of silos. They discussed the impediments to getting it done.

So Scowcroft unsheathed his sword. He said he'd talked to Rumsfeld about changes, including taking budgetary authority away from Defense and giving much of it to an enlarged DCI at CIA.

Though Scowcroft assumed that Rumsfeld had reported their conversation to Cheney—there's nothing that Don and Dick don't share—he answered the question anyhow.

"Don was strongly opposed to my notions," he said simply.

And Dick nodded. And then they both knew everything—too much, maybe. Each man could count dozens of people who'd opposed Don over the years—sometimes with sound ideas—who were now dust. Kissinger railed against him. The old bull Nelson Rockefeller, a Vice President himself—who was gutted by Don, with Dick's help, in the seventies—often deemed Rumsfeld "beneath contempt."

"Dick, look," Scowcroft said. "My proposals would be disruptive. There's no question about it. If you think this is a bad time for it, I'll just fold my tent and go away. I don't want to. And it seems to me this is something that ought to be put on the table right now. Now's the time!" He paused. "But I'll be guided by you. . . ."

Cheney paused for a moment, assessing the landscape. He was now entertaining bold strategies in the use of U.S. power—an invasion of Afghanistan as step one, regime change in Iraq as step two. Scowcroft, with his staunch realism, was unimpressed by the sweeping ideas of Paul Wolfowitz, Rumsfeld's deputy, who believed that American power could be used to replace rogue regimes with U.S.-friendly democracies, especially in the troubled Arab world.

Brent, with his modest portfolio, had now set himself on a collision course with Don Rumsfeld. The forty-first President's man versus the forty-third's.

"No, go ahead, submit the report to the President," Cheney said, after a moment. Scowcroft said he'd submit it in draft form, to give them all a little wiggle room. And then the two men—old friends, from countless battles—rose and shook hands.

What's in that handshake, and half-smile? What does it feel like as they pull apart?

Because that was the last meeting Brent Scowcroft would ever have with Dick Cheney.

At the massive Omaha processing center for First Data, Bob Mueller's troops had settled in. They were deep inside a Fortune 500 company, a place where federal agents had never roamed so freely, prowling through First Data's massive computer banks. The company, with its headquarters in Denver, accounts for nearly half of U.S. charge volume, and is involved in charging activity in countries around the world.

In these early days of panic—and fear of a "second wave" attack—that span was seen as a virtue. There was, after all, so much to check, starting with the names of all the hijackers. Each Atta and Hanjour, around the world, needed to be checked, and followed. Billing addresses were matched with charging history, locations matched with dates. Is this the right Atta, or another one? If he's the right one, then his spending could create the spine of a thousand companion searches, nightflares lighting a dark path. One might illuminate the path of another known terrorist, or a financier, or a safe house, or a place that terrorists frequent. At least, that was the way it was supposed to work.

To understand this moment, and what was driving the actions— some of which could infringe upon civil liberties and privacy rights— it is important to understand how little the U.S. counterterrorism effort had, at this point, to rely on and how desperate they were. There was not one significant human intelligence, or humint, source inside the al Qaeda operation. There was no evidence of al Qaeda operatives, or supporters, inside the United States. The Atta team of nineteen had managed to enter the country, operate within it, communicate with al Qaeda leaders, and execute the worst domestic attack in U.S. history, and investigators still didn't know *how*!

U.S. officials, in both law enforcement and intelligence, were essentially blind and waiting, with dread, for a "second wave." The thinking was to act first, work out logistics later. Yet when FBI officials first sat down with First Data in the days after the company had called the bureau, they felt that they had some precedents to rely on.

There is a long history of American companies, often large, notable companies, working in secret concert with the U.S. government. Western Union, in fact, had been at the front of that procession. A company Western Union bought in the 1860s called the American Telegraph Company banned messages in cipher during the Civil War at the behest of the War Department. During World War II, all U.S. telegraph companies forwarded copies of international cables to the federal government. The program, "Operation Shamrock," continued after the war and was unknown to Congress and top intelligence officials.

Every day, a courier would leave NSA's headquarters in Fort

Meade, Maryland, and board a train for New York City. The clerk would copy onto magnetic tape all international telegrams from the day before that had been sent by three major companies—ITT, RCA Global, and Western Union—and bring the tape back to Maryland for analysts to pore over. This collection of foreign intelligence also involved U.S. citizens and was blocked when it was uncovered, along with other intelligence abuses, during post-Watergate congressional investigations of CIA in the mid-seventies. Shamrock, and similar abuses in the wiretapping of U.S. citizens—some of whom were opponents of the Vietnam War—was the impetus for the passage of the Federal Intelligence Surveillance Act in 1978, and the creation of the so-called "FISA Court." Congress determined that any surveillance involving a U.S. citizen would have to be reviewed and approved by the court. The law was graciously written, allowing for a three-day lag time, so that eavesdropping could be authorized by the President in an emergency and reviewed later. For the next twenty years, the court was, essentially, a rubber stamp—handling nineteen thousand applications in its history, and refusing only five.

In White House strategy sessions in September and October of 2001, officials from FBI, CIA, and NSA—in consultation always with the Vice President—looked in desperation at what tools might be available for the unfolding battle. It broke into two large sectors: telecommunications and finances. The two would fit together, like the clasp of left and right hand, to lay the foundations of a worldwide matrix.

On one side was NSA, which had been working to expand and perfect its sigint capabilities in an era of galloping communications technology. By 2001, U.S. citizens made approximately 1.2 billion landline calls a day and 800 million cell phone calls. E-mails had been growing by a trillion a year for the past five years. This raging river of noise and digitalia gets channeled through the huge telecommunications "switches" of companies such as Global Crossing, Worldcom, AT&T.

Yet their switches in the United States handle more than just this country's traffic. Modern communications travel at all but unfathomable speeds across the globe to find the fastest path to their destination. That means a call—or e-mail—between France and Spain may pass though Oregon; and digital packets, shooting through the network, may carry a bundle of messages from Islamabad and Israel. Borders, in this realm, are meaningless; location matters not at all. NSA black boxes sitting on a wide array of telecom switches in the fall of 2001 could gather calls and e-mails from much of the planet. Which is what they did, as NSA computer technicians furiously worked to perfect the algorithms for "search and sort" engines to manage the flow. This is what was explained to each party's leaders and representatives on both the House and Senate Intelligence Committees in October 2001—four from each party, the so-called "gang of eight."

According to reports of several attendees at these briefings, administration officials explained that the system would be used to hunt known or probable terrorists, their supporters, and their financiers. It could also handle broadly wrought searches, like massive keyword searches for those who were speaking about terrorist operations and—as was already under way—all calls between the United States and Afghanistan. Some concern was voiced by congressional Democrats about civil liberties, but informed questions were difficult to pose: the program was so secret that they couldn't even consult their staffs.

That same month, October, Bush signed a secret presidential order allowing the NSA, with its telecom helpers, to carry forward what had already begun and continue to eavesdrop on U.S. citizens. The FISA Court was ignored. The specific legislation reads that the court will be the "exclusive" arbiter of issues pertaining to domestic surveillance of agents of "a foreign power." It would, no doubt, have proven logistically challenging for the administration to work with the court—creating, essentially, warrant applications to eavesdrop on the communications of thousands of U.S. citizens being surveyed by the "blind eye" of the NSA's sleepless computers, some of which were citizen-to-citizen calls. Clearly, a smaller but significant number of Americans were graduating to higher categories of surveillance based on what they did or said. In fact, the administration didn't consult the court on that smaller number, either. According to an intelligence source with intimate knowledge of the NSA program and these early days: "The thinking was that going to the FISA Court, or trying to alter the 1978 act, would somehow expose, with leaks, or just from questions that we'd have to answer, what our system's capabilities were. Once you take that first step, the rest falls into place—including a fear that if we just talked to FISA about the smaller subset that drew our increased interest they'd feel obligated to trace the legal issues to the huge pool of level-one searches. Either way, we just went ahead."

That was one part of the worldwide matrix, the communications side—what people said or wrote. The other side was what they did. That, in large measure, meant what they bought, where they bought it, and, generally, where they brought it home. For this, the administration relied heavily on First Data. Covenants with other credit card processors in the United States and abroad meant that—much like the large telecom switches—everything could be invisibly blended; a borderless world of transactions. Western Union had similar sharing arrangements for wire transfers, which often involve banks and various financial institutions. To clear or trace transactions, large companies generally have access to one another's back office processing units. It's all interconnected. You just need a universal passport—like the one Western Union possesses.

Once these two parts, two rivers, were merged after 9/11, the data rose to flood stage. Millions of communications dispatches from NSA swamped CIA and FBI. The former did its own frantic sifting—something CIA automatically does, looking for that actionable bit of gold. FBI doesn't sift well. It's oriented to gather evidence for prosecution—every bit, every drop, is saved, and doled out for a next step. Much of the flow went through FBI, with key information brought to the First Data computers—FBI's own in-house search engine. In the first few weeks after the attacks, thousands of financial searches were conducted based on initial communications leads from NSA. They cascaded into one subset, then another, of increasing interest, priority

. . . and effort, by agents rushing, first, to produce paper. In the FBI, every action must be "papered." That means documented in some legally defendable fashion—something worthy, if need be, of an appearance in court.

The legal umbrella, as of October 26, was the newly passed USA Patriot Act. The act allowed for a vast expansion of surveillance within the United States, including the searching of financial and personal records, and "sneak and peak" provisions, permitting citizens to have their activities monitored without their knowledge.

The favored mechanism used by FBI was something called the "national security letter," a legal figleaf created for espionage and terrorism investigations in the 1970s as a way to get around consumer privacy laws. It allowed the FBI to review the customer records of suspected foreign agents secretly. On balance, maybe a few hundred would be issued annually.

After 9/11, Justice Department lawyers suggested that the letters be used in a new, expanded way. They noted that the letters could be issued on the simplest, thinnest suspicion—no real evidence needed. An NSA hit was plenty. Scores of top managers, including special agents in charge of many field offices, could issue the letters. And they issued them in a flurry—at a rate of thousands a month—snatched and used like tissues during cold season.

Not that there weren't good old-fashioned subpoenas as well. There were. Thousands were issued, approved by the fistful, at the federal court in Omaha. A special FBI–First Data facility was soon set up near the company's processing center, a place where agents and company technicians could commune and tap into the great computers—and beyond, into the world's financial system—in respectful sanctity. Omaha, for a time, produced more subpoenas than any other courthouse in America.

As to sensitivities of congressional oversight of this vast enterprise, a moment in late October is revealing.

Members of the Senate and House Intelligence Committees entered a secure room in the Capitol for a briefing on the "war on terror." Officials from Justice, Treasury, CIA, and FBI were due to testify about the "financial war."

Dennis Lormel hovered in the back of the empty gallery, talking to a colleague. There was a delay—a Senate vote was holding things up. He'd be going third or fourth. With him on the panel would be a top financial enforcement official from Treasury named Jim Gurule, who had jurisdiction over the Office of Foreign Assets Control, or OFAC. As a peace offering of sorts—since First Data was an FBI partner— Lormel had let some officials of the Secret Service, which handles credit card fraud, come by First Data. They were, after all, experts in trolling the planet of card charges.

Lormel squinted from a distance as he watched Gurule begin to set up. There was an easel. Gurule unsheathed a visual aid for his presentation: a large chart showing how First Data was accessing and organizing financial information across the globe.

Lormel, all 220 pounds, rushed him from across the room. "Are you fuckin' crazy? Get that sign out of here. No one is supposed to know about this. *And, Jesus, it isn't even a Treasury operation!*" Gurule was stunned. He took down the poster and hustled it out of the room.

Congressional oversight of covert activities is a principle that distinguishes the United States from other countries. It is an ideal that is central to the checks and balances—the counteracting ambitions, as Madison and others had attested—that prevent abuses of power. In this case, and scores of others, those fighting the "war on terror" decided it was an unaffordable luxury.

In that day's testimony—and many to follow—no one uttered the name First Data.

And so a vast search-and-seizure machine, with a financial body and a communications head, was constructed and fired up to match the challenges of this man-on-man war.

History will ultimately judge that machine, and those who encouraged it to be built—from the President on down—against words written with ink quills more than two centuries ago. The Fourth Amendment of the Bill of Rights to the U.S. Constitution ensures that *"The right of the people to be secure in their persons, houses, papers, and effects, against unreasonable searches and seizures, shall not be violated, and no Warrants shall issue, but upon probable cause, supported by Oath or affirmation, and particularly describing the place to be searched, and the persons or things to be seized."*

It is often called the most forcefully written of the amendments. You can feel the founders' ardor, a don't-tread-on-me fierceness of spirit in the declarative phrasing. They had, after all, just completed a successful insurgency against the controlling authority of Great Britain; they were used to being "violated" in Boston and Philadelphia, Concord and Hoboken, and to not being "secure in their persons." The words "probable cause" are among the most oft-spoken and colloquial of any in the document: they regulate, artfully, the collision point between citizens and their government under the proposition that reasonable people will be able to agree, for the most part, on that standard.

Whether reasonable people agree or not with this particular course of action—and the expansion of presidential authority it entails—will be debated for years; maybe, even, for as long as the so-called "war on terror" lasts. What is known and indisputable? As this machine searched the landscape, it swept up the suspicious, or simply the unfortunate, by the stadiumful and caught almost no one who was actually a danger to America.

CHAPTER TWO

BEYOND SUSPICION

The "dark side" is a complex, shape-shifting term—its meaning altered by tone and inflection. When Cheney spoke about it on national television a few days after the attacks, he had given it a note of resignation—*this is what we must do, where we must live, like it or not.*

There is, however, always a choice in such matters, in the actions that ultimately define character. The character of an individual or a nation.

The debate as to man's better and lesser angels is, of course, as old as human sentience. While mindful of that, the improvisational challenge at hand meant, in those seminal months after 9/11, this age-old dilemma would be unsealed for reappraisal. Maybe there was something we'd missed—maybe we could indulge man's brutish impulses, or embrace those who have, as a path to noble ends. If we kept our eye always on the worthwhile end—the sunlit uplands of a safe and secure America—we could navigate any valley.

An early journey into shadows was under way in mid-October, 2001, as Ben Bonk, CIA lifer, quietly entered a baronial home on Regent's Park in London for a meeting he hoped would be the start of something.

The house belonged to Prince Bandar bin Sultan, a nephew of

Saudi Arabia's de facto ruler, Crown Prince Abdullah, and, for eighteen years, the kingdom's ambassador to the United States. At fifty-two, Bandar, a close confidant of both Bushes, is a man of profound complexities, a cheery, educated man of enormous appetites. An omniscient observer could have spotted him recently walking the sidelines of an NFL game, dining and smoking cigars in the West Wing, and channeling funds to a family that may have inadvertently been supporting 9/11 hijackers, almost all of whom were Saudis. A sharp eye might spot a driver stopping by Riggs Bank in Washington on a certain day each month to pick up a suitcase with $50,000 in cash that Bandar doles out to friends, relatives, and Saudi operatives in the United States.

He is also a man who gets things done, and he builds relationships that rest on his consistent effectiveness. This day he was brokering an important sit-down at his house. He welcomed Bonk and ushered him into a stately parlor. Waiting there was an elegant, hand-tailored, smiling embodiment of the "dark side."

"Exciting, about those Spartans," said Musa Kousa.

Bonk laughed. "Yeah, we waited a long time. Since Magic." Ben was at Michigan State in those glory days—he graduated in 1976, the year before Magic Johnson arrived. Kousa, a rabid basketball fan, was a few years ahead; he was at MSU studying for a master's degree in sociology in 1973. His thesis, handed in a few years later, was a keeper, the kind that professors make a copy of and stick in a drawer. It wasn't so much the trenchant analysis, though there was some of that in 209 pages with footnotes. It was the research. Kousa, born in Tripoli, Libya, to a prominent family, had been able to interview his subject: Moammar Gadhafi.

Time past, time present. For both men, it was a very long way from East Lansing, Spartan Stadium, and MSU's green and white.

Bonk spent nearly two decades traveling the world for the CIA, especially the Arab world; he married briefly, divorced—like so many agents—and moved up quickly through the agency's ranks. By 2000, he was deputy director of the CIA's Counter-Terrorist Center—a soft-spoken, steady counterpoint to the flamboyant Cofer Black. Ever reliable and precise, it was Bonk who, along with Deputy Director John McLaughlin, camped at Bush's ranch in September 2000—two months before the election—to carefully tell the Republican nominee state secrets. Bonk grimly informed Bush that during the coming four years, Americans would certainly die in terrorist acts planned or simply inspired by bin Laden.

The most vivid example of terrorism against the United States before 9/11 was the December 1988 explosion of a Pan Am jet over Lockerbie, Scotland. It killed 270 people, mostly Americans—including 35 students from Syracuse University.

Bonk's fellow Spartan, Musa Kousa, almost certainly helped plan that attack.

That, at least, is the consensus of every significant intelligence agency in the West. Kousa had gone from Lansing to Libya to work for Gadhafi. By 1980, he was head of the Libyan Mission in England—essentially Libya's ambassador to the United Kingdom. In an extraordinary interview with *The Times* of London, he told the reporter that Libya supported the IRA and that two Libyans living in London should be killed. He was summarily expelled from the country. Soon thereafter, the two Libyans were found dead in their London apartment; other Libyan dissidents, opponents of Gadhafi, were killed across Europe in the coming year.

The Lockerbie flight took place in an era when Gadhafi was looking to be a player on the world stage. Like bin Laden, terror was his means. By the mid-eighties, Ronald Reagan was calling Gadhafi the most dangerous man in the world. He was the dictator of a rogue state. The United States bombed Libya in 1986—an attack that killed Gadhafi's daughter and injured two of his sons—in retaliation for his having bombed a nightclub in Germany. Onerous unilateral sanctions were placed on the country. Kousa, then deputy head of intelligence, was soon implicated by the French and British intelligence in a second disaster: the blowing up of a French airliner, UTA 772, over Niger in 1989. The death toll was 170.

In 1998, George Tenet, just a year into his directorship of the CIA, and John McLaughlin flew to Jiddah to meet with Bandar. In the ambassador's sprawling home, which McLaughlin describes as "like Disney World—with flying monkeys and giant TV screens," Bandar mentioned he'd chatted recently with Gadhafi. "I think he might want to talk. He's tired of being alone."

A year later, Musa Kousa slipped into Geneva. Bonk and he met there. What became clear to Bonk as one decade bled into the next was that the Libyans had grown tired of being excluded from the world community. They were unable to send their privileged sons abroad to U.S. colleges, and were suffocating under sanctions that limited everything from dry goods to key parts for oil refineries, many of which had slipped into disrepair. Bruce Riedel, on Clinton's National Security Council, soon became engaged on the policy side, beginning discussions about settling Lockerbie. All of it had to be handled in utmost secrecy. The silence was for a reason: families of the Lockerbie victims had long since organized into a fierce, somewhat unruly advocacy group, lobbying for arrests, sanctions, and anything that would amount to a facsimile of justice. Notice of a dialogue with the monsters from Tripoli would have summoned a righteous explosion from families whose loved ones looked on from pictures on nighttables, from home movies and fading memories.

But that was all before 9/11. The United States and its Western allies were now in need—in need of intelligence. Kousa, twenty-one years after his expulsion from England, stepped off the plane at Heathrow and was soon greeted by a delegation: top officials from the diplomatic and intelligence arms of both Britain and America. He had in his arms dossiers with the names and locations of Islamic terrorists in Europe, North Africa, and the Middle East.

And back they went—now a sizable crowd—to Bandar's place, a neutral ground, courtesy of the Saudis. A month after 9/11, and three days after the United States began bombing the Afghanistan refuge of al Qaeda, the two daunting campaigns of the "war on terror"—stop the terrorists and global disarmament—were on display in Bandar's elegant parlor. The morning meetings between Kousa and William Burns, the assistant secretary of state for Near East affairs, dealt with payments to the Lockerbie families, whether the Libyans would admit culpability for the attack, and a quid pro quo of disarmament. Libya was widely known to have chemical weapons of mass destruction, and maybe biological agents. Kousa, told that all of it would have to be given up, was noncommittal but attentive. His country was run by one man—and that man needed to agree to all of this.

It was, in fact, in the late afternoon that Musa and Ben finally sat down and chatted about Mateen Cleaves, point guard on Michigan State's 2000 team, how he dominated Florida in the NCAA Championship game—giving the school its first national title since Magic led them over Larry Bird and Indiana State in 1979.

It wasn't just throat-clearing. To understand the "war on terror," and the ethical dilemmas of dealing on the "dark side," you need to be at this table, inside the mansion of an ambassador from the home country of fifteen of the nineteen 9/11 hijackers, talking to a smiling, stylish gentleman who allegedly killed a planeful of passengers before they had a chance to put down their tray tables. There are families of those kids on the Lockerbie flight who—if they happen to read this short passage—may vomit. Or curse. This man, Musa Kousa, and his boss, inhabit their nightmares. Can such behavior—the slaughter of innocents—ever be forgiven? Does being able to sit and talk basketball with a representative of the U.S. government represent a kind of absolution? Is someone who commits such atrocities fundamentally different from a general who calls in an airstrike on a village, or on a terrorist's house where children may be sleeping?

But America was in need. A second wave of attacks was anticipated, and U.S. intelligence assets in the Arab world were thin. They needed expert eyes—and expertise comes in many guises.

"Look, Musa, you can put Lockerbie past you," Ben said. "We want it settled. You want it settled. We need to move past that now."

Kousa seemed relieved—he'd waited years to hear what Bonk had just said. The Libyans were ready to pay—and pay handsomely—

reparations to the families of those who died. "We want to get past it, too, Benny."

Then Bonk got deadly serious. "Everything has changed after 9/11," he said. "Two things. We're going to need you to give up your destructive weapons. And, most importantly, we'll need assistance to fight the terrorists."

Yes, Kousa understood. He knew, like much of the rest of the world, that the United States was facing formidable opponents in bin Laden and Zawahiri. And he had a name ready for Bonk, a gift: Ibn al-Sheikh al-Libi, a Libyan operative of al Qaeda. "He could be important," Kousa said. Bonk made note of the name. Details from Kousa were sketchy, but he believed the operative was in Pakistan. Other names mentioned were mostly Islamic fundamentalists in various countries who were enemies of Libya, a regime, officially Muslim, which the Wahabists considered apostate and corrupt.

Then Bonk went fishing. He gently proferred the name of an organization—Ummah Tameer-e-Nau (which means "Islamic revival"). The group, based in Pakistan, had just become an area of acute interest to the United States. UTN housed several dozen members of Pakistan's radicalized elite, including engineers, physicists, chemists, assorted military men, and members of the country's all-embracing secret police, the Inter-Services Intelligence, or ISI. Its activities, though, seemed largely humanitarian—bringing medical services and relief to residents of Pakistan's impoverished neighbor, Afghanistan. But one of the organization's founders was Mahmood, the Pakistani nuclear scientist.

"Ever hear of them?" Bonk asked.

Kousa paused for a moment, as though considering what he should—or shouldn't—say. "They approached us," Kousa said, "about whether we wanted their help in building a nuclear bomb." The group's primary though unstated goal, he added, was to spread nuclear technology to the Muslim nations of the world.

Bonk, practiced in the arts of misdirection, managed not to betray how intensely interested he was in what Kousa just said.

While policy makers in the White House and the Pentagon were quietly planning the invasion of Iraq, another, parallel experiment in disarmament had officially begun.

In this case, it meant traveling to the dark side to exchange precious elements—actionable intelligence, hefty reparations, destructive weapons, and international acceptance.

"Let's meet again soon," Bonk said.

Kousa just smiled.

Bonk returned to the CIA with this prized disclosure. Mahmood, quickly, was placed in proper context—atop the murky UTN, a relief agency wrapped tightly around seeds of destruction.

The so-called "war on terror" is about making friends, in some cases unlikely friends, by finding avenues for concerted, consensual action. In the weave of state-to-state alliances, and rivalries, it's not as easy as it might appear. But UTN spelled opportunity. It was a transnational organization with a visible footprint, albeit from relief work, and no official state sponsor. That meant each state could go after UTN, like a body attacks an alien organism.

Once its secret nuclear designs were discovered, the United States contacted cooperative intelligence services across the globe. The French, the British, the Saudis, and the Sudanese, all began digging. Information was shared through the "intelligence channel"—a thoroughfare for information between services that, in theory, would always be open.

UTN's network, in fact, was spread across a variety of Arab countries. The names of other UTN members were quickly unearthed. Those names were passed along to other services, as well.

And now the evidence was sufficient to press ISI to move. It was all handled through the intelligence channel—the less fanfare the better.

Grenier called ISI. He laid out some information on Mahmood's UTN network.

Agents from ISI apprehended Mahmood and Abdul Majid on October 23 and brought them in for questioning. With prepping from CIA, the Pakistani intelligence service suddenly had plenty to inquire about.

On Wednesday, October 24, a tall, rangy, prematurely gray-haired man ducked his white mop into Jim Pavitt's office.

Pavitt, who runs the CIA's Directorate of Operations, ran around his desk to greet him. "Rolf! The man I've been looking for."

Old friends? Brothers in arms? Of course, but Pavitt had something to sell, and Rolf Mowatt-Larssen had, for weeks, been trying to gather intelligence, CIA-style, on what it was.

They'd known each other for nearly twenty years—Pavitt the case officer who worked Europe and Asia and moved up the ranks to become DO.

For his part, Rolf Mowatt-Larssen—West Point graduate and former Army paratrooper, six tours for CIA over sixteen years, including station chief in Moscow twice during the end of the eighties and the tumultuous mid-nineties, and onetime boss of Valerie Plame—was surprised to be back on the seventh floor. He had thought his days in upper management were over four months earlier when he'd finished a year on Director Tenet's staff. He was ready to get back into the field, and at forty-six, as one of the most experienced station chiefs in the network, he had taken what he wanted: the Beijing station. China—America's rising challenger.

The calls had started coming a few weeks after 9/11. He and his wife were hip-deep in CIA language class for Chinese, and the cell phone kept ringing. They needed him back. There was a job—an ops job, but different. He made a few calls; got a sense of the situation these days on the seventh.

Pavitt was in pitch mode. "It's the most important job we got . . . heading chemical, biological, radiological threats. . . . You'll be the man . . . blank check, anything you want . . . it's the save-the-world job."

Mowatt-Larssen listened, as CIA ops guys learn to listen—half-smile, betraying nothing. He'd done some checking. The Counter-Terrorist Center under his old friend Cofer Black had nearly one thousand people. Chem, bio, rad, currently had four. Four people on something that, if there was a disaster, could change our way of life.

Pavitt went on for a while, kicking into preacher mode.

"History is beckoning, Rolf! Will you do this? *Will you?*"

Mowatt-Larssen paused, half because he was thinking it over, half for effect.

"Okay, Jim, I'll do it."

Done. In a second they're up as Pavitt speed-walked Rolf down the hall to Tenet.

They hugged. Tenet's a hugger. He was welcoming Rolf back into the family. A family that had been traumatized while one member, Rolf, was away. That was why his return, at this key moment, was so revealing. Everyone needed to explain themselves to him, to explain what had changed, what abided, and then voice their feelings. An agency legend, called back into the upper ranks, needed to be convinced, afresh, of decisions that were already well along.

Tenet and Mowatt-Larssen walked the halls. Tenet is better in motion—he's constantly trolling hallways, in what is commonly called George's "walkabouts." Rolf, a half-head taller, ambled by his side.

"We're behind the eight ball here," Tenet said. "UBL either has a bomb now or won't rest until he has one."

Rolf nodded, scribbled a few notes in a small pad, an old habit. George walked a bit more. "My gut instinct is we're in big trouble," he said.

This is also what Tenet does: he thinks out loud, thinks it as he talks it, searches forward in verbal leaps and lunges. He did it, time and again, with Bush. Internal administration memos often highlight the importance of verbal briefings of this President, how, one such memo states, "the last verbal briefing" on a particular issue "will carry the day." Tenet's thought-talk, raw and transparent, helped Bush see how ideas are formed, underlying evidence and conclusions reached. It was audible cognition. For a nonreader like Bush, that added dimension was salvation.

Cheney, while bemused by Tenet's manner—by his headlong passion, his storytelling as analysis—was always wary. Double-check him, he'd tell his chief of staff, Lewis "Scooter" Libby. Every word. Meanwhile, Condi Rice—precise, sometimes halting in speech, always checking the pool's temperature before diving—hated it. Tenet was the cannon-baller, always soaking her. She'd talk to aides about "Tenet's bullshit."

But, as they walked, Rolf could see Tenet digging for something. They stopped. This is the thing you wait for.

"Listen to me, Rolf," Tenet said, grabbing his arm. "You've got to be wrong."

"What are you talking about?"

"You're gonna be wrong sometimes, okay? You've got to be. You've got be *so far out in front* on this WMD issue, calling the shots, spotting potential threats, that you're the one that's wrong—not me, not anybody. You've got to *protect* us, you've got to protect the country on this one . . . in terms of being way out front. Listen, if you're *too* far out front, and you get picked off when things don't pan out, well, that's the price you have to pay."

Rolf looked at Tenet, nodding, egging him on: ". . . How do you mean?"

"You've got to be wrong—not analytically wrong . . . but just way out front . . . You see, all our failures are because we failed to anticipate. Intelligence failures follow a failure of anticipation. They come from only following the information you know and not worrying about what you don't know."

He grabbed Rolf's other bicep and squeezed, eye-to-eye. "You need to be passionate—passionate *about what you don't know.*"

Two days later, Mowatt-Larssen sought a second opinion—on being "passionate about what you don't know"—from an old friend, Cofer Black. Black greeted him, all pirate's smile and bluster, studiously theatrical.

"You're fucked. I'm fucked. We're all fucked," Black opened, absently shuffling papers on his desk. "Nine-eleven's happened and you've got the worst job, the WMD job. You can't win at that one, no way. We're both going to go down in the long term. If something happens, we're fucked. If nothing happens, we're fucked. We get no credit, only blame. So don't be smug and happy that you're in this particular, big-fuckin'-deal job. Because you're now screwed, just like I am."

They sat down to hash it out, two CIA warriors. Guys who would do whatever was needed, and often had. Mowatt-Larssen had been twice thrown out of the Soviet Union, an honor of sorts, for running so close to the edge. He'd played a fierce game of chess with the Soviets, move and countermove, even meeting once a month with the head of KGB over vodkas. They'd play "one question." Each got one question: the other would have to answer honestly, or not at all. No lying. It was a trust-building exercise, a sizing up of the enemy, and the way Mowatt-Larssen had recruited scores of undercover agents. Black was similar—charming and, when need be, ruthless—but with a different recent history. He'd started working Islamic radicals before almost anyone else. He'd tracked bin Laden. He was among CIA's first major designees on the field of battle. Bin Laden's victory he took as a personal defeat, and he wanted revenge.

"The classicial recruitment approach is not going to work with these guys, Rolf," he said, referring to the CIA's long-standing techniques for building relationships with the enemy and then co-opting them. "The classical European model—it has no application here. You don't know shit about al Qaeda. These guys are hard. They're already prepared to die. Think in terms of kidnapping, extreme interrogation methods—the ugly stuff."

Black liked Mowatt-Larssen and respected him. They were essentially talking about whether there was a bridge between eras: the post–World War II to pre-9/11 period, mostly dominated by a vast game of snooker with the Soviet opponent, and the post-9/11 era—just over a month old—in which they were facing an international network of suicidal Islamic ideologues.

Mowatt-Larssen moved first. "When you're talking about torture, the question is, who sets the standard of evidence required for taking so-called 'expedient action'?"

"What do you think the standard should be?" Black countered.

"Evidence," Rolf said, "is the keyword. Because a lot of people are suspected of knowing things that they may not. If your assessments of who should know what are not sound, you could end up hurting a lot of people—and creating a lot of new enemies."

Black nodded, looked to slice toward marrow.

"Fine," he said. "What about a case where a person may know something about the status of UBL and a bomb? And finding out what he knows could save a lot of lives. Then what's your standard, buddy?"

Black poked a finger at Mowatt-Larssen. "What do you do then?"

Though the "war on terror" was, as French president Jacques Chirac said, a war of a "new nature," America's invasion of Afghanistan was more of a bridge, a construct of new ideas and old, pulled together, Apollo 13–style, with duct tape and some bravado. CIA teams went in first and began working with tribal leaders. Money flowed freely. Old mujahedeen warlords signed on. The enemy, al Qaeda, was concentrated in a single refuge, supported by a ruling regime, the Taliban, so that the conventional model of one country violating the sovereign borders of another could apply.

The U.S. footprint was small—only 300 or so Special Forces troops, supported by targeted air power, to guide and fight alongside Afghan forces. They met with token resistance. Kabul, the capital, was abandoned, as the Taliban and al Qaeda forces fled into the rugged hills to set up guerrilla bases. Some simply fled for the Pakistani border to the south.

On November 11, Pakistani officials, assisted by CIA operatives, caught the man Musa Kousa identified—Ibn al-Sheikh al-Libi—in Pakistan. It was the first significant capture, albeit of a midsized character, in the "war on terror."

The news traveled from the Pakistan CIA station to Langley, and it was put on the agenda for the 5 p.m. meeting. It was still relatively early in the new era, two months along, and the meeting was still relatively small—about a dozen top CIA officials and a periodic visitor from Defense or State. The meeting had been started by Tenet in 1999, but its importance became evident after 9/11. Tenet, after all, was spending much of each day downtown, tied up with meetings in the White House or Capitol Hill or other departments. His role was keeping the rest of the government apprised of what CIA was doing, and why.

Deciding what CIA *should do,* and why, was left for 5 p.m. Tenet almost always made sure to get back to Virginia in time. The meetings started, always, with a "threat matrix" from the Counter-Terrorist Center, or CTC, that was monitoring the action around the globe. At this point, CTC was receiving approximately 17,000 items of intelligence a week, including nearly 2,500 cables daily from CIA's overseas stations. It was, by far, the world's single largest collector of intelligence on terrorism. Coordination was another issue. Even with a thousand employees, there was more arriving than could be examined or assessed.

They moved around the room. Mowatt-Larssen gave a report on WMD issues pertaining to nonstate actors. Hank Crumpton, a twenty-year veteran of CIA's clandestine service who headed up the agency's Afghanistan campaign, gave a report on developments in the war. Then there's Phil, "Nervous Phil," who gave a report on the global intelligence matrix he oversees—a vast experiment in blending sigint and land-based data to track terrorists across the planet. Tenet calls the run of reports his CINC briefing—for commander in chief—and appraises what he hears for possible presentation to the real CINC, usually at the next morning's briefing.

This day, as the reports ended, Tenet started the group discussion. The capture of al-Libi was just a starting point. More high-value captives would, it was hoped, be on the way while lesser-value captives were building up rapidly in Afghanistan. What would be done with them?

Tenet reported on a recent conversation with Rumsfeld. The two men lunched together every other week, alternating between CIA and DoD, a catered meal in each man's conference room—a calibrated arrangement, like so much else in the competitive relationship between the two agencies. A recent subject served at lunch was incarceration. What to do with the prisoners whom the joint force of CIA paramilitaries and U.S. Special Forces were collecting in Afghanistan, a spoil of the swift victories across the country? Some prisoners, mostly unlucky soldiers of the Taliban, were being passed to commanders of the U.S.-supported Northern Alliance. But more would be coming, some of them—they hoped—valuable operatives of al Qaeda.

Tenet told Rumsfeld that CIA was already deep into efforts that were beyond its traditional menu, having to marshal and supply forces in the effort to capture or kill bin Laden, while hunting terrorists in dozens of countries.

Rumsfeld was unmoved. "We are not getting into the prison business," he told Tenet. Of course, the vast Department of Defense, with nearly 3 million employees, did run prisons—military prisons. But, no, Rumsfeld and Tenet both understood that the incarceration of terrorists was different from rounding up captives from battle, who might soon enough be released. It was enough that CIA was leading the charge in Afghanistan, with the Pentagon in a supporting role. There was no way America's proud military would be left with the thankless job of terrorist jailer for CIA.

When Tenet recounted all of this to his team, there were moans of disbelief.

"Once again, we're the default—left holding the bag," said one.

"This is not what we're good at," said another.

One top CIA manager asked if anyone knew anyone who'd been involved in the U.S. corrections system. At least they'd have some experience.

"As the numbers rise, where the hell are we going to put them?" asked A. B. "Buzzy" Krongard, the former chief of Alex Brown and

Sons, the investment firm, and who was now CIA's executive director, a sort of chief operating officer at the agency, its number three job. Suggestions came from various directions. Put captives on ships off-shore? Find some unaffiliated island?

Again, the interrogation issue came up, this time with a dozen top CIA managers present. "A successful interrogation may yield all the important, operational information we're bound to get," said Ben Bonk. "We need somewhere to try what we can to make them talk." Countries were identified where captives might be housed—some close allies, some partners we'd rather not be seen with in public.

Around they went, in this meeting and other five o'clock meetings in the coming weeks. Would the CIA run these facilities, or a host country? Unclear. What were the standards to guide the interrogations? Tenet sounded a cautionary note to Scott Mueller, a career lawyer who had recently arrived as general counsel, and his deputy, John Rizzo, the agency's longtime legal guide. "We need guidance from Justice and the White House on what we're allowed to do," he told them. "We need consensus before we budge."

After one meeting, Ben Bonk and several DO chiefs huddled in the hall with a friend, a chief of operations who remains undercover. "Whatever we decide," the older man, quiet and terse, told the group, "make sure we don't start something unless we know how we plan on finishing it."

On November 16, Mohammed Atef, al Qaeda's military commander, died in an airstrike in Gardez, near Kabul. He and other al Qaeda members were in a hotel that was blown to rubble. The damage was done by a delicately armed Predator, a drone aircraft. The hesitations about the arming of Predators that characterized the years prior to 9/11 were now just a memory. The drones were being built and armed from September 12 onward with all deliberate speed. Atef, a former Egyptian police officer, had assumed military command of al Qaeda in

1996, had planned the attacks on the U.S. embassies in Nairobi and Tanzania in 1998. He was a key organizational force within al Qaeda—moving money and making decisions on resource allocation and priorities.

Almost as important as his death, however, was what was hauled from the rubble of the hotel: documents and precious videotapes. One was a homemade twenty-minute "casing" tape, showing several sites in Singapore—including U.S. military sites and the city's subway system—that had been targeted for attack by Jemaah Islamiya, al Qaeda's arm in Southeast Asia. Another video revealed assassination plots on leaders who were to attend an upcoming Persian Gulf summit. Freezing the tape, investigators were able to isolate shots of nearly fifty al Qaeda operatives.

The following week, Tenet filed into the Oval Office in the mid-morning with Hank Crumpton. Of all the CIA briefers in this period, Crumpton was the marquee player—a twenty-year CIA veteran from Athens, Georgia, with a syrupy drawl, a long history in the clandestine service, and a master's degree in international public policy from Johns Hopkins. He headed up the CIA's Afghan campaign from Langley.

The President and Vice President assumed their usual positions—Bush on the wing chair near the fireplace; Cheney in the one next to him. Crumpton crouched on the floor between the wing chairs. His father was a surveyor and topographer, and Crumpton—a map aficionado—created a new, detailed offering for each briefing, renderings of battle sites and landscape, names of key actors, and arrows to show where the action is likely to head next.

Bush and Cheney leaned forward, hovering, each, over Crumpton's shoulders as he explained "the most important engagement thus far"—the battle, a few days before, at Tarin Kowt, seventy miles north of Kandahar. Crumpton talked about how a local politician, Hamid Karzai, had infiltrated enemy lines and directed fifty tribesmen, assisted by eleven U.S. Special Forces soldiers and well-timed air support, into defeating 700 Taliban fighters. Bush was impressed. "Tell me more about what this Karzai did," he said.

Crumpton did, describing Karzai—a Pashtun who could unite the country's north and south—as "the linchpin" of both military and nation-building efforts.

But, a few days later, at the end of November, Crumpton, back with another map, showed Bush how the campaign's prime goal—to capture bin Laden—was in jeopardy.

With Cheney looking on, Crumpton—relying on detailed, urgent reports from CIA teams in Afghanistan—showed the President the terrain around Tora Bora, where bin Laden and about a thousand fighters had settled.

He laid out the array of problems. The White Mountains, where the caves were located, were filled with tunnels and escape routes, Crumpton said. Bush asked about the passage to Pakistan. Musharraf had assured the administration, in a deal that involved U.S. aid of nearly a billion dollars, that his troops would seal off the passages into Pakistan, the most logical escape route. Crumpton, using his map, showed how the border between the two countries was misleading, that the area on the Pakistani side of the line was a lawless, tribal region that Musharraf had little control over. In any event, satellite images showed that Musharraf's promised troops hadn't arrived, and seemed unlikely to appear soon.

What's more, Crumpton added, the Afghan forces were "tired and cold and, many of them are far from home." They were battered from fighting in the south against Taliban forces, and "they're just not invested in getting bin Laden."

A few days before, on November 26, a force of about 1,200 marines—by far the largest U.S. force in the country—had settled around Kandahar, three hundred miles east of Tora Bora. Crumpton, in constant contact with the military's CENTCOM center in Tampa, Florida, had told General Tommy Franks over the past week of the concerns of the CIA's managing operatives in Afghanistan that "the back door was open." He strongly urged Franks to move the marines to the cave complex. Franks responded that the momentum of the

CIA's effort to chase and corner bin Laden could be lost waiting for the troops to arrive; and there was concern marines would be mired in the snowy mountains.

As Crumpton briefed the President—and it became clear that the Pentagon had not voiced the CIA's concerns to Bush—he pushed beyond his pay grade. He told Bush that "we're going to lose our prey if we're not careful," and strongly recommended the marines, or other troops in the region, get to Tora Bora immediately. Cheney said nothing.

Bush, seeming surprised, pressed him for more information. "How bad off are these Afghani forces, really? Are they up to the job?"

"Definitely not, Mr. President," Crumpton said. "Definitely not."

Thanksgiving was approaching, and Tenet felt his frustration growing about what was happening, or not happening, with the two Pakistani scientists. He told Mowatt-Larssen he wanted results, that he wanted the situation wrapped up "in a few days."

"This is an emergency situation," he said. "Why can't we get our arms around it?"

More information, bit by bit, had been collected on Mahmood and UTN, though the Pakistanis were of only modest help. Mahmood and Majid were in custody and then, suddenly, freed, then reapprehended. Their families and friendly Pakistani professionals pushed for their release. Mahmood claimed physical infirmity. So they came in for questioning with government officials and returned home to their families for the evening. Not surprisingly, they revealed nothing. Tenet felt it was time to call upon the collected forces of America's IC, or intelligence community: time to get the word out.

He summoned principals from the intelligence community to his conference room for an emergency meeting. The attendees included Bob Mueller, director of the Federal Bureau of Investigation; representatives of the Defense Intelligence Agency; and Lieutenant General

Mike Hayden, head of the National Security Agency, America's eaves-dropping network, a global web as thick as a layer of atmosphere.

"The nightmare is here," Tenet told them. He described the meet-ing around the campfire, and the participants. Everyone could connect the dots. He told them the intelligence was evolving—the outlines were clear—but everyone needed to help find puzzle pieces and fit them together.

The men were grim. It was decided that each agency would lend key players to a joint operations group headed by Mowatt-Larssen—a task force that would convene the next day. Mike Hayden said he'd gather all pertinent signals intelligence over the last ten years—sigint about uranium and plutonium transfers, theft or loss of bomb-building materials, and the known, and suspected, intentions of vari-ous terrorist groups—and have it ready by morning. He'd also send over a team of analysts.

Bob Mueller, a former U.S. Attorney who had been director of the FBI for just a month, arriving a week before 9/11, sat glassy-eyed. He had a job that was utterly untenable. Find any terrorists who might be on American soil. Protect the homeland—whatever that meant—and understand the enemy well enough to predict their next move. He was having trouble, like so many people at that point, just keeping the names of the nineteen hijackers straight.

"George, how much does one of these things weigh?" he asked.

Tenet, who had already consulted some leading nuclear scientists about the array of possible devices—simple versions of what someone could do with a softball of plutonium—did his best to answer.

"I mean, how big, or small, could it be?" Mueller persisted.

"How might you transport it?" The questions kept coming.

After a perplexed moment, everyone realized what the FBI direc-tor, learning on the fly, was doing. He wanted to tell his army of agents *what to look for.*

The hard fact was none of them really knew.

* * *

Vice President Cheney and Condoleezza Rice were already in the Situation Room on a late-November day, speaking quietly, as Tenet and a briefer spilled into the mahogany chamber.

That was Tenet's style—forward, emotionally urgent. Condi looked up, impatiently. George and she were an impossible fit— a tough-talking New Yorker, polished presentably by Georgetown University Jesuits and years of political seasoning; and a fierce academy-bred achiever, alone at forty-six, bemused and appraising, cool, and sealed each morning in a snug Oscar de la Renta.

"All right, let's get started," she said. "I know we have a lot to talk about."

Tenet nodded. Cheney and Rice had been getting regular reports on the deepening investigation of Mahmood, his deputy Majid, and UTN, the organization Mahmood helped found. Now it was time to lay out all the findings—the emerging threat—for the Vice President. It was clear to Tenet that, at this point, Cheney was in charge of much of the administration's foreign policy. He would clearly be in charge of this most critical area: WMD.

"Mr. Vice President, this is the thing we all feared the most," Tenet said. "This changes everything."

He listed the particulars: this meeting around the campfire might offer a glimpse into the dreaded "second wave," which everyone in the know was losing sleep over. UTN has tentacles in Afghanistan, Pakistan, and Saudi Arabia. The Libyan disclosure was particularly troubling. How many other nations had received UTN's offer? Cheney sat for a moment, saying nothing. "We have to deal with this new type of threat in a way we haven't yet defined," he said, almost to himself. "With a low-probability, high-impact event like this . . . I'm frankly not sure how we engage. We're going to have to look at it in a completely different way."

Tenet cued his briefer, who went into the specifics of the group of Pakistani elites that supported Mahmood. The Pakistanis had now called in six members of UTN for questioning. It was a group with diverse skills. Mahmood's field was enriching uranium. At least one other member was an engineer, with expertise in bomb design and manufacture. But the suspects were handled casually, respectfully, and questioning was yielding little. The Pakistanis had even attempted polygraph tests. The tests were administered imperfectly; the results showed deception. Cheney listened intently, hard-eyed, clamped down tight. When the briefing finished, he said nothing for a moment. And then, he was ready with his "different way."

"If there's a one percent chance that Pakistani scientists are helping al Qaeda build or develop a nuclear weapon, we have to treat it as a certainty in terms of our response," Cheney said. He paused to assess his declaration. "It's not about our analysis, or finding a preponderance of evidence," he added. "It's about our response."

So, now spoken, it stood: a standard of action that would frame events and responses from the administration for years to come. The Cheney Doctrine. Even if there's just a one percent chance of the unimaginable coming due, act as if it is a certainty. It's not about "our analysis," as Cheney said. It's about "our response." This doctrine— the one percent solution—divided what had largely been indivisible in the conduct of American foreign policy: analysis and action. Justified or not, fact-based or not, "our response" is what matters. As to "evidence," the bar was set so low that the word itself almost didn't apply. If there was even a one percent chance of terrorists getting a weapon of mass destruction—and there has been a small probability of such an occurrence for some time—the United States must now act as if it were a certainty. This was a mandate of extraordinary breadth. Everyone sat for a moment, rolling it over in their minds, sketching the implications.

Cheney broke the silence, moved to specifics. "Can we trust the Pakistanis to come clean on this?" he asked. The scientists had been arrested, released, put under house arrest, and kept in a kind of loose abeyance. Mahmood's family had claimed he was sick, and others— including key members of Pakistan's ruling elites—had pressed President Musharraf to leave the old scientist be.

"No, not really," Tenet said. "Despite our pressure, it's still a fluid situation." Everyone agreed on that.

"George, you're going to have to go," Condi said, and smiled sympathetically. "Sorry. There's no second option."

Then it was all but over. Tenet would start, immediately, making preparations.

"You'll represent the President," Cheney said, looking gravely at Tenet. "Your words will be his."

The primary directive guiding policy from September 12 onward was to find the terrorists, wherever they might be, and stop them. It prompted the military strike into Afghanistan—al Qaeda's refuge—and the action plans of the broadened, unleashed CIA in eighty countries. It was the impetus behind the USA Patriot Act, extending the government's legal powers across America; behind the Treasury's campaign to squeeze institutions for what had been proprietary financial data to be used as a kind of "monetary intelligence," or *finint;* and behind the FBI's frantic actions to round up anyone suspicious . . . and ask questions later. The problem of *find them* preceding *stop them* pushed everyone into the intelligence business.

But a further expansion of the American mission was at hand. With revelations about bin Laden and his Kandahar campfire, the government's action plan was rapidly widening to officially include an old standby: disarmament.

Every U.S. administration since World War II had fretted over the spread of weapons of mounting destructiveness. The fear prodded the United States, and other nations, to give up a measure of sovereignty to international agreements, a series of them, and to divide into counterbalancing coalitions: NATO and the Warsaw Pact. The concept of mutually assured destruction had long locked America and the Soviets into a dance of conflict and, at day's end, constraint.

That bipolar balance—and the way it enforced order among

nation-states on all sides—was all but gone by 2001. Nothing had risen to replace it. States still mattered, of course, but, small, medium, and large, they were beginning to act across disparate regions of the globe in a loosened, entrepreneurial fashion, testing boundaries.

In large measure, the U.S. policy makers felt similarly unbound at the start of 2001. In its early months the Bush presidency departed from America's long-standing credo of muscular internationalism—of leading the community of nations primarily by relying on persuasion rather than force. A new mission had been born in neoconservative think tanks and in the pronouncements of Cheney, Rumsfeld, Wolfowitz, Feith, Perle, and others during the 1990s, as they pined in exile. The idea, simply stated, was to be unashamed, and unfettered, in the use of power, now that America finally stood alone as the world's only superpower. Global accords on everything from greenhouse gases to international courts, many of which had long ago been designed and encouraged by the United States, now were seen as constraints, the threads binding Gulliver. Such agreements were for lesser countries. They were to be shaken off—which was what happened in early 2001 when the Bush administration took over.

But what would an unbound Gulliver do? In a memo sent to NSC principals during the first week of the administration, Rumsfeld did his best to characterize what the mighty America now faced. Under the heading "National Security Policy Issues—Post Cold War Threats," he wrote: "The post Cold-War liberalization of trade in advanced technology goods and services has made it possible for the poorest nations on earth to rapidly acquire the most destructive military technology ever devised, including nuclear, chemical and biological weapons and their means of delivery. We cannot prevent them from doing so." Six pages later, after noting how competitors like "China, Russia, Iran, Iraq, North Korea or others are investing" in such destructive capabilities, Rumsfeld wrote how we must devise strategies to "dissuade nations abroad from challenging" America. The focus, in those days, was largely on state-based threats.

September 11, 2001, would herald the arrival of the nonstate actor. The only thing that was sudden was his destructive debut, the moment of shared recognition. The nonstate, or transnational, actor had been waiting impatiently in the wings. The primacy of states and borders had been eroding steadily for decades, and more swiftly after the bipolar U.S.-Soviet structure gave way. The new transnationalists, like bin Laden and Zawahiri, said, in essence, that state-based power was illusory, or at least overstated. The duo had operated within countries and between them, recruiting thousands of jihadists, training them, and organizing them into a flexible, global network. They had inflicted damage on the American mainland that no hostile state had dared. They were carrying forward destabilizing ideas to a worldwide constituency. Their point was that the march of globalization meant that borders didn't matter, and states even less so.

Though governments still possessed almost all of the world's destructive weapons—and the ability, in general, to make decisions as to who would live, and how, in the lands they controlled—the evidence about bin Laden and the Pakistani scientists now ignited U.S. urgency on the long-standing issue of disarmament. The conventional idea that even a rogue state wouldn't be suicidal enough to use a weapon of mass destruction on the United States or its allies now seemed moot. A rogue state might slip a nightmare weapon, or a few pounds of enriched uranium, to a nonstate actor—*a transnat*—if it could be assured that the weapon's country of origin was undiscoverable. And why not? Let the terrorist do the dirty work that some secret sponsor would never do on its own, but maybe had dreamed of: *Bring America to its knees.* Cheney's response: If there was even a one percent chance of such an act occurring, we must act as if it's a certainty.

So, while attacking the terrorist haven in Afghanistan, and looking to find and destroy the enemy wherever he may be, a companion idea swiftly took hold: the rogue state was even more dangerous, now that a new silent partner had been found.

Who, after all, might bin Laden, or his imitators, meet with next around the campfire?

* * *

The blue Air Force 707 flew like a crazed crop duster into Islamabad on the morning of December 1.

On board, Tenet, Mowatt-Larssen, and a chief analyst for WMD, all of them clutching their seats, Tenet whooping.

The undercover analyst, Leon, had for the past five years been slowly building a CIA specialty shop in CBRN—chemical, biological, radiological, nuclear. He'd produced glossy booklets on various threats and the delivery systems, how to detect them, what to do to neutralize them. He was a studious desk jockey, an expert on issues that had until now been largely theoretical.

Meanwhile, there was cause for panic among a small group of Pakistan's security forces, with American dignitaries, in an official U.S. plane, arriving on only one day's notice. They were flying into dangerous territory. U.S. troops were in Afghanistan. The battle was raging on Pakistan's border. There were riots in Karachi. Islamist radicals, some with black market Stingers, could be waiting. Musharraf was told to alert almost no one about the meeting, not even close aides. The plane swerved, then dipped into a nosedive toward Islamabad Airport.

Tenet slipped into what looked like a security van. Mowatt-Larssen was placed in the lead car—the limo—as decoy, and the motorcade swerved through Islamabad, past monuments to the great victory of building a nuclear bomb, an event that marks the nation's ascent into the first rung of world powers, equal, now, of the hated India, and the first nuclear power among the Muslim nations of South Asia. In a country that lives on six dollars a day, this was a point of pride.

The motorcade passed the U.S. Embassy, picked up the ambassador—Wendy Chamberlin—and proceeded to the palace. President Musharraf, in his khaki general's uniform, met the delegation outside, led them up the marble staircase to his chambers. A slight, precise man—slender, maybe five foot eight—he is standing testimony to the principle that size doesn't matter in affairs of state. Nor does volume.

He is quiet, but always appraising, with a gentle laugh—all of it conveniently misleading. Musharraf came into power in 1999 in a military coup and had governed since with ruthless efficiency. His power comes from knowing things first, and then acting swiftly, often harshly.

He passed out silver boxes to his guests, each containing a business card—*Pervez Musharraf, President of Pakistan*—and they alighted on a settee and clustered chairs. A silver tea service arrived, cups were poured, and everyone nodded affably.

On the plane, the trio had worked over final lists of demands—things that Musharraf would have to do. First, of course, would be presentation of the bad news. The guiding principles, as the Air Force jet dove toward Islamabad, came from Tenet: "There is no cultural nuance here. There are things he must do. We don't care what Musharraf thinks."

But, of course, they did. Deeply. Tenet placed his cup on the table and gathered himself. This is what he does as well as anyone in the U.S. government: ingest a long list of tactics and goals, and then metabolize it. On cue, all of it emerges in noise, and motion, and sweat. He makes it all very personal.

"We have trouble, big trouble—trouble for you, trouble for us," he started, and laid out the campfire story, by now well practiced. The intentions of those involved. The capabilities. The threat . . . to everything and everyone. "Al Qaeda has said for years that they want a nuclear device. Now it is within reach. That is an unacceptable situation for the United States. Intolerable."

Musharraf took in every word, didn't budge, no expression.

Then he spoke. "This is not possible, Mr. Tenet. It took Pakistan many years and a great deal of money to produce the devices we have. What you are talking about—al Qaeda producing a bomb—is implausible."

"If it was implausible, the President wouldn't have sent me here," Tenet said.

"My key adviser on these matters has discussed such things with me—about whether terrorists can create a device—and he tells me it is not a threat."

That "adviser," of course, is A. Q. Khan, who was being tracked and tapped for the past two years by an entire CIA team. Tenet knows the adviser is Khan. Musharraf may assume Tenet knows this, but may not know what the CIA, at this point, knows: that A. Q. Khan runs a global business that sells nuclear technology to states hostile to America.

Tenet turned to Mowatt-Larssen. They'd expected this resistance. Musharraf needed to be educated about the latest thinking. On the plane, they had called this part "Hit him with the two-by-four."

Rolf described the current state of availability, by theft or on the black market, of enriched uranium, or plutonium, and the latest designs for small, portable bombs, bombs of various sizes, shapes, and firepower. Musharraf listened, intently, until after a few minutes his posture became less defensive.

"What about other states that might have bomb materials, unsecured materials, which the terrorist could get?" he asked—a key sign that'd he accepted the premises.

Tenet took over, again, to test a new set of propositions that now guided U.S. policy.

"It is increasingly a matter of intent that we need to be concerned with. If a group, or state for that matter, *wants* to build a nuclear weapon," Tenet said, "the President feels we need to act."

The underlying question is, what could a sovereign nation, and its dictator, be convinced to do on behalf of the United States, especially in a country with strong anti-American sentiments—sentiments that were being stoked by what the United States felt it must do in combating Islamic terrorists? It was the post-9/11 question—one with built-in contradictions for an administration that embraced, from inception, the idea that international agreements like the Kyoto Protocol tied the hands of the world's only remaining superpower. Power was useless if left unused, the thinking went. The United States, the President said, "must be a force for good." Americans focused on "good." Much of the world focused on "force," on being handled.

Tenet began to list the things America needed, starting with the immediate, official arrest of both men. No more catch and release. The United States would need to be involved in the interrogation of both men, and would supervise polygraph tests. Mursharraf reluctantly agreed, but said no one must find any of that out.

Among the supporters of Mahmood was a prominent Pakistani politician whom Musharraf knew well. Tenet also wanted him arrested. Musharraf balked. "If you have evidence on him, let me see it. Otherwise, I cannot do this."

Some demarcations were immediately visible. Musharraf could help—he would arrest the scientists, and keep them in custody. But he couldn't afford to do much if it was seen as at the behest of the United States—that would leave him vulnerable domestically. These lines would define many such encounters, with many countries, across the region in the coming years.

Everyone rose. Tenet left a packet with the list of demands, including the major ones the Pakistani just agreed to. He and Musharraf clasped hands.

"The President needs to be assured you will not let your country's scientists act on behalf of bin Laden."

"You have my assurance."

Top officials of CIA and FBI settled in the Vice President's office. Condoleezza Rice joined them. It was mid-December. The Vice President looked particularly agitated. For the past few weeks, he'd been overseeing all the key events in regard to the Pakistani nuclear threat, the disaster scenario made real. The Pakistani nuclear scientists were imprisoned and being interrogated. The pressure on Musharraf—making him directly accountable—seemed to be working, as the Pakistani president cracked down on UTN and its supporters. The organization was under attack and many of its members were now in prison. What's more, the polygraph testing was now being headed by an American, one of the leading experts in the practice, and bearing fruit. When hooked to the polygraph, a now-incarcerated Mahmood gave up key details.

Around the August campfire, he and Majid had talked to bin Laden and Zawahiri about the global struggle against imperialists and crusaders, of how they are all guided by the will of Allah, how the coming months would be days of great change and excitement.

Then they talked about nuclear logistics. Mahmood drew diagrams of various nuclear bomb designs, simply structured, transportable, and effective. Bin Laden and Zawahiri pressed him with "how to" questions. Mahmood went into a lengthy discussion of how to enrich uranium, his forte, by constructing a complex cascade of high-speed centrifuges that turn raw uranium into gas, and then an enriched form. It would cost hundreds of millions, he told bin Laden, beyond what most countries, and any terrorist network, could manage.

Mahmood told interrogators that bin Laden, unfazed, stopped him. "What if you already have the enriched uranium?"

Was it a question, or a statement? That was not clear. Either way, the clarification of these specifics fueled Cheney's darkest fears. But today's meeting would add a new thread of nightmare intelligence: *anthrax.*

The age-old killer had been formally introduced to the American psyche two months before. On September 18, four letters containing anthrax were mailed to NBC, the *New York Post,* and other news organizations. Letters to Democratic senators Tom Daschle and Patrick Leahy were mailed on October 9. The words "Death to America, Death to Israel, Allah is Great" were written on a note in two letters to the U.S. Senate. The nation—just a few weeks after 9/11—was stunned. Five people died, twenty-three others were infected; the Senate office buildings were shut down on October 17, after thirty-one congressional staffers tested positive for exposure. While al Qaeda was initially suspected, by mid-November, FBI investigators were pointing toward a domestic source. They thought the culprit might be a disgruntled scientist with anthrax experience, but they had nothing definitive.

As the FBI searched, records from an al Qaeda camp in Durunda, Afghanistan, were being shipped to Langley. The camp had been bombed by the U.S. military in November. Documents found in the rubble sat for a few weeks until a CIA analyst in Leon's division, a woman with particular expertise in biological agents, happened across something that startled her. The documents were plans for a biological-processing facility. There were detailed manuals pertaining to the handling of a variety of biological agents. The special focus was on anthrax. Zawahiri, the documents indicated, was heading up the bio program himself, joined by Mohammed Atef, al Qaeda's military commander and the key allocator of resources. Though it was not clear whether or not they had yet obtained or manufactured anthrax, the al Qaeda program was well along.

When Cheney was briefed on the matter, he immediately called today's meeting of FBI, hitting dead ends with its investigations, and CIA, now identifying an indisputable foreign threat.

As one participant recalled, "It was one of the toughest, no-bullshit meetings I've ever attended."

The years weighed on Cheney—the frustrations with analysts offering their balanced assessments, their caveats and disclaimers, the wearying decades of intramural combat inside the federal behemoth. The one percent rule freed him from that. It was all about identifying a probable enemy, a suspect—and getting to that enemy before it got to us. If, in fact, the anthrax letters were born of plans and possibly materials in Afghanistan, it would mean that the enemy—an al Qaeda bio-attack team—was currently operating in the United States.

"I'll be very blunt," the Vice President started. "There is no priority of this government more important than finding out if there is a link between what's happened here and what we've found over there with al Qaeda." He stopped. "I need to know everything each of you know—and I need to know it now."

The FBI team made its offering. CIA followed.

Then Cheney and Rice fired questions at both. How do we know that? What are you planning next? Who are we after?

It wasn't about evidence—that was for the slow-footed, for lawyers building cases. This was about action. The one percent rule had found its next application. First there was al Qaeda in league with nuclear scientists. Now Zawahiri was heading up a bioweapons program, at the same time the country was in an anthrax panic. Cheney wanted targets. "Who do we hit first?" he asked CIA.

They knew only so much. The answers started to be: "I'll get right on it." There was much work to do.

Cheney then looked hard-eyed at both, natural, institutional enemies. He turned to FBI. "You see any foreign connections whatsoever in your investigation, you have to share it with those guys down the river. Are we clear!" The FBI officials nodded, knowing not to speak.

He turned to CIA. "You guys down the river. If you can help the bureau in any way, you better do it—and not just the minimum. You cross all the lines. You tell them everything. Make sure nothing's left out."

He got up—meeting's over—and looked at both groups with disdain. "You guys don't cooperate for shit. Well, I'll be damned if that's going to happen here."

George W. Bush was sitting in the Oval Office receiving reports on progress throughout much of each day. He was now, as he often liked to say, "a wartime president." Whether he had changed after 9/11, or had simply discovered qualities that had lain dormant, he had surely found his métier. Bush had long been comfortable making quick decisions without the luxury of precedent or detailed study and investigation. In his first nine months, this had prompted concerns among some senior staff in the White House, members of the cabinet, and seasoned hands in Congress—*was he reading the materials, was he thinking things through?* Now, a staccato rhythm of swift decisions seemed to be the thing needed. There was no precedent to what had been done to America and what the country now faced, and that was liberating. The moment demanded improvisation, a demand that freed Bush. Left unfettered, and unchallenged, were his instincts, his "gut," as he often says, and an unwieldy aggressiveness that he'd long been cautioned to contain.

Other top officials soon learned what Tenet knew when he called in Cofer Black. Military or intelligence advisers who'd killed men—the more visceral, the better—knew that tales of combat would be readily received by a leader who was most focused, always, when he could make things *personal.* Tactile. Visceral. The President himself designed a chart: the faces of the top al Qaeda leaders with short bios stared out. As a kill or capture was confirmed, he drew an "X" over the face. "Making progress," he'd joke, ruefully.

On that score, he'd had a particularly glorious Presidential Daily Briefing in early December. An Afghan military chief told CIA operatives that Zawahiri had likely been killed in an air attack near the eastern city of Jalalabad.

Tenet excitedly made the report to Bush at the morning briefing. Bush grabbed a lead pencil with the presidential seal, marked an "X" across the wide, meaty, bespectacled face of the Egyptian, a man whose importance to the Islamic jihad movement all but matched that of bin Laden. There was rejoicing in the Oval Office.

By that time, bin Laden was settling in the high-altitude labyrinth of Tora Bora, one that CIA knew well from the 1980s, when it had supported mujahedeen fighters, and bin Laden himself, in their battle with the Soviets.

The B-52s had started saturation bombing in late November— shaking the hills with massive, 15,000-pound "daisy cutters," the world's largest conventional bombs, which create a mist of ammonium nitrate and aluminum that ignites and incinerates everything within a radius of 600 yards. But the key, as with much of the Afghan campaign, would not be just force, but targeting. A team of four CIA operatives, supported by a dozen Afghan tribesmen, scaled the mountains in darkness and set up an observation post overlooking the cave complex. It was an extraordinarily risky maneuver. From that vantage, they could not be seen—detection would have meant swift and certain death—but could see everything. They opened communication with the base camp, and transmitted key coordinates to U.S. bombers. The bombs began to devastate bin Laden and his forces. The team started monitoring close-in communications between bin Laden and his commanders, which they transmitted to translators at the base camp. This was precisely the moment the United States had pressed inexorably toward. Three months after he had left New York and Washington in flames, a desperate bin Laden was finally cornered.

As the moment of glory approached, however, concern grew at Langley. More appeals came from CIA to send forces to surround the caves—about a 15-square-mile area. A fierce debate was raging inside the upper reaches of the U.S. government. The White House had received a guarantee from Musharraf in November that the Pakistani army would cover the southern pass from the caves. Bush, Cheney, and Rumsfeld felt the Pakistani leader's assurance was sound. It was, in fact, a key strategic bequest—a contribution from the so-called "policy level"—to the broader campaign.

Classified CIA reports passed to Bush in his morning briefings of early December, however, warned that "the back door is open" and that a bare few Pakistani army units were visible gathering near the Pakistani border. None had crossed into Afghanistan, a fierce tribal area Pakistan had always been reluctant to enter. Musharraf, when pressed by the White House, said troop movements were slow, but not to worry—they were on their way.

On December 15, bin Laden got on his shortwave radio. He praised his "most loyal fighters"—about 800 strong, at that point, tucked throughout the complex of caves—and said "forgive me" for drawing them into a defeat. He said the battle against the "crusaders" would continue "on new fronts." Then, he led them in a prayer, and slipped away.

With a small band, he escaped on horseback toward the north. The group, according to internal CIA reports, took a northerly route to the province of Nangarhar—past the Khyber Pass, and the city of Jalalabad—and into the province of Konar.

That day and the next, much of the remaining al Qaeda force of about 800 soldiers moved to the south toward Pakistan.

Now, as Christmas approached, more bad news was coming. Zawahiri was most likely alive as well, even though his wife and children had died in the bombing around December 1.

Tenet delivered the bad news. "We'll keep looking, Mr. President," he said. "That I can assure you."

"Hate to do this," Bush said, as he took an eraser from his desk and rubbed it across the "X," uncovering Zawahiri's face. Again, he and the doctor were eye-to-eye, while, in the next box, Osama bin Laden looked on with his feline smile.

Three months after 9/11, 250 al Qaeda soldiers had been killed or captured, while another 800 had escaped and largely disbanded, including almost all of al Qaeda's senior management and Mullah Mohammed Omar, the one-eyed leader of the Taliban regime.

By mid-January 2002, a few hundred captives deemed to be the most valuable were transported to Camp X-ray, a makeshift prison at Guantánamo Bay, Cuba. It would be managed by the Pentagon—which had, against its will, met CIA in the middle. The U.S. military would be responsible for handling the general array of Afghan captives. CIA would be responsible for highest-value captives, who might provide the most valuable "yield" during interrogation.

Of course, at this point there was only one of them—al-Libi. And FBI fought CIA over what to do with him. The FBI sent agents to Afghanistan with experience in interrogating al Qaeda members linked to the 1993 World Trade Center bombing, a process of surprising suspects, who were prepared for barbaric treatment from infidel captors, with favors in exchange for information. It had been a suc-

cessful method: productive relationships were developed. The CIA—
under pressure from the White House for immediate, actionable
information—claimed there wasn't time for such a measured approach. The debate went up to Mueller and Tenet, and Tenet—
appealing directly to Bush and Cheney—prevailed. Al-Libi was
bound and blindfolded for a trip to Cairo, where he'd be handed over
to Omar Suleiman, Egypt's intelligence chief and a friend of Tenet's.
On the tarmac in Afghanistan, an FBI agent would recall years later to
Newsweek, "the CIA case officer goes up to him and says, 'You're going
to Cairo, you know. Before you get there I'm going to find your
mother and I'm going to f— her.' So we lost that fight." The victory
for CIA meant that the Egyptians—with their command of the language, knowledge of al Qaeda, and brutal inclinations—would fill the
void of a U.S. interrogation policy that was still in formation. The CIA
would get oversight positioning, be able to offer questions and receive
regular reports of disclosures and progress.

Ben Bonk met in London in January with Musa Kousa, a meeting
again brokered by Prince Bandar at his house overlooking Regent's
Park. Bonk had with him a picture of al-Libi.

"That's him," Kousa said. "You've got the right man."

At this point, American intelligence about al Qaeda—the nature of
the organization and its activities—was still in the early stages. In a battle in which virtually every suspect carried several names, and moved
easily and often between countries with porous borders, positive IDs
were elusive. We didn't know who they were, or where.

All of this remained largely invisible to the American public, which
was focused on what it could see, on what could be measured. There
were few U.S. casualties. While whispered regrets surfaced inside the
government that Donald Rumsfeld and General Tommy Franks had
not ordered American troops to block off various escape routes from
Tora Bora, the public was overwhelmed by images, powerful ones, of
the Stars and Stripes flying in Kabul and Kandahar, which satisfied a
profound longing. It's hard to recall when America wanted a victory so
much.

To many in the intelligence and military communities, however, it was clearly the end of the beginning. The forced marriage between CIA and the Department of Defense—CIA side by side with Special Forces, intelligence matched with force—was now largely complete, and everyone returned to their buildings.

Rumsfeld told a group of senior Pentagon aides, "I never again want our army to arrive somewhere and meet the CIA on the ground." To a gathering of top generals in "the tank," the Joint Chiefs' secure conference room, he was even more succinct: "Every CIA success," he told them, "is a DoD failure."

The "war on terror?" Again, definition by default. It wasn't a war in Afghanistan—at least not for long. We'd flushed al Qaeda from its haven, a positive outcome, but already visible as prologue.

"We knew they'd scatter to Pakistan, or Iran, or Somalia, or Sudan, or Syria, or Yemen. They might go to Indonesia. We just had to then isolate where they might be going, as a first step," said Deputy Director McLaughlin, looking back. "Once they dispersed, that was really the start of the "war on terror" as we know it. A war that we were just then learning how to fight—and the one we're still fighting."

George W. Bush was ready to fight a different war.

On January 29, the President stepped to the podium before the U.S. Congress, the nation, the world, as the most powerful man in modern times.

He stood atop an Imperial America—the world's sole, if reluctant, claimant to empire—with an approval rating, measured in various polls, that hovered at an astonishing 90 percent.

The Afghan enterprise now stood upright, successfully cast in juxtaposition to the ruinous experience of America's fallen competitor, the Soviet Union. They'd spent their limited treasure and 15,000 lives fighting the CIA-supported mujahedeen, before retreating northward in humiliation. America did not make the mistake of embracing convention and sending its fighting vehicles and young warriors by the expected tens of thousands into treacherous rocky mountains. It had fought an intelligent war, if maybe a bit too clever. Two goals had been achieved, at modest cost. Al Qaeda, "the Base," had been forcefully ousted from its base. The regime that harbored it had collapsed, its leaders fleeing for the hills to join the geopolitical underclass of "guerrilla."

Karl Rove—the President's alter ego and strategic subconscious—told political operatives at a Republican National Committee meeting in Austin in mid-January that the historic public affirmation of Bush's handling, thus far, of the "war on terror" would surely translate into equally historic gains in the 2002 midterm elections. "We can go to the country on this issue," Rove said, "because [the voters] trust the Republican Party to do a better job of protecting and strengthening America's military might and thereby protecting America."

The more important question—more important than any poll, then or since—was, what did the President actually know at that point? And how, precisely, was that knowledge sufficient to guide a variety of historic decisions?

Bush knew, based on classified CIA assessments, that catching many of the high-value targets would be a daunting challenge. Bin Laden had escaped from an area around Tora Bora of roughly 15 square miles, to a vast, lawless tribal region along the Pakistan-Afghanistan border that stretched for 40,000 square miles, the size of Kentucky. Other al Qaeda managers may have scattered to places, Tenet told Bush, like Iran or Syria, Yemen or Sudan, where the reach of the United States was limited. There were many faces untouched on the chart the President held in his hand each morning.

Bush also knew a great deal that the public had little idea about. That included the threat posed by a potential union of the Pakistan nuclear scientists—and their organization—and Osama bin Laden. That included the threat of al Qaeda having possibly housed a bioweapons manufacturing facility. He and Cheney felt those threats deeply, as well as the lack of any clear solution.

Meanwhile, a quiet, steady offensive within the administration had moved steadily forward. The neoconservative civilian leadership of the Pentagon had bided its time while the CIA and a small footprint of U.S. Special Forces had seemed to prove the lessons of "military transformation"—what a small, targeted, "smart" force could do, a test Donald Rumsfeld had long hoped to conduct himself.

Afghanistan was a prelude, in the view of those atop the Pentagon. Plans for the invasion of Iraq, officially begun in November, had already moved through several iterations.

There was no deliberation. The Cheney Doctrine had quietly prevailed. *It was not about analysis. It was about our reaction.* Brent Scowcroft was no longer welcomed in the White House. Colin Powell, of the Scowcroft school of realists, was being steadily marginalized. George H. W. Bush—the only man on earth with any relevant experience of what a president should know about sending the U.S. military into Iraq—was not consulted.

But no matter. The lessons the President had learned since the attacks were not ones that could be taught. Yes, all Americans had experienced the trauma of 9/11—but only one man had experienced it in the unique role of President, leader, protector. No one could ever really understand what that felt like—granting Bush an exclusive emotional domain. No one, except maybe Cheney. There were issues between the two men in the first nine months. Cheney was skilled; the President was just learning. In the spring of 2002, Bush asked Cheney to pull back a little at big meetings, to give the President more room to move, to take charge. Bush asked Cheney not to offer him advice in crowded rooms. Do that privately. Cheney did.

Now, things seemed easier. They worked more effectively together than they ever had before, a left hand and right, complementary, picking up each other's rhythm. While the President focused on tactics, on the personal, and looked, always, for a path to action, Cheney thought through the broad sweep of geopolitics, of global affairs.

And those theories would begin to redirect U.S. energies—fully now matching the prime, *find them, stop them* directive of the "war on terror" with a second track, an audacious alongside idea: the humbling and disarmament of rogue states.

The President, Cheney felt, needed to make his stand on behalf of the ancient and still prevailing world order. Old verities could yet be grafted to the altered landscape. States mattered. Terrorist organizations, it was decided, couldn't sustain themselves over long periods of time to do large-scale operations if they didn't have the support of states. There was a response to be found in the state-to-state dance of force and diplomacy, upon which American power was built over a century and still rested. The cease-and-desist sent to Afghanistan's Taliban regime had been executed, for all to see. If a state "harbored" terrorists, willingly, it could now predict the consequences and alter its behavior accordingly.

But it shouldn't stop there. The need to "dissuade nations"—as Rumsfeld liked to put it—from acting inappropriately had to be active, forceful, and consistent. It was now the policy of the United States.

As members of Congress sat down after welcoming the President with a standing ovation, George W. Bush fully articulated that policy and told them who should be most concerned about it:

"Iraq continues to flaunt its hostility toward America and to support terror. The Iraqi regime has plotted to develop anthrax, and nerve gas, and nuclear weapons for over a decade. This is a regime that has already used poison gas to murder thousands of its own citizens—leaving the bodies of mothers huddled over their dead children. This is a regime that agreed to international inspections—then kicked out the inspectors. This is a regime that has something to hide from the civilized world.

"States like these and their terrorist allies," he went on, "constitute an axis of evil, arming to threaten the peace of the world. By seeking weapons of mass destruction, these regimes pose a grave and growing danger. They could provide these arms to terrorists, giving them the means to match their hatred. They could attack our allies or attempt to blackmail the United States. In any of these cases, the price of indifference would be catastrophic."

A few top officials at the White House, CIA, FBI, Justice—and those with the highest-level security clearances—applauded as the

President spoke, knowing what was driving those words. It was not only 9/11, not only a campfire in Kandahar, not only a bioweapons lab in Afghanistan. It was also freedom, finally, from slow-footed, hedged, evidence-based analysis. There was certainly a one percent chance that such regimes might have weapons of mass destruction and might give them to terrorists. We, then, must act as if it's a certainty.

"We'll be deliberate, yet time is not on our side. . . . I will not stand by, as peril draws closer and closer. The United States of America will not permit the world's most dangerous regimes to threaten us with the world's most destructive weapons."

And then the President offered something beyond Cheney's portfolio, something more personal than the sweeping ideologies. In an evidence-free realm, he would draw his certainty from the deep well of faith. This was all him:

"Those of us who have lived through these challenging times have been changed by them. We've come to know truths that we will never question: evil is real, and it must be opposed." The crowd erupted.

"Beyond all differences of race or creed, we are one country, mourning together and facing danger together. Deep in the American character, there is honor, and it is stronger than cynicism. And many have discovered again that even in tragedy—especially in tragedy—God is near."

The most prescient—and insightful—reaction to the speech came from a man whose sourcing inside the White House was impeccable: the conservative columnist Charles Krauthammer.

"If there was a serious internal debate within the administration over what to do about Iraq, that debate is over," he wrote in *The Washington Post* a few days later. "The speech was just short of a declaration of war."

CHAPTER THREE

NECESSITY'S OFFSPRING

"Gentlemen, we are at war."

Tenet, naturally theatrical, knew when to pause, to let a line sink in.

While the President, the Vice President, and the Pentagon were preparing for the next stage—an invasion and occupation of Iraq—Tenet was getting down to the business of fully, and finally, fighting the "war on terror" as it was originally, fitfully defined. *Find them, stop them.*

The architecture was already clear. CIA would be offense. FBI would be defense. Justice would set the rules, some of which were meant to be broken. He would have to do some things that he'd rather not see on the front page of a newspaper. When, if, they appeared, he hoped he'd have a defendable position.

"This," Tenet continued, "is a challenge unlike any other we've faced. It is a challenge which redefines the way we work, the way we think, the way we act.

"It is a challenge which has cut deeply into my country's psyche."

Another pause.

"This is not a passing phenomenon. It is a challenge that will outlive everyone in this room."

Everyone in that room was an intelligence chief—an extraordinary collection of them, twenty or so—representing the world's "English-speaking peoples."

This designation of kinship, popularized by Winston Churchill in speeches designed to deepen an alliance with America as World War II approached, had for decades provided a cooperative context for a group of like-minded nations: the United States, Canada, Great Britain, Australia, and New Zealand.

Intelligence chiefs from these nations had assembled, irregularly and informally, for a few decades. Sometimes the DCI came. Often not. Tenet changed that when he assumed the post in 1997, taking over from John Deutch, who never had much taste for meetings like this. A firm rotation was developed. Everyone came, led by the vanguard of the American intelligence community.

This year, it was New Zealand's turn to host, and a procession of planes—unmarked Gulfstreams, mostly—alighted at Queenstown Airport on Sunday, March 10.

Everything, of course, was different at this meeting. The long-standing goal to cooperate and coordinate—to match the group's generally solid concert on sigint with the increased sharing of humint—would now be lifted to divine mission. Cooperation was now survival.

So, on Monday morning, the team that would fight the global "war on terror" settled in for a long day at the end of the earth: an inconspicuous stone house on the edge of a resort on an island with more sheep than people.

"We must work as one," Tenet said, once his opening was complete. "As for CIA, I can tell you this. There is nothing we won't do, nothing we won't try, and no country we won't deal with to achieve our goals—to stop the enemy. The shackles, my friends, have been taken off."

Then they dove in. Tenet and Pavitt with Lieutenant General Mike Hayden, head of NSA, guided the proceedings, offering updates, though much of the best news had already been passed, week by week, in regular array of cross-border communications—calls, cables, and secure packages.

Now everyone was in one room to talk it through, to hear of progress and plot the near future. Tenet told them that they felt they were closing in on a prize, an actual al Qaeda manager, Abu Zubaydah. That was the first order of business. Yes, they'd picked up some mid-sized lieutenants—like Ibn al-Sheikh al-Libi, who'd run the al Qaeda training camp in Khalden, Afghanistan. A couple of others—Abu Faisal and Abdul Aziz—were picked up in December, both mid-level al Qaeda players.

But just two weeks earlier, in late February, he told them, there had been a break. A Pajero jeep was stopped by militiamen at a checkpoint in Chapri, a town near the Afghan border. The town has an archway, passage to the Pakistani tribal frontier. The jeep carried some very tall women, three of them, wearing burkas, and four men. The group was arrested and sent off for interrogation in Kohat. The disguised men were unforthcoming, but the driver, who was Pakistani, was bribable. The passengers were bound for Faisalabad, Pakistan's teeming central mill town. The driver gave up the name of his Faisalabad contact, who soon enough was found and gave up the fact that Zubaydah was in town.

Pavitt said that CIA operatives, matched with Pakistani intelligence teams, were sweeping Faisalabad, and had narrowed the search to a dozen or so houses.

Everyone in the room knew of Zubaydah, a thirty-year-old Saudi-born Palestinian. He'd been ever present on sigint for nearly two years. His name was intoned by operatives at all levels, by new recruits, foot soldiers, and wannabes throughout South Asia and the Mideast. It wasn't always clear what Zubaydah was doing, or where he fit in the wider organization. Just that he seemed to connect people.

Sigint among these closest, English-speaking allies had, over the past fifty years, been tugged by goodwill and advancing technology into an ever-tightening weave. The system, called Echelon, developed during World War II to intercept radio communications, had grown with each step of the technological revolution. Largely managed out of Fort Meade by the NSA, with 38,000 employees worldwide, and by the British out of the Government Communications Headquarters (GCHQ) based near Cheltenham, England, the system catches an estimated 3 billion communications each day that are carried by radio, satellite, telephone, faxes, and e-mails. Automated computer analysis sorts the intercepts. It is essentially one system—with shared satellites, fiberoptic pipes, listening posts, and devices placed at telephone switching stations—that has firewalls built within it.

Even as technology has raced forward, the statutory framework of each country, among a family of almost identical democracies, has stood firm on rights of privacy. Essentially, that means there is a prohibition against any of the governments eavesdropping on its citizens without probable cause and a subpoena—the type that the United States would generally seek through the FISA Court. The long-standing concern with Echelon is that its primary purpose is to provide member countries with a capability to spy on foreigners and that the firewalls within the system—to prevent domestic spying—are a sort of honor system rendered in computer code. Nearly a trillion communications collected annually are searched, allocated, and stored on the basis of these complex codes. Leading computer engineers have trouble deciphering them.

At this meeting, Tenet described such constraints among "the shackles" that would, at the very least, be loosened, if not in practice discarded. What the new era demanded, he said, was creative partnerships. A country may not be able to tap the lines of its own citizens without legal authorization. But there's nothing to stop it from listening in on some other country's citizen, and then filing very thorough reports to that foreign citizen's government. Just as long as the report does not hand over the specific raw matter—the sigint dispatch of nouns and verbs—the letter of various privacy laws would stay intact.

Spirit of the law *be damned.* If necessity is the mother of invention, those in the room were now necessity's sons and daughters. "What this meant," said one foreign intelligence chief a bit later, "is that the privacy laws of the leading democracies would, essentially, be skirted. The idea was: This is war. This is what is demanded."

Around the room they went, realizing, each of them, that intelligence in this war was as important as a bullet in a gun or a plane that strafes. In the corner, FBI chief Bob Mueller watched silently, taking mental notes, trying not to think—as the discussion swirled—the way he had his whole life, like a prosecutor building a case. He already understood that the FBI would need to find some bridge between intelligence and law enforcement.

Mueller offered a brief "my focus is law enforcement, not intelligence" disclaimer to the group, and said little else. "I'm here as an observer," he added. He had already given ground to Tenet on the interrogation issue. Now he would look the other way on issues of the use, or misuse, of signals intelligence. His job in the "war on terror" was to *not do* certain things.

Lunch was served. People milled about in slacks and polo shirts, comrades in arms. Intelligence services, in any democracy, tend to be of modest size and conflicting profile. Secrets, and surveillance, are counterpoints to so many cherished freedoms, such as privacy, dissent, and government accountability. Over sandwiches, several participants discussed the oddity of working with countries like Pakistan—an authoritarian regime with a secret police force of significant size and vast latitude. Yet, in a way, one foreign intelligence chief told his American counterpart, "that could work to our advantage."

After lunch, Tenet picked up the thread. "We're going to have to work with others in a way we haven't before," he said, and then he ticked off "Egypt, Syria, Russia—very much Russia . . . China, Pakistan and Saudi Arabia and India."

Each country chimed in. The Brits were strong with Pakistan and Algeria. Australia had leverage with India and Indonesia. Who had relationships that were active and productive? How could all those relationships be shared?

"Risks are going to have to be taken," Tenet implored them. "These countries are our partners now, like it or not. We're going to have to shed old habits and old mind-sets."

Pavitt laid out the particulars—the progress on specific innovations since 9/11. Tens of millions had been spent, with hundreds of millions more expected, to establish Counter-Terrorist Intelligence Centers, or CTICs, in more than a dozen countries that were not generally considered all that friendly to the United States. It was a delicate dance, as a fragile trust with local intelligence officials was built, day by day, on grants of helicopters, eavesdropping equipment, and bulletproof vests, making local intelligence officials feel like princes. The CIA had already sent specialists to train local forces in Yemen and Morocco. "We're going to be working with intelligence agencies that are utterly unhesitant in what they will do to get captives to talk," said Pavitt.

One foreign intelligence chief interjected with a question: "How do we know what we should or shouldn't tell some of these foreign services? Especially ones we've traditionally had trouble trusting?"

"In most cases, tell them everything—because they already know more than you," said Tenet, his voice rising. "Without them, and their help, we have no fucking global effort. We'd be walking through the Arab world wide open and half blind. The key for us, at this point, is understanding that we don't know shit."

On March 17, a team of CIA operatives, joined by FBI agents, quietly slipped into Faisalabad: a town of more than 5 million, about twice the size of Chicago. But to most American eyes, it is an endless and indistinct urban sprawl, with each few blocks repeating a standard cluster—mosque, with attached school; row of shops, with adjacent dump; cluster of cement homes, next to tented slum and open sewer—that repeats itself a thousand times across the dusty plains of central Pakistan. The average income, roughly six dollars a day. The accepted religion, fierce Islamic orthodoxy.

The parents, like all parents, have dreams for their children and schemes to boost them to a better life; their prides-and-joys—ragged and smudged with clay dust—kick soccer balls, or collect artifacts to play house, and, like all kids, laugh more than they should.

An invisible electronic net was draped over this human array. It was localized in the northwest part of town. Thousands of phone calls a day were being monitored from a few selected neighborhoods. The methods for doing this, these days, are as varied as offerings in a Nokia catalog. There are the catchall sensors, attached to trunk lines and telephone switching systems, that sweep the 0s and 1s of digital communications for certain combinations of words; there are relentlessly generated algorithms from satellites and cell phone stations, that triangulate, in some cases from a satellite to Earth, using points of contact to show a caller's location. Then there are agents poised in front of this house or that with radar guns, like electronic vacuums, sucking in all emanations from what might be a "safe" house that is no longer safe. This river of noise is routed through translators in Pakistan and, in some cases, the United States, appraising ears whose job is to know a direct hit when they hear one.

The hit came toward month's end. Two calls to mysterious numbers in Afghanistan. Numbers that might or might not be linked to bin Laden or, if he was alive, Zawahiri, came from a particular house in Faisalabad.

On March 27, a group of agents from the CIA, FBI, and the Pakistani intelligence service, ISI, dressed in bulletproof vests, strode into the office of the Faisalabad police chief. They needed some of his officers for a few routine arrests for immigration violations. Operational secrecy, here, is difficult. The ISI and the Pakistani military are filled with al Qaeda and Taliban sympathizers. For this operation, only a handful, less than a dozen people, were apprised of the particulars, including Musharraf. Among the "illegal settlers" they'd be rounding up, one was of special interest, the police chief was told. The agents then passed out photos of the pleasant-looking, dark-haired young man, studious, with wire-rimmed glasses. This was Abu Zubaydah.

In the hours after midnight, the intelligence teams were joined by more than a hundred police officers, a small battalion that surrounded the Shabaz cottage, a three-story gray cement villa in a suburb of Faisalabad. Wiretaps and intercepted e-mails convinced agents that Zubaydah might be with a dozen others in this fortress—the house of a rich widow—which was surrounded by an eight-foot wall, topped with electrified barbed wire. Outside, behind a nearby house, CIA agents debated strategy with the local police chief: if the goal was to capture Zubaydah alive, should they surround the house and settle in for a siege, or storm it?

By 3 a.m., a decision was made. A Pakistani assault team clipped electrical wires, vaulted the walls, subdued three sleeping guards, and kicked open the front door. Zubaydah and three others grabbed Saudi passports, handfuls of cash, and ran up the stairway. Up on the roof, cornered, they took a running leap over the barbed wire and dropped 25 feet to the roof of a nearby villa. Police were waiting. A struggle ensued, with Zubaydah yelling at the Islamic officers: "You're not Muslims!"

"Of course we are," one of the policemen replied.

"Well, you're *American Muslims*!" Zubaydah spat.

That was the end of the talking. One of Zubaydah's deputies—a Syrian named Abu al-Hasnat—grabbed an AK-47 from one of the officers and began firing. Zubaydah was hit in the leg, stomach, and groin. Al-Hasnat was killed. Three officers were wounded. Through the night, twenty-five suspected al Qaeda operatives were swiftly rounded up in the neighborhood, about half of them from inside the Shabaz cottage.

By morning, with Zubaydah under guard at a nearby hospital, authorities were boxing up what they considered the most precious discovery of the night: a trove of computers, disks, notebooks, and phone books, about ten thousand pages in all. A loaded van then sped to the Faisalabad airport, where a U.S. Air Force plane waited to fly the riches back to Washington. A major capture, accomplished—*finally*.

All that was left to do was write the press releases.

★ ★ ★

"Come 'awn, ladies, we don't want to be late—it's not every day we get to go on a field trip."

Dan Coleman smiled at the ladies as they passed, twelve sisters in data input boarding a Bluebird bus, humming outside FBI headquarters in the predawn of a mid-April morning.

The women love Dan. Anyone would love him. He's a tough, fat man, with a high voice and gently appraising eyes, as good a pair as the FBI has. They'll flash from time to time, indignant Irish hazel, but only at higher-ups—foolish preening bosses, who look damn good but not much else.

Dan, fifty-two, is one of about two dozen or so public servants in the vast U.S. government who really know al Qaeda, and have for some time. CIA, surely, has a few; FBI has its share. Among all of them, Dan is in a category of one. He was the FBI's first case agent on Osama bin Laden in the mid-1990s and helped start the bureau's OBL unit. Inside FBI, Coleman is known as "the man who introduced Osama bin Laden to America."

Coleman worked all angles of the 1993 World Trade Center bombing and the prosecutions that flowed from it. He traveled far and wide to all the global hot spots. He worked the Islamic fundamentalist cells in Brooklyn and New Jersey, jihadists under the sway of Sheikh Omar Abdel Rahman, the blind sheikh, who was once a competitor to Zawahiri to lead the Egyptian Islamic Jihad. Instead, Rahman ended up in America, set up shop in Jersey City, and created havoc. Dan and the FBI guys in New York closed the net on this group with a sure and steady beat, working sources, making arrests, cutting deals when needed, and building evidence—bit by bit, then by the ton. That's what works in court, especially in a nation ruled by laws, not men. Patrick Fitzgerald, then a federal prosecutor out of New York, handled many of the prosecutions. The whole community—from Rahman on down—is now in jail. They're not going anywhere. As one of his jobs, Dan keeps in touch with various former al Qaeda informants—like Jamal al-Fadl, an up-and-coming Islamic terrorist who was caught, put under federal protection, and became the star informant of various prosecutions.

For Dan Coleman, knowledge of this long history is both a blessing and a burden. He can recite events, stretching back to the 1980s, when bin Laden was wooing Western patrons for support in fighting the Soviets in Afghanistan, and al-Zawahiri—captured in a sweep of Islamic radicals who were thought to be linked to the assassination of President Anwar Sadat—was being radicalized inside Egyptian torture chambers. With the string of attacks since the mid-nineties, with the embassy bombings in Kenya and Tanzania in 1998, the bombing of USS *Cole* in 2000, Coleman and a handful of U.S. agents watched the duo's organization grow in capability and confidence. They knew who they were up against.

To dwell on that, though—on all one has learned in the years prosecuting al Qaeda—affronts the emotions that surround the 9/11 attacks: the sensory shock, the newness of it. It supports the belief that it could have been prevented, the "what ifs" that no one wants to hear about.

What was wanted from Coleman in 2002 was to be there, at the ready, when someone from "on high" needed context and counsel. So Dan left his home in South Brunswick, New Jersey, a few weeks after 9/11 and moved to a one-bedroom rental across from FBI headquarters in the not so nice, slow-to-gentrify part of downtown Washington near Chinatown. He was on call twenty-four hours a day. Questions came from the White House, down the chain of command through Mueller and his deputies. Dan, though just a case agent—not a manager, or a guy with graduate degrees, with a twenty-dollar haircut and a trim blue suit—was a guy who had answers, something in short supply.

The Bluebird van rumbled across the Memorial Bridge on its way to Virginia, a stately bridge with golden statues—*Arts of War* on one side, *Arts of Peace* the other—that empties into the foothills beneath Arlington Cemetery. Dan called his wife, Maureen, even though it was early. Like married couples do, they talk about nothing, which is everything, and then about the kids. They have a bunch—three teenage boys, a daughter at Seton Hall, and their oldest, Danny, halfway around the world in Afghanistan, a U.S. Army Ranger. Seeing the rows of white grave markers as the Bluebird swung alongside Arlington made Dan think of how worried they are about Danny, and how they knew so little. "Look, Maureen," he said. "Hearing nothing is a good sign."

The van soon pulls onto the campus of the CIA and the women get out, a dozen African-American women looking this way and that. Several had worked as secretaries and data input specialists at FBI for more than twenty years, but none had ever visited the FBI's companion agency and arch rival in Langley.

The animosity and distrust between FBI and CIA has a long and impressive history—bespeaking differences, members of both agencies often quip, as great as between cats and dogs. Even in this analogy, both see what they want or need to see. FBI's riff: we're tough and earnest, loyal and true to task, while the CIA is fussy and feline, double-dealing and unreliable. Then there's CIA's counter: we're shrewd, intuitive, and sharp-clawed—moving alone, often quietly, but getting the job done—while the FBI is filled with dumb animals, built to fetch.

But now, both FBI and CIA agreed, was a time of special needs, demanding special measures. A lack of coordination between the two agencies was already, just six months after 9/11, being cited as among the key lapses that allowed the attack.

While the President was resisting calls to create a bipartisan investigatory commission of the type impaneled after Pearl Harbor and presidential assassinations, inside CIA and FBI internal investigations were well under way. The gaps were clear. The CIA didn't share the names of all suspected terrorists with the bureau. The FBI, geared toward prosecuting *committed* crimes rather than prospective ones, wouldn't have known what to do with the names had they been passed to the appropriate field offices.

Yet even if FBI and CIA were now ready to share everything—as they were ordered to do, day and night, by half the policy makers in Washington—there was a "process problem." The two agencies view information in starkly disparate ways: CIA drives to know what is knowable, and make educated guesses about what's not, and move on.

It does, no doubt, sometimes act on that information, with the recon-stituted CIA arguably the most action-oriented in modern history. But its role is still to advise the actors, the policy makers, from the President on down. FBI seeks the knowable as well, but always with an eye on the raison d'être for all collected information: arrest and prosecution.

That means each handles streams of information differently, fact by fact. CIA tends to sift quickly, panning for the gold of a telling insight, a key connection. The amount of information collected—if you fold in the National Security Agency; the National Reconnaissance Office, which handles overhead satellite recon; and the National Geospatial-Intelligence Agency, which aggregates the mapping, charting, and ge-odetic functions of eight separate organizations of the defense and intelligence communities—is simply beyond human scale. Sifting is necessity, a survival mechanism.

FBI comes from a different direction: it views information as, one hopes, evidence. It tries to frame an issue—a set of characters, a sus-pected crime—to guide the streams of fact. It creates vast, man-made lakes of evidence—evidence that must be assessed, categorized, and then organized into a form that can shine brightly someday in court.

Coleman is an oddity, an FBI guy who can sift as swiftly and artfully as the best CIA analyst—and then put what he finds into a format that the FBI can use, if need be, as evidence. In other words, intelligence meets prosecution in the head of a wisecracking fat guy with asthma from Jersey. To win the "war on terror" you need a few thousand Dan Colemans—organized in a loose horizontal structure, like Silicon Val-ley Internet geeks in 1996—ready to marry acuity and with ingenuity. Not likely.

Of course, the span of insight between Dan Coleman and an NSA search algorithm is almost unfathomable. Which is another part of the problem in a battle where information is weaponry—knowing what a nugget of gold *actually looks like.* It doesn't glitter on its own. FBI inves-tigators had been interviewing Coleman and others through the win-ter, seeking context on several key NSA dispatches that had been discovered in the days after 9/11. Most notable among them were calls

NSA had collected in 2000 from San Diego to a number in Yemen. The Yemen number was for the daughter of a man who, Coleman told investigators, "was the uncle of half the violent jihadists we knew of in the country." This was the number—so familiar to Coleman from his work prosecuting al Qaeda that he knew it by heart—the 9/11 hijacker Khalid al-Mihdhar had called while he hid out in San Diego. In fact, Coleman and other FBI al Qaeda specialists had even placed an order with the NSA back in 1998—that any calls between the Yemen line and the U.S. be passed to the bureau—that the NSA didn't fill. "For us," Coleman said, "anyone who called the Yemen number is white-hot, a top suspect."

The dilemma was not just with the sharing of information, which CIA and NSA rarely did. It was also replicating and spreading the contextualized insights that experience and study had built into only a few people in the vast U.S. government. Or in Coleman's patois: "It's a longer jump than you might think for information to become knowledge and then wisdom. As the technologists say, there's no easy way to find a scalable solution for that—you can't replicate someone's brain—and one person can only review so much stuff."

In this case, one guy supported by twelve data-input women. This morning's field trip was part of a negotiated program between the agency and the bureau.

The Zubaydah trove had arrived. CIA was already reviewing it. Dan was there to get an early look. And then, with his team, create a takeaway copy and carry it, literally, back to FBI.

You'd think there'd be an easier way to do this. But, like so much else in the government, this was a fix for yet another broken process. The problem was that CIA—the main branch carrying forward the "war on terror"—wouldn't or couldn't or, in any event, *didn't* create a database that was easily shared with a wide array of other federal agencies. There was a system that provided a so-called "broad platform" for easy entry, with access codes and wide applications. It's the Pentagon's system—code-named "Harmony"—which many other agencies can tap into. CIA wouldn't sign on.

So, they sat, Dan and his team, going through the computer files from Zubaydah's safe house in Faisalabad, and notebooks, and folders of jotted-down ideas, and names. Some of it was valuable. Names; phone numbers; contacts. Each one would be run down. Each one was a solid lead, and maybe golden. The team would capture it in a precise, indexed, and retrievable FBI fashion. Then Dan could bring it back, disk by disk, to the bureau and send it off to the right players inside of FBI. In the "war on terror," getting the right information tagged and off to the right place is as important as loading weapons with ammunition.

Then Dan saw the prize: Zubaydah's diary. It was extensive, stretching back more than a decade—a winding path through Zubaydah's life. He was born in a Riyadh suburb but spent his teens on the West Bank. In 1987, at sixteen, he joined the Palestinian uprising. He eventually migrated to Afghanistan in the last days of the war with the Soviets. Somewhere in this period—in Afghanistan, it is believed—he received a severe head injury. Dan didn't think much about the head wound report—something he'd heard a year before—until he read the top secret diary, which had been translated by a CIA team in the first few days after the Shabaz cottage was cleaned out.

In it, Zubaydah wrote of his exploits in the voice of three people: Hani 1, Hani 2, and Hani 3. Hani 1 was a boy, really, ten years younger than the youthful Zubaydah's real age. Hani 2 was the same age as Zubaydah; and Hani 3 was ten years older. Zubaydah wrote impressions of countless days—years, all told, of meeting with potential recruits, and his reactions to events and news reports—from all three perspectives. Each Hani had a distinct voice and personality. What was being observed, by three pairs of eyes, meanwhile, was often less than compelling—what people ate, or wore, or trifling things they said . . . in page after page after page. Zubaydah was a logistics man, a fixer, mostly for a niggling array of personal items, like the guy you call who handles the company health plan, or benefits, or the people in human resources. There was almost nothing "operational" in his portfolio. That was handled by the management team. He wasn't one of them.

As disappointing as what was in the diary, Coleman's trained eye noticed what wasn't. The CIA had long suspected that the ubiquitous Zubaydah was involved in the August, 1998, bombings of the U.S. embassies in Africa. He looked for entries in the summer of 1998 in Zubaydah's diary. Nothing . . . nothing but nonsense.

For those in the innermost circles of intelligence and policy, spring 2002 would be a time when new lessons about the "war on terror" were being learned, some of them quite troubling.

The President's approval rating in April was still at historic highs, a blue sky, with only one small cloud of public puzzlement: neither of the top leaders of al Qaeda, namely, bin Laden and Zawahiri, nor Mullah Omar, the Taliban leader, had been captured or killed.

This had prompted various statements—from the President on down—that capturing bin Laden or Zawahiri was not all that important, starting with a long discourse on the subject by Mr. Bush on March 13 at one of his rare solo press conferences. "We haven't heard much from him," he said about bin Laden. "And I wouldn't necessarily say he's at the center of any command structure. And, again, I don't know where he is. I'll repeat what I said. I truly am not that concerned about him."

But, in this period, notes from the President's daily briefings indicate that Bush asked about bin Laden and Zawahiri virtually every morning, and often several times a day. One CIA official, familiar with the agency's interactions with the White House, comments, "Bush was obsessed with both of them."

Similarly, what had happened at Tora Bora—how the CIA's advice was ignored, and how both the civilian and the uniformed leadership of the U.S. military had miscalculated badly, allowing bin Laden to escape—was indisputable for anyone with involvement and the right security clearance.

On April 17, *The Washington Post* printed the first, preliminary report suggesting how the U.S. Army had failed to surround the Tora

Bora caves and that such a move might have prevented bin Laden from escaping. That day, at a press conference, Donald Rumsfeld disputed that assertion, saying he did not "know today of any evidence" that bin Laden "was in Tora Bora at the time, or that he left Tora Bora at the time, or even where he is today."

That was also false.

Yet when something of such extraordinary news value is cloaked, in part or wholly, under the ever-widening designation of "classified," the set of creative options available to a White House is vast.

This, in fact, was a perfect White House to take advantage of such opportunities. Its innovations in "message discipline" dated from well before 9/11. President Bush and his team experimented, from the first, with new ideas of how to control communications emerging from the White House, and the administration at large.

There are several moving parts. To prevent anonymous leaks—the traditional method for officials to pass information to members of the press and, through them, to the public and others in the administration, including the President—the Bush team issued government cell phones to a wide array of officials and mandated that they be used. This way, they were able to monitor incoming and outgoing calls from both office phones *and* mobile phones. What's more, they issued strict orders, with penalties that could include immediate dismissal, that no one should speak to a member of the press without permission—permission that was generally controlled by the White House communications office.

Karen Hughes, who oversaw that office and met each morning with her team of several dozen media officers from across the government, was convinced that the mainstream press was dominated by political opponents, and in any event was attracted to "conflict" stories. Her idea was, as much as possible, to ignore the major newspapers, magazines, and television networks, all of which had become accustomed, over decades, to having regular meetings with a sitting president. No more. Their access would be limited and carefully managed. What's more, the President would have only about one third as many individual press conferences as Bill Clinton, or one fifth as many as the first Bush. The goal was to keep this President away from impromptu exchanges with informed questioners, never one of his strong suits.

Informed questions, however, could also be killed at their source. They were winnowed, steadily, by a broadened standard of what is classified. The initiative was a pet project of the Vice President, who'd long believed that public and congressional scrutiny of presidents was weakening executive power. With Cheney's guidance, documents were being classified at twice the rate of the previous administration.

In all, though, this multipronged strategy to help messages flow unencumbered had been wearing thin by August 2001. Mr. Bush's approval rating hovered in the low 50s, below the norm for a modern president so early in a first term. He was being criticized for being overly managed, disengaged, and overwhelmed by the demands of the job.

All of that was swept away by 9/11. Mr. Bush's response in a series of heartfelt actions and brilliantly constructed speeches was a tonic to a nation naturally impelled to circle behind a leader in a crisis. Though much had changed, the foundation of the original message-control strategy remained intact. Now, it could readily support patriotic, "united we stand" calls to arms, powerful ones. Approval ratings soared. The public, and Congress, acquiesced, with little real resistance, to a "need to know" status—told only what they needed to know, with that determination made exclusively, and narrowly, by the White House.

While the select few on the House or Senate Intelligence oversight committees could review this raging river of classified information, the most sensitive materials were shown only to the two ranking members—one from each party—on each committee. Yet there was much that even they did not see.

In short, 9/11 allowed for preparation to meet opportunity. The result: potent, wartime authority was granted to those guiding the ship of state. A final, customary check in wartime—demonstrable evidence of troop movements or casualties, of divisions on the move, with correspondents filing dispatches—was also missing once the Afghanistan engagement ended. In the wide, diffuse "war on terror," so much of it occurring in the shadows—with no transparency and only perfunctory oversight—the administration could say anything it wanted to say. That was a blazing insight of this period. The administration could create whatever reality was convenient.

Messages, of all kinds, could finally stand unfettered and unchallenged—a kind of triumph, a wish fulfillment, that could easily overwhelm principles of informed consent and accountability.

Accountability, in fact, was shrunk to a single standard: prevent attacks on the U.S. mainland. As long as there were no such attacks, little else mattered.

What, for instance, did all of this mean upon the capture of Zubaydah? A freeing of rhetoric for the "wartime" President to say what he felt desperately needed to be said.

Which Bush did, first, in a speech at the Greenwich, Connecticut, Hyatt Regency on April 9, 2002. "The other day we hauled in a guy named Abu Zubaydah. He's one of the top operatives plotting and planning death and destruction on the United States. He's not plotting and planning anymore. He's where he belongs," the President said to raucous cheers from a roomful of Republican Party contributors. Then, he quickly bridged to a wider, state-based issue. "History has called us into action, and this nation is responding. You've got to understand my mind-set and what we think. We've got to act on behalf of the little ones. We've got to secure the world and this civilization as we know it from these evil people. We just have to do this. And that includes making sure that some of the world's worst leaders who desire to possess the world's worst weapons don't team up with faceless, al Qaeda–type killer organizations. We owe it to the future of this country to lead a coalition against nations that are so evil and, at the same time, desire incredibly evil weapons."

This message—and the characterizing of Zubaydah as the "chief of operations" for all of al Qaeda, a putative "number three" to bin Laden and Zawahiri—would be a drum the President, the Vice President, national security adviser Condoleezza Rice, and others would beat relentlessly that April and the months to follow.

Meanwhile, Dan Coleman and other knowledgeable members of the tribe of al Qaeda hunters at CIA were reading Zubaydah's top secret diary and shaking their heads.

"This guy is insane, certifiable, split personality," Coleman told a top official at FBI after a few days reviewing the Zubaydah haul. "That's why they let him fly all over the world doing meet and greet. That's why people used his name on all sorts of calls and e-mails. He was like a travel agent, the guy who booked your flights. You can see from what he writes how burdened he is with all these logistics—getting families of operatives, wives and kids, in and out of countries. He knew very little about real operations, or strategy. He was expendable, you know, the greeter . . . Joe Louis in the lobby of Caesar's Palace, shaking hands."

This opinion was echoed at the top of CIA and was, of course, briefed to the President and Vice President. While Bush was out in public claiming Zubaydah's grandiose malevolence, his private disappointment fell, as it often would, on Tenet—the man whose job he'd saved.

"I said he was important," Bush said to Tenet at one of their daily meetings. "You're not going to let me lose face on this, are you?"

"No sir, Mr. President."

Back in Langley, Tenet pressed subordinates over what could be done to get Zubaydah to talk. His injuries were serious, but he'd been moved from a hospital near Faisalabad to several locations in central Pakistan. The CIA found some of the finest medical professionals in America. CIA agents alighted at their medical offices and soon they were on flights to Pakistan.

"He received the finest medical attention on the planet," said one CIA official. "We got him in very good health, so we could start to torture him."

Tenet's months of pressure on his legal team, and their pressure on the White House counsel's office, created a chain reaction of legal response. As captives were flowing into Camp X-ray in Guantánamo, the White House and Justice Department had produced some preliminary guidance on interrogation. Most noteworthy was a memo from White House counsel Al Gonzales in late January 2002, asserting that the Geneva Conventions regarding prisoners of war did not apply to the United States in the treatment of detainees captured in Afghanistan.

The first application of the new rules, however, would be to Zubaydah. The combination of forces was less than optimal: the value of his capture had already been oversold to the American public; and Zubaydah wouldn't talk. Tenet was pushing his staff at CIA for a surprise, a breakthrough, which he could then deliver to Bush—evidence that would, after the fact, support the President's public statements. It was a pattern that would be repeated many times in the coming years.

For those at CIA, like professionals in the so-called "policy apparatus" across the government, moments like this had a subtle, corrosive effect. Everyone in the top ranks of CIA understood the Cheney Doctrine, and how it articulated an impatience with the slow-footed evidentiary process when facing a dire mandate for action. But that, mostly, pertained to the internal debates over why or how to act. Misleading the public for no apparent reason except short-term political gain seemed willful and self-interested.

And ensnaring.

"Around the room a lot of people just rolled their eyes when we heard comments from the White House. I mean, Bush and Cheney knew what we knew about Zubaydah. The guy had psychological issues. He was, in a way, expendable. It was like calling someone who runs a company's in-house travel department the COO," said one top CIA official, who attended the 5 p.m. meeting where the issue of Zubaydah came up. "The thinking was, why the hell did the President have to put us in a box like this?"

What they'd soon realize was that this was the President's management style. A way, as he would often quip, to push people "to do things they didn't think they were capable of."

★   ★   ★

"Recognized us yet?" asked Khalid Sheikh Mohammed—al Qaeda's real operational chief—and laughed.

Yosri Fouda, senior correspondent of Al Jazeera, stood dumbstruck as Ramzi bin al-Shibh then reached out to shake his hand.

It was April 19. Fouda, his blindfold just removed, blinked, suppressing disbelief, as he scanned the two men and the bare-walled apartment: the Karachi "safe house" of al Qaeda.

The lithe, smiling man shaking his hand, Fouda *did* recognize: bin al-Shibh had been on wanted posters across the world since the previous fall when his Western Union wire transfers to Zacarias Moussaoui were discovered. He was seen as connected, in some indelible way, to the 9/11 hijackers—most probably as a paymaster.

As for Khalid Sheikh Mohammed, it took a moment for Fouda to place the face. For those who carefully followed violent jihadists, as did Fouda—star reporter for *Top Secret,* an Al Jazeera show that had done many reports of late on Islamic terrorists—Mohammed was known among a wide cast of possible al Qaeda operatives. Years before, the FBI discovered he was the uncle, and a facilitator, of Ramzi Ahmed Yousef, one of the men convicted and imprisoned for the 1993 World Trade Center bombing. Mohammed had been indicted for a 1995 Philippines-based plan to crash U.S. airliners into the ocean, a plan that never saw fruition. The U.S. government offered a reward of $5 million for information leading to his capture, and published a picture of a young, doe-eyed, bearded man. The man in front of Fouda was beardless, and heavy. But the eyes were the same.

"They say you are terrorists," Fouda offered. Bin al-Shibh smiled, and backed away.

"They are right," Mohammed replied, firm and matter-of-fact. "That is what we do for a living."

It had taken two weeks of cryptic messages, and meetings with shadowy intermediaries, to bring Fouda 4,000 miles from the London bureau of Al Jazeera to this apartment—a journey that started with an

THE ONE PERCENT DOCTRINE ■ 103

early-April call to his cell phone in London. The man on the other end wondered what Al Jazeera was doing for the anniversary of 9/11 and asked Fouda for the number of a secure fax line. A few days later, a three-page fax arrived, outlining some specific suggestions for a three-part documentary celebrating the attacks—what it might include, key facts that had been overlooked, and a list of sympathetic experts on 9/11 and its effects to whom Fouda might speak. More on that last point arrived forthwith: instructions to board a plane for Islamabad and a meeting that his contact quipped would be "top secret." Fouda told some specifics of what had happened to one friend—swore him to secrecy—and created a cover story for his bosses (he was working on the next segment of a project called "The Road to Camp X-ray"). He then headed for Islamabad. There, he received instructions to travel to Karachi and get a room at the Regents Plaza Hotel, where an anxious middle-aged man met him in his hotel room and offered more details of what awaited. He said that "Sheikh Abu Abdullah"—a name for bin Laden—was alive and well and regularly watched Al Jazeera, often from videocassettes of taped broadcasts. Bin Laden, the contact said, "told us to take Robert Fisk" (an author and journalist for the *Independent*) "to Oum-Abdullah [bin Laden's wife] and to take Yosri Fouda to the brothers."

So it was that the next evening, Fouda found himself saying prayers in a hideout with Khalid Sheikh Mohammed and Ramzi bin al-Shibh, and a few of their deputies.

As the hour grew late, there was an odd dance of pleasantries and negotiations, tea and terms. Al Qaeda would supply camera and tape; Fouda would never reveal their whereabouts, or how their appearances differed from the few existing photos of each man. He had to swear to all conditions on a Koran. He was told he would again be blindfolded for a direct trip to the airport when he was finished.

It was time to turn in. But first, Mohammed, clearly the man in charge, had to clarify why Fouda—in his ostensible anniversary project about 9/11—had been brought here.

"I am the head of the al Qaeda military committee and Ramzi is the coordinator of the 'Holy Tuesday' operation," KSM said. "And yes, we did it."

At that point, a reporter for Al Jazeera had more prized information than did the collected forces of the world's greatest power and its allies.

Welcome to the "war on terror." Information, powerful information, is now doled out as democratically—horizontally and indiscriminately—as on the Internet. Everyone can play.

And Fouda, feeling lightheaded, slipped into his bedroll for a night of fitful sleep.

On Wednesday, April 24, the catering staff at the Intercontinental Hotel in Houston spun from their duties to behold a surreal sight: Dick Cheney—leg propped high from a recently implanted shunt behind his knee—flying through the kitchen in a motorized wheelchair, wingtip poised as a battering ram.

"Get the door!" someone yelled.

And someone did, thank God, as Cheney flew through, and cut hard left to the private banquet room, rubberized wheels squealing on the parquet.

It was late afternoon, with so much to do—so many preparations—and so much at stake. Crown Prince Abdullah, Saudi Arabia's de facto leader, was in town, but reluctantly. The next day, the livid Saudi ruler would meet Bush in Crawford, in what was being dubbed a "showdown" between the Islamic world and the West.

This was the preliminary dinner, the softening-up dinner with Cheney and Rumsfeld, who'd flown in to hear out the Saudis before tomorrow's big meeting at the ranch.

Relations between the Kingdom of Saudi Arabia and the United States were in tatters. The Saudis had been stewing for more than a year, in fact, ever since it became clear at the start of 2001 that this administration was to alter the long-standing U.S. role of honest broker in the Israeli-Palestinian conflict to something less than that. The

President, in fact, had said in the first NSC principals meeting of his administration that Clinton had overreached at the end of his second term, bending too much toward Yasser Arafat—who then broke off productive Camp David negotiations at the final moment—and that "We're going to tilt back toward Israel." Powell, a chair away in the Situation Room that day, said such a move would reverse thirty years of U.S. policy, and that it could unleash the new prime minister, Ariel Sharon, and the Israeli army in ways that could be dire for the Palestinians. Bush's response: "Sometimes a show of force by one side can really clarify things."

Abdullah might not have known all the specifics of that policy shift, but he, and the rest of the Arab world, had watched the outcome—a situation that worsened month by month for the Palestinians.

And, month by month, his anger grew. In any administration, this would have caused consternation. Since the fall of the Soviet Union, the fitful love-hate relationship between the United States and Saudi Arabia remained, arguably, the planet's key diplomatic dialogue. The United States depends on Saudi Arabia for 15 percent of its oil imports and, since a meeting between King Ibn Saud and Franklin Roosevelt in 1945, has been locked in a bargain that would make Faust wince: We'll protect you, Saudi royal family, as long as the oil flows . . . and do whatever the hell you want with the billions.

It is an arrangement that has unfolded into a sort of global stage play, with dizzying plot twists. The Saudi family managed its way to entrenched power by combining limitless riches with an embrace of Islamic fundamentalism, a devil's pact of their own. Over the past forty years, they have channeled an increasing share of their oil proceeds to radical clerics in Saudi Arabia (along with imams in other Arab countries and a few in Southeast Asia) to build and lead vast religious fiefs of soaring, ornate mosques and schools and child armies trained for a life of fierce faith. Those Saudi clerics, in a mendacious bargain—the third of this triptych—have supported the Saudis as guardians of the Holy Sites, Mecca and Medina, and looked the other way as the royal family—now about 25,000 strong—repressed opponents and explored new heights of modern-age consumption, with Gulfstreams, golden palaces, and graduate school degrees.

This strange round rosy of Western oil gluttons, Saudi princes, and angry imams was managed, with utmost attentiveness, by a succession of modern American presidents.

And, quite artfully, by the elder Bush. Saudi Arabia, long the key military base for U.S. forces in the region, was a staging platform for the 1991 Gulf War, which defanged Saddam Hussein, an opponent of many oil oligarchies. Those countries were grateful. Oil prices remained stable through the nineties. Imams built their mosques. George H. W. Bush, once out of office, tended his relationship with the Saudis—on behalf of himself and his firm, the Carlyle Group—like a gardener might a strain of rare orchids. So, on Tuesday, it was logical that the former President start the week's festivities with a lunch at *his* Texas home in the Houston suburbs. Bandar and Prince Saud al-Faisal, the Saudi foreign minister, came, Barbara was there, and Bandar's wife, the elegant Princess Haifa, and they hashed it all out—how the world had changed seven months before in a way that would have left Gibbon or Shakespeare gasping—and shook their heads about how bin Laden and his minions could have risen so fast and struck so deeply, prompting all the players to fall down in ashes.

Bandar understood, however, that this was a special event—bringing in the former President—and that G.H.W. would have fewer insights than one might expect into the mind-set of the current President. Bandar had known both men so well for so long. He knew—long before even the most informed American—that the relationship was cool and distant, not even what one would expect of a father and son; that the son didn't consult the father—even though he was, quite possibly, the most valuable adviser presented by modern history—and that this meeting was a special event set up by Cheney, over the forty-third President's reluctance, as a rhetorical act, a golden chance to remind the Saudis of their long-standing ties to the Bushes and America.

The discussion of strategy between the elder Bush and the Saudi princes was wistful, largely about a world washed away by 9/11, and also a generational passage. Privately, the current President had railed against his father's alliances, and his mistakes. Living, and leading, in reaction to his namesake was a guiding principle. In a defense of his tilting toward Israel, for example, Bush told an old foreign policy hand, "I'm not going to be supportive of my father and all his Arab buddies!"

Bandar and the elder Bush both knew that the meeting in Crawford could be bumpy. If it managed to go well, the delegation planned to stay in Texas a few more days and, on Friday, visit the George H. W. Bush Presidential Library in College Station. If it didn't go well, Abdullah planned to head directly back to a summit of Arab leaders to deliver the bad news . . .

"I hope to see you Friday," the former President said.

"Me too," said Bandar.

Dinner the next night with Cheney went less well . . . now that the angry Crown Prince had arrived. That evening, Abdullah vented while Cheney sat, nodding. He knew from various State Department reports and intelligence summaries that the Saudis were so displeased with America's Mideast policy, they were ready to lead Arab countries in using oil as a weapon against the United States—a step akin to a declaration of war. Abdullah told other Arab leaders that he'd come to represent the gripes of the entire Arab League, which had had a meeting in March that Yasser Arafat could not attend because Sharon had him isolated and under siege in his Ramallah compound. Israeli tanks and helicopter gunships had descended on the West Bank on March 29 after a series of Palestinian bombings. "It is children against tanks," Abdullah fumed, while President Bush, in the midst of all this, called Sharon "a man of peace."

"How could he have done that?" Abdullah asked, incredulous, not expecting an answer from Cheney, who just took it. Rumsfeld, joined by General Richard B. Myers, Chairman of the Joint Chiefs of Staff, tried to change the subject, telling Abdullah that the U.S. Army was much more powerful now than it was during the Gulf War. Myers reviewed highlights of the U.S. victory in Afghanistan.

"But bin Laden escaped," Abdullah said, darkly.

"Yes, yes he did, but we're closing in on him," Cheney said, to Abdullah's skeptical gaze.

And, finally, it was over. A helicopter soon was waiting to bring the Vice President to Crawford. With visible relief, he wheeled his chair around, summoned Scooter Libby, and beelined for the exit.

On Thursday, Bush pawed the driveway with the tip of his shoe, and nervously checked his watch. Outside, a scrum of reporters and photographers waited at a safe distance, in one of those strange moments of forced intimacy that are part of presidential life. Bush waited. They waited, watching him wait. Is it important that a President who hates to wait is kept waiting? It could mean nothing, or everything.

Speeding across the Texas prairie, Abdullah was in the front of a speeding bus—head of a plush caravan of buses he had bought for today's meeting—sharing a cigarette with the driver. In the back, Powell, Bandar, Saud, and Bob Jordan, the U.S. ambassador to Saudi Arabia. Powell and Bandar, both raconteurs—full-living men at ease in the world—swapped stories. Hail fellows, well met. What's happening today? Their jocular tone said, "Nothing special. Business as usual."

Of course, it was anything but. Abdullah had never met Bush the younger, and was unimpressed by what he had seen at a distance.

Now, the distance between them was 100 yards. Bush stood, solitary, in the driveway of a modest house on a vast plain. Abdullah apologized for being late. "No problem, none at all," Bush said, after his ten minutes of standing at attention.

It was a large crowd to fit into the den of the house—Condi and Harriet Miers, Andy Card and the Vice President, on crutches, and Scooter Libby, who, one guest later said, "was there to hold Cheney's leg." Before any words were spoken, Abdullah had pictures to show. Lights were dimmed in the President's den and, for fifteen minutes, they watched a video Abdullah had brought of mayhem on the West Bank, of American-made tanks, bloodied and dead children, screaming mothers.

Then, wordless, they all filed out to the President's glassed-in porch, for the venting of hostilities.

The Saudis had specific demands. Abdullah had recently offered his own peace plan: a two-state solution, a recognition of Israel by the Arab world—and, also, a nonstarter about the return to the 1967 borders, leaving East Jerusalem as the capital of a new Arab state, and a host of things he expected in terms of the crisis on the West Bank. The United States, now deep into the "war on terror," had its own set of issues. Though Saudi Arabia was home to fifteen of the nineteen hijackers—and to bin Laden—the kingdom was being less than cooperative, barring the United States from interviewing the families of the hijackers and blocking efforts to trace terror finance, most of which tracked through the country's labyrinth of charities and hawalas. First, though, the Saudi started on their list—a long one, which included the United States distancing itself from Sharon, and acts that would support the Palestinians.

Bush listened, but not really. This was not where he wanted to be. He was marking time. "Let's go for a drive," he said to Abdullah, after a few minutes. "Just you and me. I'll show you the ranch."

And they marched off, in midsentence, to Bush's pickup truck, leaving behind a phalanx of slack-jawed advisers with what one later called "monarchy blues"—a realization, as he described it, that "ideals of representative government fade at moments like this into a feeling that things haven't changed all that much since foreign affairs were the affairs of kings—how they got along, or didn't, determined the fate of nations."

Bouncing in the cab of the Chevy pickup—Bush, wearing a suit and tie for the visit of a foreign leader, Abdullah in a tweed jacket over his gown—they seemed to get along just fine. Bush loves doing this: showing the 1,600-acre ranch, cutting this way and that over the central Texas scrub in the pickup, making snap decisions on which path to take, where to go first, and last. There are seventeen varieties of trees. He pointed them out, told Abdullah of his love of the land, his desire for peace. They stopped and talked at one of Bush's favorite spots. They saw a wild turkey.

Then, after an hour or so, they were back for lunch. And everyone settled at a long table on the glassed-in porch—Colin, Condi, Andy Card, Cheney, Bandar, Bush, Saud, Abdullah, and Jordan—and Bush asked Abdullah if he could say a prayer. Abdullah nodded, and Bush prayed, and then they ate beef tenderloin and potato salad, brownies and ice cream.

Abdullah, dabbing his lips, snapped to attention as the brownies were cleared—as though he'd lost track of what had brought him here—as did Bandar and Saud. They had eight items on their list. They needed deliverables—something to bring back to the roiling Gulf that would ease the Arab world. Would Bush back up his words with actions? Was he on Sharon's side, or was the United States still interested in supporting its Arab friends? Was America any longer the region's honest broker?

But the discussions could get no traction. The Saudis wanted pressure on Sharon to release Arafat from confinement in Ramallah. Saud went over possible steps the United States could take. Bush stared blankly at them. They went down the items. Sometimes the President nodded, as though something sounded reasonable, but he offered little response.

And, after almost an hour of this, the Saudis, looking a bit perplexed, got up to go. It was as though Bush had never read the packet they sent over to the White House in preparation for this meeting: a terse, lean document, just a few pages, listing the Saudis' demands and an array of options that the President might consider. After the meeting, a few attendees on the American team wondered why the President seemed to have no idea what the Saudis were after, and why he didn't bother to answer their concerns or get any concessions from them, either, on the "war on terror." There was not a more important conversation in the "war on terror" than a sit-down with Saudi Arabia. Several of the attendees checked into what had happened.

The Saudi packet, they found, had been diverted to Dick Cheney's office. The President never got it, never read it. In what may have been the most important, and contentious, foreign policy meeting of his presidency, George W. Bush was unaware of what the Saudis hoped to achieve in traveling to Crawford.

But Crown Prince Abdullah did learn something. He'd had his first George W. Bush encounter: visceral, emotive, nonsubstantive, and faith-based. He left befuddled, but oddly moved—by their ride together in the pickup; by the things Bush said he loved as they drove, and how he desperately wanted to work together, to bring peace to the Mideast; by the fervent prayer before lunch, and by the way Bush grabbed hands, firmly, with undisguised yearning, as they parted. "I have tears in my eyes, Mr. President."

"I do, too," Bush said. "I do, too."

Zubaydah's injuries—gunshot wounds to the leg, groin, and abdomen—had been successfully treated by the finest U.S. physicians in late April and early May. The doctors repaired internal bleeding, a fracture, and organ damage.

He was stabilized by mid-May and, thus, ready. An extraordinary moment in the "war on terror" was about to unfold. After months of interdepartmental exchanges over the detainment, interrogation, and prosecution of captives in the "war on terror"—as well as debates over which "debriefing" techniques would work most effectively on al Qaeda—the United States would torture a mentally disturbed man and then leap, screaming, at every word he uttered.

The eight-month lead-up to this moment—where legal theories were marshaled after 9/11 to allow for "flexibility"—is a short story of preparation meeting desperation.

Through the late fall of 2001, deliberation between lawyers at CIA,

FBI, Justice, and the office of the White House counsel had attempted to frame an all but certain future: a time, up ahead, when the United States would have captives, maybe lots of them.

The questions were of a type lawyers almost never get to pose, even in ethics seminars at law school. Can you kill an al Qaeda suspect once he's in custody? No, was the consensus—it would be too profound a violation of international law. Not that it wasn't discussed. Everyone did agree that you'd want to hold prisoners as long as possible—they're too valuable as sources of intelligence and, maybe, too danger-ous to release. The goal of lawyers across the government was to lay the legal parameters wide enough to provide options, prerogatives, and maximum flexibility. Who knew what lay ahead?

A question posed by CIA and the Justice Department in September 2001—should captives go through the U.S. criminal justice sys-tem?—was answered by Bush on November 13, when he signed an executive order stating that "Given the danger to the safety of the United States and the nature of international terrorism . . . I find con-sistent with section 836 of title 10, United States Code, that it is not practicable to apply in military commissions under this order the prin-ciples of law and the rules of evidence generally recognized in the trial of criminal cases in the United States district courts." The captives would be tried in military courts.

That would certainly provide latitude. The schedules of such pro-ceedings were often fluid—based on military judgments as to the value of holding, or interrogating, a prisoner. And if a captive was an "enemy alien"—meaning not a U.S. citizen—he or she would be hard-pressed to file a strong habeas corpus petition in U.S. federal courts.

The companion question, of what could be done to captives while in custody, became a pressing issue at the end of 2001. A few high-value captives had been picked up, and by January 2002, hundreds of assorted prisoners, mostly low-rung al Qaeda or Taliban soldiers, began to arrive at Guantánamo Bay. A memo drafted on January 9, 2002, from John Yoo—a deputy assistant attorney general who'd marshaled legal analysis to support the Vice President's expansive view of executive prerogative—asserted that the Geneva Conventions governing the treatment of prisoners of war did not apply to al Qaeda or the Taliban. He and his co-writer, Robert J. Dellahunt, reasoned that al Qaeda, as a nonstate actor, is not a party to the international treaties of war, nor was the Taliban so "intertwined" with al Qaeda as to make the two indistinguishable. The memo went on to state that the President was not bound by international law because it is not formally recognized in the U.S. Constitution and that, in any event, the resolution on September 14 gave the President "sweeping authority with respect to the present conflict."

This memo created quite a bit of havoc among government lawyers, prompting sharp retort from the State Department that such analysis was "seriously flawed." The President did not agree. On January 18, he sided with the "sweeping authority" position that Geneva didn't apply and passed that proviso to the Pentagon. This drew a concerned response from Colin Powell—the most experienced military man among the President's senior officials. The Geneva Conventions protected all soldiers, of all types, Powell asserted. If we threw them away, we'd be harming our own men and giving up a precious perch of moral probity.

The President called upon his White House counsel, Alberto Gonzales—his trusted legal arm since his days as governor of Texas—to explain to Powell the authorized policy on the matter.

"As you have said," Gonzales wrote to Bush, "the war against terrorism is a new kind of war. It is not the traditional clash between nations adhering to the laws of war that formed the backdrop for [Geneva Convention III, on the Treatment of Prisoners of War]. The nature of the new war places a high premium on other factors, such as the ability to quickly obtain information from captured terrorists and their sponsors in order to avoid further atrocities against American civilians, and the need to try terrorists for war crimes such as wantonly killing civilians. In my judgment, this new paradigm renders obsolete Geneva's strict limitations on questioning of enemy prisoners and renders quaint some of its provisions requiring that captured enemy be afforded such things as commissary privileges, scrip (i.e., advances of monthly pay), athletic uniforms, and scientific instruments."

At the same time, a parallel debate was unfolding as to tactics: *what worked.* The battle over al-Libi, won by the CIA when the captive was "rendered" to the torture chambers of Cairo, didn't end the debate.

It continued to rage between Langley and FBI headquarters in Washington, where the bureau's agents—especially those with experience questioning al Qaeda operatives—wanted to get at Zubaydah, even if they were convinced he was mentally unbalanced.

"These guys are involved in a lifelong conspiracy," said Dan Coleman, who had experience with almost all the star witnesses of the FBI's prosecutions during the 1990s. "The CIA wants everything in five minutes. It's not possible, and it's not productive. What you get in that circumstance are captives and captors playing to each other's expectations, playing roles—essentially—that gives you a lot of garbage information and nothing you can use."

Inside of the FBI, Mueller and his deputies thought hard about whether access to the high-value suspects—if bought by compromising the FBI's "debriefing" standards—was worth the price. "If it is discovered that the FBI is involved in extra-legal methods," Mueller told one top deputy, "it will haunt us for years in every courtroom."

As to the underlying issue of effectiveness, of determining what works, the FBI had ammunition to support its "meeting expectations" critique of the CIA's brutal, impatient techniques. Agents passed around copies of a training manual that was discovered in November in the ruins of Mohammed Atef's bunker in Kandahar. It informed al Qaeda recruits that if they were captured, they'd face torture, dismemberment, and certain death.

What the captives didn't expect, FBI interrogators knew from experience, was respect and judiciously offered favors. Coleman and FBI interrogators had successfully plied prisoners—like Wadi el Hage, a key player in the 1998 embassy bombings, or Jamal al Fadl, a close aide to bin Laden and Zawahiri who turned into a witness-stand star—

with Chinese food, porn, and, in one case an operation for a captive's wife. Agents were present when the grateful wife told her husband, "Now, you tell them whatever they want." He did.

CIA's counterpoint, however, was one that had adherents among an army of self-styled amateurs on interrogation in the U.S. government, from the Oval Office on down. No one has time to build "relationships"—a word that was repugnant to those who viewed al Qaeda operatives as evil incarnate. In the debate between Mowatt-Larssen and Cofer Black, the impatient institutional energies of the U.S. government had settled on Black's position; do everything, and quickly.

Choices made, Zubaydah now recovered, it was time, in May of 2002, to test boundaries.

According to CIA sources, he was water-boarded, a technique in which a captive's face is covered with a towel as water is poured atop, creating the sensation of drowning. He was beaten, though not in a way to worsen his injuries. He was repeatedly threatened, and made certain of his impending death. His medication was withheld. He was bombarded with deafening, continuous noise and harsh lights. He was, as a man already diminished by serious injuries, more fully at the mercy of interrogators than an ordinary prisoner.

Under this duress, Zubaydah told them that shopping malls were targeted by al Qaeda. That information traveled the globe in an instant. Agents from the FBI, Secret Service, Customs, and various related agencies joined local police to surround malls. Zubaydah said banks—yes, banks—were a priority. FBI agents led officers in a race to surround and secure banks. And also supermarkets—al Qaeda was planning to blow up crowded supermarkets, several at one time. People would stop shopping. The nation's economy would be crippled. And the water systems—a target, too. Nuclear plants, naturally. And apartment buildings.

Thousands of uniformed men and women raced in a panic to each flavor of target. Of course, if you multiplied by ten, there still

wouldn't be enough public servants in America to surround and secure the supermarkets. Or the banks. But they tried. The FBI generally kept its various alerts secret. But word drifted out to the media,
time and again, considering the thousands who were involved.

Every morning, the President was briefed at eight, by Tenet and his
staffers. At eight-thirty, Mueller and his team arrived. "First comes offense, then defense," the President said one morning as the two made
their switch-off. The sports analogy, a favorite of Bush and Tenet, both
avid sports fans, easily stuck. It made sense. In the main, *find them, stop
them* mission of the "war on terror," there were, essentially, these two
squads on the field. Most other players in the government were in
supporting roles. Justice set the rules, though legal prosecutions, per
se, were not expected to be pertinent any time soon. An array of agencies, from Immigration and Naturalization to Customs to the Federal
Aviation Administration, handled homeland security, loosely overseen by former Pennsylvania governor Tom Ridge. But it was a confused, ad hoc effort and not yet housed as a department. The Pentagon
was mopping up in Afghanistan, and preparing for Iraq.

CIA and FBI were slotted into the roles and rhythm that would
abide, in large part, for years. CIA sounded the alarm; FBI ran, wild-
eyed, from the building—a dog given a scent, but little more. Where
should they start sniffing? No idea. Start with *everywhere.*

Zubaydah said that al Qaeda was close to building a crude nuclear
device. This sent shock waves through the government. But it was un-
confirmable.

A tried-and-true maxim: the only intelligence of value is that which
can be independently confirmed. Interrogators, sending home one
open-ended alert after another, pressed Zubaydah for the verifiable.
They needed a body, a colleague. The captive wouldn't give up one.

Then there was a small break. A CIA interrogator, according to
sources who monitored the program, was skilled in the nuances of the
Koran, and slipped under Zubaydah's skin. The al Qaeda operative believed in certain ideas of predestination—that things happen for rea-

sons preordained. The interrogator worked this, pulling freely from the Koran. Zubaydah believed he had survived the attacks in Faisalabad, when several of his colleagues were killed, for a purpose. He was convinced that that purpose, in the fullness of time, was to offer some cooperation to his captors, something a dead man couldn't do.

And he did cooperate. He gave up one body: Jose Padilla.

Padilla, a Brooklyn native, had moved to Chicago as a boy. He eventually drifted to south Florida, where he converted to Islam. He left the United States for Egypt and later was being trained by Mohammed Atef when the al Qaeda military leader was killed in Afghanistan in November 2001. Padilla migrated over the border to Faisalabad, and talked with Zubaydah about some of his improbable ideas. He wanted to build a small nuclear device and detonate it in America. Padilla was not credible on that score—he was untrained in even the rudiments of such matters—but was encouraged by Zubaydah to pursue other projects. He was then passed along to a true operational commander to discuss what was possible.

The code name for that chief was Mukhtar, Arabic for "the Brain." The name Mukhtar had popped up many times at the NSA on sigint over the past two years, including on some key sigint intercepts connected to 9/11. After a bit, Zubaydah said that Mukhtar's real name was Khalid Sheikh Mohammed.

This was the biggest break in the interrogation. As for Padilla, it was made clear to Zubaydah that this disclosure would mean nothing unless he was caught—flesh-and-blood proof of Zubaydah's cooperation. The captive told his interrogators how he could be found and, a few days later, Padilla was spotted in Pakistan. Agents followed him. He was bound for America. On May 8, Padilla stepped off a plane at O'Hare Airport in Chicago. FBI agents met him at the gate.

On the seventh floor at CIA, most of the participants felt satisfied they'd chosen right in not putting captives like Zubaydah into the U.S. justice system.

"Imagine him sitting with a lawyer," John McLaughlin said at one five o'clock meeting in May where the modest disclosures from Zubaydah were discussed. "That would be an utter cop-out. We would never know what we missed."

On the issue of interrogation, Zubaydah represented a first test, with results that could now be reviewed. It seemed as though the FBI—and those inside CIA advocating a gentler model of interrogation—might be right. That sort of traditional, subtle "debriefing" seemed to have worked. But as to "extreme methods"—their worth, their deficits—a counterpoint was offered. "Did it work," a DO chief said, "because he was tortured first? That's the problem. Once you go down this road—and try everything—it's hard to know what worked."

Week by week, it was turning into the springtime of alerts. The faint outlines of al Qaeda were talking shape. In Langley, a preferred metaphor was of a puzzle. A vast puzzle. Of course, it was a puzzle you assembled without seeing the picture on the box, or knowing the size. "The first steps," John McLaughlin would tell the senior managers, were to find "edge pieces." That way, you start to create the frame. The frame sets boundaries, then leads you inward.

It was clear that the huge terrorist-catching machine—NSA and the telecom partners, First Data and various financial backrooms—needed high-quality inputs to perform; otherwise they just thrashed, undirected, and caused damage in many directions. At the NSA, the phone numbers and e-mail addresses found at the Shabaz cottage were lighting up troves of cables. All sigint collected around the world since 2000 with the keyword "Mukhtar" was reassessed under the known identity of Khalid Sheikh Mohammed.

The phone numbers, computers, CDs, and e-mail addresses seized at Zubaydah's apartment now—a month after his capture—began to show a yield. This was not *garbage in,* like so many of the First Data searches. These higher-quality inputs were entered into big Cray supercomputers at NSA; many then formed the roots of a surveillance tree—trunk to branches to limbs and buds. Each bud grew, in seconds, into another tree.

The key assessments were then passed to the basement of CIA, where the most promising telecom links were matched with their companion impulses in the world financial system. In the sub-terrain, "Nervous Phil," the CIA's matrix master, and a team of connection specialists—most of them women—worked long days and slept on couches. Nervous Phil, like his friend Dennis Lormel at FBI, realized that the key would be to reverse the inefficient process of massive key-word searches, or credit card runs on anyone with an Arab surname who rented a truck. That was, as they say, using the wrong end of the telescope. On the other hand, tracking the impulses on a specific hot credit card, or bank account, or phone line, could light up a global grid in real time. This was human sentience, writ large by technology. Tag the beasts, the terrorists, and see where they go. Don't seize them. Follow them. Two possible suspects shop at the same bodega in Wembley? Get CIA to call MI5 and get an agent into the neighborhood. Three suspicious men use the same storefront bank in Munich? Find the parent corporation. Start weaving spiderwebs, the gossamer threads that display on drop-down screens, or posters, or easels, who is connected to whom.

It was a game of critical mass, steady but slow. The landscape only starts to take shape when there are enough hits, enough lights to display a density of connections, a density that reveals terrorist hot spots.

In the meantime, it was dot to dot. A captive at Guantánamo Bay—Juma al-Dosari, a Bahraini in his late twenties—had been under interrogation that yielded a disclosure. Al-Dosari had been swept up among the captives in Afghanistan in the fall. It took U.S. investigators a few months to figure out that he was an al Qaeda recruiter who had been to America a year earlier, in April 2001. Under interrogation, "Juma" revealed that he had met with a group of men in Lackawanna, a western New York town with a large Yemeni community, and that he had tried to recruit them.

One of the New York men had, in fact, come to the attention of the FBI not long after Juma's springtime visit. An anonymous letter the bureau received said that a group of men from Lackawanna had traveled to Afghanistan to "meet bin Laden and train with him." Shortly after the letter was received, one of the men returned from Afghanistan and was questioned by the FBI in Buffalo. The man's explanations seemed plausible; he was stable, educated, married, with several children, and the FBI essentially filed the report away, periodically checking on him and compatriots in the Lackawanna community. But al-Dosari's interrogation revealed an alias for another man who was in Lackawanna, and was now at large: Kamal Derwish. Derwish had been born in Buffalo, returned with his family to Yemen as a boy, and, after a stint in Saudi Arabia, had come back to the Buffalo area in 1998 as a man of twenty-five. He was the spiritual leader of the Lackawanna group and had led them to the al Farooq training camp in Afghanistan in May 2001.

Knowing his alias, U.S. sigint operators were able to locate communications he'd had with Saad bin Laden, Osama's son, and Tawfiq bin Attash, one of the planners of the 2000 bombing of the USS *Cole.* They also learned that he'd received advanced weapons training in Afghanistan and, in the mid-nineties, had fought in Bosnia with Muslim rebels.

This set off alarms. Derwish was dangerous, hooked in closely with al Qaeda's operational decision makers and—as a spiritual leader and charismatic guide—was a neat fit for the role of cell leader. Conclusion: Derwish's cell must be the men in Lackawanna.

On May 17, the information was passed to the FBI's Radical Islamic Task Force and then to the Buffalo field office. After months of questions from Bush to Mueller—"Are there terror cells in America?"—the FBI director finally had his answer. Yes, Mr. President, we think we've found a cell in, of all places, Lackawanna, New York, a depressed town on the edge of Lake Erie.

★ ★ ★

Meanwhile, Zubaydah was still talking—maybe nonsense, maybe not. There was almost no way to tell. The Brooklyn Bridge has been targeted, he told his interrogators. So has the Statue of Liberty. Yes, both of them.

The FBI tried to keep the information tightly held. But it was leaked internally to the New York City Police Department, which had its own counterterrorism division.

At the end of May, the city was put on high alert.

In public, Vice President Dick Cheney defended the alerts. "We now have a large number of people in custody, detainees," Mr. Cheney said on CNN's *Larry King Live*, "and periodically as we go through this process we learn more about the possibility of future attacks. And based on that kind of reporting, we try to be very cautious and alert people when we think there's a reason to be concerned about a particular subject or target."

Donald Rumseld went before a subcommittee of the Senate Appropriations Committee on May 21 to talk about the military budget. What was most noteworthy, however, was a short disquisition he offered on "the threat."

"In just facing the facts," he said, "we have to recognize that terrorist networks have relationships with terrorist states that have weapons of mass destruction, and that they inevitably are going to get their hands on them, and they would not hesitate one minute in using them. That's the world we live in."

He went on to discuss how terrorists were linked to Iran, Iraq, Syria, Libya, North Korea, and "one or two other" countries, all of which were developing weapons of mass destruction. Terrorists, he said, were intent on gaining nuclear, chemical, and biological weapons, and would succeed, eventually, despite U.S. efforts to prevent them. "We are going to be living in a period of limited or no warning," he added. He said al Qaeda terrorists were in the United States, "and they are very well-trained."

Such comments, flowing from the administration for the past several months, were having the expected effect. A CBS News poll released just before the Rumsfeld testimony and the New York City alerts showed 33 percent of those surveyed said they believed another terrorist attack was "very likely." A week before, only 25 percent held such a view.

While the array of alerts, and cryptic, fearful public pronouncements, were fueling a diffuse public concern, deep inside the administration, and at uppermost levels of security clearance, the fires of fear raged.

Rumsfeld's last comment about "very well-trained" terrorists in the United States was a direct reference to the deeply classified information about Lackawanna, which was not disclosed publicly for several months. His comments about linkages between terrorists and rogue states—or states, like Pakistan, with uncontrollable elements within them—were the vapor trail of repeated, often urgent reports about the Kandahar campfire and the anthrax trail.

On the first score, there was progress. President Musharraf had moved forcefully against the Pakistani nuclear scientists and UTN, the organization they represented. Sultan Bashiruddin Mahmood's later interrogations—and polygraphing by the CIA—indicated that no radiological materials had actually been passed by the scientists to bin Laden. While the polygraphs confirmed and deepened the account of the campfire meeting, they also were particularly helpful in directing Pakistani intelligence agents to members and supporters of UTN, including several who were funding sources in the United States. Especially after the Americans expressed their displeasure that Pakistani troops had not assisted as promised in corking escape routes from Tora Bora, Musharraf had acted with particular vigor with regard to UTN. By late spring 2002, many of the organization's members were imprisoned, and Mahmood—still a widely known scientist in Pakistan—was under permanent house arrest.

The anthrax issue was more complex. There seemed to be more labs, and wider capabilities, than originally thought. Rolf Mowatt-Larssen was chasing ghosts—traveling to Pakistan, Afghanistan, Indonesia. As to radiological, chemical, or biological agents finding their way to terrorists, the Vice President's belief was that it was an issue of when, not whether.

All these reports helped fuel Rumsfeld's sense of futility as to America's ability to stop the spread of destructive weapons and keep them from terrorists. That futility was the fuel that drove the plans to invade Iraq . . . as soon as possible.

Cheney's ideas about how "our reaction" would shape behavior—whatever the evidence showed—were expressed in an off-the-record meeting Rumsfeld had with NATO defense chiefs in Brussels on June 6. According to an outline for his speech, the secretary told those assembled that "absolute proof cannot be a precondition for action."

The primary impetus for invading Iraq, according to those attending NSC briefings on the Gulf in this period, was to make an example of Hussein, to create a demonstration model to guide the behavior of anyone with the temerity to acquire destructive weapons or, in any way, flout the authority of the United States.

In Oval Office meetings, the President would often call Iraq a "game changer." More specifically, the theory was that the United States—with a forceful action against Hussein—would change the rules of geopolitical analysis and action for countless other countries.

Yet reports about bin Laden and the Pakistani scientists, or al-Zawahiri and his anthrax program, did not connect neatly with these ideas. These were nonstate actors dealing with two freelance scientists on homegrown projects.

This disconnect added pressure to prove the Saddam–al Qaeda link. Early doubts voiced by CIA about any connection between the two were duly noted and largely ignored by the Vice President, Don Rumsfeld, and their respective staffs.

Their own intelligence units, after all, were hard at work. In Deputy Defense Secretary Paul Wolfowitz's arsenal by the late spring of 2002 were a variety of visual aids—including posters with linkage charts of Iraqi officials and their potential connections to Mohammed Atta and other al Qaeda operatives—which he carried to high-level meetings.

An area of intense analysis by Defense Under Secretary Douglas Feith's unit at the Pentagon, with support from Cheney's office, was how quickly after the 9/11 attacks one could see joyous demonstrators crowd the streets of Baghdad. In briefing after briefing, questions swirled, based on what was visible on various Arab satellite channels. Could such an effusion—complete with signs—be spontaneous? If not, how long would it take to plan and orchestrate? Would that not mean that Hussein knew of the attacks in advance?

CIA would then commit a team to digging out the answers, present them, and then get new versions of the questions. No pressure, in any overtly articulated way. Just repetition.

"What became apparent," said the DI chief Jami Miscik, "is that some questions kept getting asked over and over and over again . . . as if, somehow, the answer would change, even without any good reason for it to change—like any new information coming in."

CIA was locked in what a White House bent on action would consider the old reality-based world—a realm of the Scowcrofts, or Powells. While CIA analysts may have understood, intellectually, the audacity of what the White House was suggesting—what the Cheney Doctrine asserted—it couldn't manage to act accordingly. At least, not yet.

CHAPTER FOUR

ZAWAHIRI'S HEAD

The digital clock buzzed at 1:10 a.m. on June 8 and Dan Coleman reached over to smack it silent. No hour to be staring, half conscious, at the stucco ceiling of a rental apartment far from home. No hour to be awake, anywhere.

He groaned upright, pulled on his jeans and a Seton Hall sweatshirt he wore at every opportunity—his daughter was a sophomore—and, in a few minutes, he was pulling out of the garage in his 2000 Oldsmobile Intrigue, jet-black, FBI issue. The streets were quiet, but the capital was lit up as always—the monuments, the Mall, the White House—and he thought of London during the Blitz, how they cut off the electricity. Should all these lights be on in the middle of the night? he wondered. Is anyone really protecting the city during the vulnerable, early-morning hours?

With open roads, he could speed to the 495 Beltway that rims Washington and onto the Dulles Toll Road, heading northwest for the Virginia airport. It was a good time to think, as the dark landscape passed, and he thought about his wife and kids in New Jersey, his asthma, which was acting up, and his oldest son, Danny, in Afghanistan, an Army Ranger who had parachuted into Kandahar. A letter

Danny had sent just that week said things were going well enough, that there wasn't much left to do. He was so happy to read that letter.

The last time he'd seen Danny was at the end of January, when he got a short leave and they had a party for him. They'd gotten word right before the holidays that he'd be coming home and Maureen insisted they keep all the lights up, and the Christmas stockings, and they watered the base of the Scotch pine about a hundred times to keep the needles on. When he got there, it would be just like Christmas Eve. And it was. God, it was. Maureen picked him up at the airport. Dan drove like a madman up from Washington for the party. It was lovely, the kid out of uniform—he always took it off as fast as he could—and looking so damn good, smiling, all matter-of-fact and blasé about the harrowing things he'd done—*No big deal, Dad. So how you been?* Just like Dan's own father, who couldn't become a cop because he was wounded in World War II, or Dan's grandfather, a cop who never made much of a deal about how tough he was. There was a code: *you did what you had to do.*

There are always a few people who—by tricks of fate and, often, bad luck—end up living more than the usual share of some larger historical moment. Across time, examples are plentiful—like the Manassas, Virginia, farmer who moved from his demolished house in 1861 to the quieter locale of Appomattox, and had the war's surrender documents signed in his parlor; or Hawaii senator Daniel Inouye, who signed up for World War II duty at a time when Japanese-Americans were being hauled into internment camps and then won a Medal of Honor in Europe with the famed "go for broke" regiment of Japanese-Americans soldiers.

Dan, in a quieter way, is one of those people: 9/11, with all its crêped effects, hanging from his rambling frame. He'd been there, of course, and sped over from FBI headquarters with a few colleagues as the towers went down. They did what they could—sweated, and tended to the injured, and screamed and cried on that day, and for days after. Then he drove the black Oldsmobile home to Maureen and they looked at each other, knowing that Danny, as an Army Ranger, would be going to Afghanistan, and he'd be the first in. By any estimate, that would be as dangerous as any assignment. Maureen said what they both were thinking: "It's not enough you couldn't stop the attack. Now our son's gonna get killed."

Dan thought of all this, what Maureen said, and then the Christmas party, then Maureen again—two memories that fit like a handshake—as the lights of Dulles Airport came into view. Built in the middle of nowhere back in 1962, it still stands alone and forlorn in the Virginia hills, lit up for its own pleasure at 2 a.m. He turned the big Olds away from the large public terminal toward the one for private planes—general aviation—and stepped out into the June night.

Waiting in the foyer of the little terminal were two men—one was a lieutenant colonel, a big guy, whom Dan didn't know; the second was a post-9/11 acquaintance named Steve, a onetime social worker who now was an intelligence officer with Delta Force. They'd just stepped off a plane from Afghanistan.

"Steve!" Dan shouted. They chatted for a precious moment or two, as Steve told Dan what Dan hoped to hear—that he'd checked up on Danny, and that he was doing fine. The confidentiality rules on this score are strict. Many Special Forces soldiers can't even write to loved ones about their location or the nature of their mission—but Steve bent things a little for big Dan, a fellow soldier in the struggle.

"He's a great kid, I hear," Steve said, and Dan nodded and laughed. "Yea, I hear that, too."

Then it was down to business.

"Well, it took a couple months, but here it is." Steve reached into a duffel bag at his feet and grabbed a round metal box, Army green with yellow letters—US GOVERNMENT—and about the size of a hat box.

He handed it to Coleman. Something rolled inside.

Dan looked at him. "So it's in there?"

"Far as I know," said Steve.

Zawahiri's head.

How does the head end up, here, at Dulles Airport? As with anything, locating a starting point is a matter of how deep you want to dig.

For the real deep drillers, you could start in A.D. 610, when a middle-aged merchant, Muhammad ibn 'Abdu'llah ibn 'Abdu'l-Muttalib, retreated to a mountain cave near Mecca for prayer and contemplation and was visited by the angel Gabriel. The angel commanded Muhammad to memorize and recite a long array of verses sent by God—passages that would eventually form the core of the Koran.

By the time of his death, twenty-two years later, Muhammad had conquered numerous opponents and established a new monotheistic religion that incorporated and, in the minds of him and his followers', succeeded, or completed, many precepts of both Christianity and Judaism.

That faith would become the cornerstone of an empire that grew from Mecca over the next two centuries to include much of the Iberian Peninsula, Central and South Asia, Africa, and parts of Southeast Asia.

One feature of that period of growth was *ijtihad,* or critical interpretation of religious teachings to find applications in one's own life and circumstances. Scholars on the Arabian Peninsula, who had embraced this practice prior to Muhammad's arrival, pushed forward a concept of *ijtihad* after his death that helped disparate peoples, with diverse traditions, find a home under Islam's umbrella.

But empire-building demands tough choices. Those in power tend to seek consolidation of victories. Two hundred years along, by the mid-800s, four major schools of thought had emerged, each providing a firm set of answers to unresolved questions in the Koran, the Sunna, and various Islamic texts, and the "gates of *Ijtihad*" were closed. The so-called "golden period of Islam" and many of the "cradle of civilization" countries that had embraced the theology would slowly and steadily fade from this point. But battles inside the religion about the right to *ijtihad*—or various interpretations of the first teachings— would rage for a millennium between, and within, the religion's two major camps, Sunni and Shiite.

This crests to present tense, or almost, with the rise of Wahhabism in the early nineteenth century, stemming from the belief of its founder, Ibn Abdul-Wahhab, that certain early, strict precepts of Islam could be tapped, in essence, for a modern-age revival of the religion. Wahhab and his followers believed "the gates" should be opened, allowing them to assert a fiery fundamentalism based on a host of literal interpretations. The Saud family, which won dominance of Arabia in battles across the nineteenth and early twentieth centuries, were adherents.

And by the late twentieth century, so were a wide array of young educated Arabs, who grew increasingly dispirited with the blunted opportunities and dissatisfactions of life in "modernist" Arab regimes, which were often oppressive and run by monarchists.

The push and shove between the modernists and the fundamentalists would define the roiling recent histories of Iran, Afghanistan, Iraq, Saudi Arabia, Pakistan, Egypt, Jordan—virtually every Islamic country—a shoving match conducted, in many countries, on the slick surface of U.S. strategic, often oil-related, interests. Among the countless educated, privileged, and dispirited young men of this latest era was an Egyptian surgeon, Ayman al-Zawahiri, who flirted with fundamentalism, and politics, until he was arrested in sweeps after the assassination of Anwar Sadat in 1981. In Egyptian prisons, Zawahiri was tortured, and radicalized, and emerged to lead the Egyptian Islamic Jihad, a group that eventually merged with bin Laden's group to form al Qaeda.

Brilliant and vicious, Zawahiri helped to focus and radicalize his wealthy, younger partner, and brought to their shared efforts a wide array of expert tacticians—engineers, scientists, computer specialists—from Egypt's educated ranks. Sigint picked up right after 9/11 had al Qaeda operatives calling the attacks "the doctor's plan." For those who'd been following Zawahiri, this was no surprise. He was bin Laden's Cheney, the older man who made sure that ideas were carried to action. Soon, the doctor became a man as sought after as bin Laden himself, and the star of pamphlets dropped across Afghanistan, once the war had started, offering a "$25 Million Reward for Information" leading to the death or capture . . .

Reports of the death of Zawahiri were constant, at least four of them in late 2001 and early 2002. Each one caused a current of hopeful anticipation to run through the White House, the CIA, and among anyone who knew anything. Each one dissolved under scrutiny.

But this one was different. A delegation of Afghan tribal chiefs said they had proof positive. Zawahiri had been killed in December—a time that corresponded to many of the reports—and buried in a wadi, a riverbed, that was soon covered in snow. U.S. military intelligence, working with Canadian Special Forces, said they'd need proof positive, of course, before delivering the $25 million. Not a problem, said the tribal chiefs. With the spring thaw, the body could be retrieved, and it was.

And that's how a jawless head ended up in a metal box that Steve, the social worker pressed into intelligence work, pushed into the meaty hands of Dan Coleman, from a long line of New York Irish toughs.

"Thanks," Dan said, though that didn't seem quite right.

Then the two of them, along with a third officer, who mostly watched, walked into an adjacent room.

"Let's take a look," Dan said.

He peeled off the top, reached his hand into the cool, moist darkness, pushed his fingers down through a bed of river mud, and lifted out the skull, a bit of skin still left around the crown.

It felt like a boccie ball. He held it upright in his palm, as Hamlet did with Yorick's. The three men looked at it, appraisingly, and all saw it at the same instant: in the middle of the forehead, the eyeless head showed an indentation. It was unmistakable: the spot where Zawahiri had a dark callus, a mark of piety, of humility, from countless hours of prostration, his head pressed to stone, concrete, wood, or simply dirt, as he committed his life to the will of Allah.

"I don't know." Dan shrugged. "Sure looks a lot like him."

They nodded. *Definitely.*

A moment later, Dan, the box under his arm, was opening the trunk of the black Olds. It was a car whose trunk was gently dusted, like the upholstery in the backseat and the floor mats and the ridge of decorative chrome around the radio, with a thin residue of white powder. Dan never had time to really clean the car after 9/11, to deep-clean it.

So, from a river wadi in Afghanistan, the head was now placed in the ash heap of a car, a rolling Made-in-America burial urn.

Driving out of Dulles, Dan felt a little crazy, his mind all over. It felt funny to have the damn thing back there. This was top secret, classified. He was under strict orders to tell no one, not even those with top clearances. But, Jesus, what if he got pulled over and searched? How would he explain the skull in the trunk?

He punched the radio. Flipped stations. Nothing. Then grabbed the book on tape he'd been listening to lately—Colleen McCullough's *Caesar: A Novel,* part of her "Masters of Rome" series. Like a lot of cops, over the years he'd had plenty of idle car time to self-educate and indulge his interests. He liked books about the Romans. Like plenty of others, he saw parallels between them and us. But what interested him most was how the Romans used their power and how clearly they saw the perils of its exercise.

He listened as the car sped toward the nation's capital, carrying the head of our enemy in the trunk.

In the giant concrete headquarters of the FBI on Ninth Street, a landlocked midpoint between Congress and 1600 Pennsylvania, the lights were on, but dimmed, inside the third-floor evidence lab. A forensic pathologist needed to receive the head and book it as evidence—and it wasn't easy getting someone there at 3 a.m. The person he'd called was a specialist in buried remains. She was also a single mom, who, some years earlier, had adopted a baby girl from Russia. Dan knew to tiptoe in; the pathologist, whose name was Missy, motioned to her left and put a finger to her lips. The girl, now eight, was sleeping soundly on the couch.

"What have we got here?" she whispered.

"A head," Dan said, with a shrug, "looking for a DNA match." It was a typically omissive conversation. For people like Dan, everyone, everywhere in the government and across America, must remain on a "need to know" basis. They know only what they need to. Not a word more.

Missy opened the box and reached in with gloved hands. "There's not very much here to get what we need" for a mitochondrial DNA test, which can identify a specific individual's DNA by testing living tissue against a match. She held it up and nosed in close, like a dentist, squinting. "Maybe there's some tissue in one of the teeth."

She put the head on a sterile mat, turned to Dan, and pulled out an evidence form. "What do I file it under?"

"265ANY-259391," he said, as she scribbled.

She looked up at him, expectantly. "The case file for Osama bin Laden?" Dan nodded, his face blank. She gave him a receipt.

They hovered there, awkwardly. Dan, Missy, Zawahiri's head, and a little girl on the couch.

"I hope it's whoever you're hoping it is," she whispered. And the head—an artifact, a talisman, of the "war on terror"—was placed into an evidence locker without a sound, so as not to wake a sleeping child.

A few days later, the FBI forensic specialists drilled through the skull to get into the anterior molar. There was a bit of live tissue. They got their sample.

DNA analysis could now begin.

The CIA was brought in, and moved into action. Unmatched DNA can determine sex and age, but for specific identity they needed a DNA match from a family member. Zawahiri's brother, Mohammed, was in custody in Cairo. A CIA operations manager called a chief at Egyptian intelligence.

He explained the situation.

The Egyptian listened. "No problem," he said. "We'll get his brother, cut off his arm, and send it over."

"No . . . Christ!" the agency man stammered. "No, just a vial of blood. A vial of blood's all we need."

The Egyptian sighed. "Fine. Whatever you want. You want blood. We'll send blood."

Yosri Fouda traveled like a fugitive, like a man who knew too much.

True enough. He had spent two extraordinary days in the Karachi apartment in mid-April with Khalid Sheikh Mohammed, bin al-Shibh, and the others, talking about the Koran, praying, and discussing 9/11.

KSM told Fouda that the planning for "Holy Tuesday" had begun two and a half years prior to the attacks. He said, "As we were discussing targets, we first thought of striking at a couple of nuclear facilities, but decided against it for fear it would go out of control."

KSM said it was decided to leave alone the nuclear facilities "for now."

Khalid Sheikh Mohammed, a Kuwaiti by birth, was clearly al Qaeda's operational chief, the tactical field commander to the more removed and ethereal bin Laden and the strategic-thinking Zawahiri. He told Fouda that there was a long line of recruited martyrs to choose from—so many, the organization had something called the "Department of Martyrs," poised to attack "infidels and Zionists."

At one point, his partner, bin al-Shibh, had shown Fouda a suitcase of his "Hamburg souvenirs"—dozens of items, ranging from Boeing brochures and flight manuals to English-language textbooks and CD-ROMs of flight simulation programs. Bin al-Shibh was, in fact, chosen as the twentieth hijacker—not Moussaoui, who had been taken off the roster because he was deemed unreliable—but he was unable to enter the United States because he was on various "no-fly" lists. He was young, elegant, and well educated—a match, in an odd way, to the sophisticated, intellectually agile Fouda—and he recited a chilling prayer for his guest: "Our words shall remain dead, like brides made of wax, still and heartless. Only when we die for them shall they resurrect and live among us."

In the end, Fouda interviewed both men at length, stayed a second night, and then was blindfolded for his departure. KSM assured the correspondent that they would pass the tapes along to him expeditiously.

But that didn't happen. Fouda waited, taking time off to reflect on what had occurred, quietly working on the project by tracing bin al-Shibh's path through Hamburg. He took part in a "Media and Terrorism" seminar in Cairo, and then flew to Beirut to interview the family of Ziad Jarrah—pilot of United Airlines Flight 93 that crashed in rural Pennsylvania. By early June, he'd still not received the interview tapes, but he did get several mysterious messages about delivery of the tapes for cash. Meanwhile, he told no one what had occured in Karachi.

The Al Jazeera headquarters in Doha, Qatar, looks and feels like a home for CNN or any Western television network, but it is subtly different in how it serves its audience and in the dilemmas it faces. While the station exerts extraordinary influence in shaping Arab opinions, it is also a vast experiment in whether the ideals of a free press can take seed in this often inhospitable part of the world.

When the station opened for business in 1996 as the pet project of a new emir—Qatar's Sheikh Hamad bin Khalifa al-Thani, who had just taken over as emir from his aging father in a bloodless coup—it was hailed by the West as a great leap forward.

The idea of a vast, pan-Arabic station was first embraced by the BBC, which had tried to launch an Arab-language service with a Saudi station in 1994—an effort that folded up in 1996.

The emir took advantage of that shortfall, hiring many well-trained Arabic-speaking journalists who'd worked for the BBC start-up. His station grew quickly, and lent a boost to al-Thani's broader mission of turning the oil-producing Qatar—a country about the size of Connecticut that also sits on 14 trillion cubic meters of natural gas—into the Switzerland of the Arab world. It would be a wealthy, neutral, and stable nation. The country's per capita GDP of $26,000 is on par with most Western democracies. The population is 95 percent Muslim, but diverse, with nearly half its citizens claiming their ethnicities as Pakistani, Indian, or Iranian. Not that there isn't a strong fundamentalist Muslim community, and some stirrings of radicalism among the country's population of 900,000. The emir, whose al-Thani family has ruled Qatar since the mid-nineteenth century, artfully walks the line between Old World theocracy and New World clout. That means odd contradictions: to wit, the emir *is the law,* and also the defense minister, in a country with an 89 percent literacy rate, universal health care, and a satellite television station.

At the start, Al Jazeera was a novelty—especially in a region where almost all television stations were state-controlled and the governments were used to having their messages passed along, respectfully.

Almost immediately, complications arose. The station criticized its own government, an act that prompted praise from the U.S. State Department in 2000. After a tough story about Jordan, the Amman bureau was closed and Jordan recalled its ambassador from Doha. The Saudis, similarly aggrieved, enforced a debilitating advertising ban against the station. In response to unflattering Al Jazeera stories, six other countries did the same. The cable channel has received some four hundred letters of official complaint.

Though the United States was often the subject of sharp-elbowed reporting on the station's news shows and arch, anti-Western commentary on its roundtables, those costs were modest compared to benefits of having an independent media source in the Arab world.

When the Afghan war started, however, that calculus—like so much else defining U.S. foreign policy—was reassessed. Nonpartisan, with sympathies for its Muslim audience, Al Jazeera reported intensively on the carnage caused by U.S. bombing runs in Afghanistan. The pictures outraged American policy makers and prompted Colin Powell to encourage the emir in his early October visit to the United States to rein in the station. Al-Thani responded with a lecture about cherished freedoms: "Parliamentary life requires you have free and credible media . . . and that is what we are trying to do."

Beyond the grisly photos—such as the burned corpses of Afghan children killed in Jalalabad—the station was also viewed as a platform for bin Laden, who first appeared on the network in 1998. Just a few hours after U.S. planes began bombing the country in early October, a worldwide audience watched Osama bin Laden, a Kalashnikov at his side, sitting outside his cave hideout and casting the battle as one between Islam and the West. "America," he said, "will never taste security and safety unless we feel security and safety in our land."

More statements from bin Laden would follow. Tapes were delivered directly to Al Jazeera at its Afghanistan headquarters in Kabul. Condoleezza Rice complained that al Qaeda was sending coded messages to adherents and supporters, and pressed U.S. broadcasters to not run broadcasts of al Qaeda tapes without a careful preview.

The frustration, though, ran deeper. Bin Laden, and al Qaeda, were showing that nonstate actors could also mount a kind of message power. The appeal of bin Laden, smiling in front of his cave hideaway, or speaking in elegant Arabic about the challenge Muslims now face from the American Goliath, was too good a show, too strong a narrative. One man and his ragtag army facing down an angry empire. The United States, which seemed to boast global media power to match its overwhelming military strength, was being bested again.

By early November, Al Jazeera was seen as bin Laden's facilitator. The President, who'd met with al-Thani when the emir visited on October 4, turned to Tenet.

It was widely known that Tenet and the emir were close. Tenet had visited Qatar many times since he became DCI. The emir, a six-foot-eight, 350-pound giant in gold-trimmed robes and sandals, was a Tenet man. They joshed. They schemed. They talked tough to each other.

This, of course, was part of the Tenet method. He had earned the trust, year by year, of leaders of Arab nations—a trust that was seen, rightly, in the first months after 9/11 as among the most precious assets of the United States.

"What's that line—you kiss a lot of frogs before you find a prince?" said CIA executive director Buzzy Krongard, about Tenet's array of relationships—with Abdullah of Saudi Arabia, the emir of Qatar, Musharraf, and on and on. "George kissed a lot of frogs."

Tenet was like the legendary salesman who would do whatever was necessary—wine and dine, stay up all night over Scotches, send notes on holidays—to win over a client. To many Arab leaders, he became an unofficial adviser, counseling them about their affairs in the complex world.

In this case, Tenet knew al-Thani was in a tight spot—pressed between his obligations to the United States and an unstable Arab world. Leaders of the various Arab states, his peers, chafed from having been bloodied in recent years by Al Jazeera and finding no comfort from al-Thani.

How could al-Thani now provide improved coverage to the United States? Tenet pressed him—to rein in the station. The emir explained that Arab leaders regularly complained to him as well. The key, in terms of either his Arab brethren or the United States, was, the emir said, a hard-and-fast rule to never get involved in issues of coverage. There was nothing he could do.

The CIA saw its options more broadly. There were discussions in late October and early November about what might be done.

As Krongard said, "It came down to a principle you'd hear again and again over the next few years about the Arab world. *Talk to them in a way that they understand.*"

On November 13—a hectic day when Kabul fell to the Northern Alliance and there were celebrations in the streets of the city—a U.S. missile obliterated Al Jazeera's office. Al Jazeera reporters, covering the city's fall, were out in the street.

"This office has been known by everybody, the American airplanes know the location of the office," said Al Jazeera's managing director,

Mohammed Jasim al-Ali. "They know we are broadcasting from there."

All that, in fact, was correct.

Inside the CIA, and White House, there was satisfaction that a message had been sent to Al Jazeera.

On the morning of June 14, 2002, Al Jazeera's biggest scoop was entering the building. Fouda, with notes and disclosures—if, still, without his promised tapes—felt he needed finally to file a report to his bosses.

At lunch that day at the elegant Diplomatic Club on the beachfront in Doha, he described the long string of events, of intrigue and encounter, to Mohammed Jasim al-Ali—essentially, the editorial director of Al Jazeera. "No way!" al-Ali shouted, his eyes wide. He said that he and Fouda needed to go up the ranks, and tell the satellite channel's vice chairman. Which they did that afternoon.

The next morning, they met with Al Jazeera's chairman, Sheikh Hamad bin Thamer al-Thani (a cousin of the emir). For a half-hour Fouda described what he had found, until the sheikh interrupted him with questions. "The tapes! When are you going to get ahold of them?" Fouda went through the saga. "How many people know about this so far?" Fouda answered, Only the people currently in the room. "Keep it quiet, and take no chances," Sheikh Hamad said. "If you need any special arrangements for your security, just let me know."

Hamad asked about Khalid Sheikh Mohammed. Two weeks before, FBI chief Bob Mueller had held a press conference officially announcing that KSM was the mastermind behind 9/11—the main disclosure from the Zubaydah interrogation. Pictures and profiles of the terrorist had saturated the media, elevating KSM to the status of international criminal, and folk hero in much of the Muslim world.

No one had heard from either bin Laden, or Zawahiri, in months—and KSM filled the void. Ramzi bin al-Shibh—the only member of the Hamburg cell who was still at large—was now placed in his proper context at KSM's side. An interview with both of them? It was the biggest scoop in Al Jazeera's history.

Fouda and his bosses talked the rest of that day in hushed tones. The anniversary of 9/11, and the planned release of Fouda's documentary, was still three months away. Much work needed to be done. The correspondent would do a good deal of it himself with a handheld camera. Anyone working on the project would be kept in the dark. It must be kept in the utmost secrecy. On that last point, everyone agreed.

George Tenet walked into the 5 p.m. meeting looking as if he were going to burst.

"I'm going first today," he said, as everyone settled. The usual protocol—of CTC's threat matrix, then the various reports—was altered.

Not today, George said. "What I have today will be the only thing we're going to care about."

It was mid-June. People settled into their chairs.

"As you know, we've had our differences with my friend the Emir," Tenet said. "But today, he gave us an amazing gift."

Then he laid it out, long, sweet, and with relish. The story of Fouda's meeting with al Jazeera's top brass a few days before, with all the key details—including the probable location of the building and who was there, the nature of what KSM and Ramzi disclosed, including operational initiatives, such as al Qaeda's original plans to hit a U.S. nuclear plant. Fouda had a good idea of where the apartment was in Karachi, and what floor he had been on. He concluded with a traditional Tenet expression of affection:

"In other words, the fat fuck came through."

Conditions were discussed in Tenet's exchange with the emir about how CIA would handle the information, said one person who was at the meeting. No one, not even Al Jazeera management, knew the emir was making the call.

For a brief moment, the conference room was celebratory. As one CIA chief at the meeting said, "This was George's private account, and he loved being able to deliver in a huge way. And we all loved him being able to do it—it was about the best intel we had up to that point."

Tenet, after all, was not a CIA lifer, not trained in the methods of intelligence gathering. He was a politician, a Capitol Hill staff chief who'd moved up at the right moment, who had impressed Bill Clinton, and had ascended to the top.

A few questions were asked as the meeting commenced. Was the emir doing this to best the Saudis—rivals who had allegedly tried to assassinate him several years before and were not cooperating with many U.S. demands? Was he attempting to curry favor in spite of the fact that his station's office in Kabul was destroyed, *or because of it*? Did a show of force, in this case, produce a desired result? Those who believe in the primacy of force said yes.

CTC gave its threat report. Hank briefed on Afghanistan, Rolf on WMD initiatives, Nervous Phil on the global matrix. Then the meeting began to break up—everyone excitedly wielding assignments based on the emir's gift. The NSA would begin to blanket certain areas of Karachi. The station chiefs in Pakistan needed to start plotting strategy for humint. CTC's vast operation could now focus all coordinated efforts on the city. The Zubaydah interrogators were given a new weapon, an ability to surprise Zubaydah with unexpected knowledge—that they knew the whereabouts of "Mukhtar," and of bin al-Shibh, too—and see if their captive might accidentally fill in some blanks. That's the way some of the best information is gleaned: a subject spills something he thinks his interrogators already know.

"No one sleeps," Tenet said, adjourning. "We're closing in."

The Situation Room—that rectangle of wood paneling and drop-down screens in the White House basement—has recently matched the Oval Office as *most storied chamber* of the U.S. government. In an odd turn of the media age, this tiny square of carpeted real estate has seized the public's imagination. The multitudes watch, hour after hour, as actors play out dramas in a replica of the room, or see images of the actual players sitting portentously in their familiar habitat. So much seems to go on there, as the President meets with his National Security Council in these days of challenge and peril.

On balance, though, little actually gets done here. Any cabinet secretary will tell you that. Sit Room meetings are often for show, a place to hold forth, to let the President hear the various crafted offerings of his major departments and then ask a few questions. At this level, almost everything is decided before the meeting commences, or in some small afterglow cluster in the hallway.

For problem solving and action plans, anxious public servants will, time and again, bypass the Situation Room for its small adjacent conference room—a place where the real work gets done.

Since late October 2001, on each Wednesday at 8:30 a.m., a half-dozen men had been gathering in this room, coffee cups in hand, in one of the most secretive and productive meetings in the U.S. government. They were an ecumenical group, loosely managed by Treasury's general counsel, David Aufhauser, an elegant Washington lawyer who coordinated the government's overall "financial war." Included were representatives from the NSC, CIA, NSA, and the White House. Others periodically dropped by. Each week, their mission was to think in new ways about how money flowed around the globe and how to use that flow against al Qaeda.

Among the President's first commands back at his special cabinet meeting on September 17 was that America fight a "financial war" against terror. Treasury officials immediately began freezing any account they could find—enough that the President could set a rhetorical challenge the very next week in the Rose Garden. "This morning a major thrust of our war on terrorism began with a stroke of the pen," he said on September 24, unveiling a list of twenty-seven entities— thirteen suspected terrorist groups, eleven individuals, and three charities—whose assets the United States had frozen, or planned to freeze. "Today, we have launched a strike on the financial foundation of the global terror network."

Not really. It was simply the launching of what Aufhauser and others dubbed the "Rose Garden Strategy"—regular announcements about the freezing of assets of organizations and individuals with Arab names.

The President's idea was to starve the terrorists—cut off their financial supply lines. "By shutting these networks down," Bush said at another press conference—this one on November 7 at a new headquarters for the financial war, or FINCEN, in Vienna, Virginia—"we disrupt the murderers' work."

Each statement heightened the pressure for results. In late October, Aufhauser had called upon forty or so representatives from various agencies to collect their top ten names of potential terror finance targets. They then met in a large conference room at the Treasury Department with their lists. Several lists included the name Pacha Wazir. Wazir was a shadowy financial kingpin from the United Arab Emirates—the open-air money bazaar of the Arab world. He ran a chain of hawalas, storefront banks, and wire transfer stations across South Asia and Europe. Over the ensuing weeks, as everyone connected their data, it became clear that he was the main money-handler for Osama bin Laden.

About this time, Aufhauser asked Dennis Lormel to start coming to the select meetings on Wednesdays. They were in slightly different areas, of course. Aufhauser, and his fellows, were trying to cut off the flow of funds to terrorists, carrying forward the President's "financial war" pledge. Lormel was trying to use money as intelligence to find and stop terrorist operations.

But their interests—and those of their departments—began to converge. Wazir was too valuable, the Wednesday group decided, to simply freeze his assets and declare victory. They took his name off a list of asset freezes and seizures that the President was due to announce in a ceremony at the Treasury Department on December 11.

Meanwhile, FBI, and its parent the Justice Department, had yet to claim a single significant prosecution. Wazir would be their first.

By early 2002, Lormel had placed an FBI team deep inside the United Arab Emirates—the small, wealthy Gulf state that is the Arab world's banking hub. Not surprisingly, wire transactions, including the $109,000 that came through the UAE to Citibank and Chase and, ultimately, the 9/11 hijackers, emanated from Dubai. UAE's central bankers decided that quiet cooperation would be the best path, and Lormel's team in the country would be their tutors about audit controls and international banking standards. In Washington, Justice Department lawyers dug through available criminal statutes on money laundering, and, each week, Aufhauser asked Lormel how the prosecution was coming. "It's coming, David," Lormel said. "Just relax. It's coming."

Meanwhile, as spring arrived, the Wednesday group was discovering, little by little, that the President might have misspoken. According to various internal U.S. government estimates, approximately two thirds of the money that supported Islamic terrorist activities originated in Saudi Arabia. To stop the flow of available funding to terrorists—to "disrupt the murderers' work," as the President said—would mean the kind of cooperation that the Saudis wouldn't, or couldn't, provide. That was always the dilemma with the Saudis: intent versus capability. In the first few months after 9/11, there was no doubt that the problem was intent. Saudi finance ministers flat out told officials in the U.S. Treasury Department that there was no money of Saudi origin supporting terrorism. They said there was no assistance they could provide.

Privately, the President called it "our Saudi problem." In the spring of 2002, a stream of delegations from State, Treasury, CIA, and the NSC traveled to Riyadh to apply pressure. The Saudis started to give ground, just a bit. A list of compacts, agreements, and joint Saudi-U.S. task forces took shape, floating forward on expressions of shared purpose and gallons of tea from silver urns.

Two things then occurred. One, the Americans realized that desire, even if it were genuine, might not be enough. A country like Saudi Arabia, which lacked audit controls and traditions of financial transparency—and where so much money was tied up in the labyrinthine accounts of nearly 25,000 members of the royal family—might lack the tools, the so-called "financial handles," to track much of the country's capital flow. There were asset seizures in the kingdom in early and mid-2002. But even getting at the sources, when that was possible, was only a first step. Money often started clean, part of the flow that supported charities and basic needs of poor residents in the kingdom, or Sudan, or Bahrain, and then became "dirty" as it coursed downstream, account to account, person to person. Once it reached the hands of a potential terrorist, it was a dirty trickle. Terrorists can be "operational" for very modest sums. The 9/11 hijacking cost a total of only $500,000 in training, travel, and expenses. Billions, meanwhile, gush through the world's black market. All a terrorist needs to do is drop a bucket in that raging, toxic river.

But help was on the way. Initiatives launched by Treasury and CIA were getting much better at tracking money as it passed through accounts across the world. International banking compacts, matched with better targeting and an interest of countries, friendly or unfriendly to the U.S., not to be designated as supporters of terror, helped make specific cooperation from, say, the Saudis less important.

For those who understood the fitful workings of the bureaucracy, the sophisticated tack was now to press forward, freeze assets, as per the President's pronouncements, and offer lip service to higher-ups . . . while quietly doing something completely different.

Money, they now all understood, was for the most part a form of intelligence. The resource features of currency were a subordinate point. The money trail would serve as a hybrid of sorts. Not actionable humint, a precious rarity, but better, in general, than the sigint, which one CIA chief calls "humint without context." The money trail—what one might call *finint*—could identify the players, the place, and, possibly, the intent.

On a morning in June 2002, the Wednesday morning group slipped into their chairs with cups of coffee.

"Dennis, where the hell are we on Wazir?" Aufhauser pleaded. "Do we have a case here, or not?"

Lormel took a deep breath. An FBI delegation had just come back from the UAE. The country's central bankers had finally agreed to co-operate in ways unheard of in the Arab world. U.S. officials could all but live inside the country's financial system, nexus for so much of the capital flow in the Arab world. The FBI delegation had come with wish lists drawn from throughout the government—including some outstanding financial trails from the nineteen hijackers. As a financial center, the UAE was anxious to adopt the sort of audit controls, and fraud prevention mechanisms, that would impress institutions in the first world, in the United States, Europe, and Japan. They wanted to learn. What Lormel and his team learned was that Wazir was responsible for handling a startling $67 million in assets for al Qaeda in just over two years.

Second, it became clear that—despite his centrality to al Qaeda's overall funding—Wazir would be almost impossible to prosecute under U.S. statutes. There were too few trails that passed directly through America and U.S. financial institutions. All Lormel could gin up were misdemeanor money-laundering violations and a few modest felonies. This was certainly not enough to catch Wazir and haul him to the United States for prosecution.

After months of investigation of Wazir, and a final download of the key information for the UAE, it was a bitter pill to swallow.

"Sure, we have a case," Lormel told Aufhauser and the group. "Just a fucking lousy one. In terms of U.S. laws, it's going to be very difficult to ever prosecute guys like Wazir. If we could include all his activities worldwide, that'd be different. But U.S. law can only bring us slaps on the wrist." Lormel ran through the statutory particulars. "It kills me to say this," he concluded, "but we're never going to get the prosecutions we want on this financial stuff."

Across the table sat Nervous Phil.

"He's all yours, Phil," Dennis said.

Phil smiled. "Our plan for Wazir," he said in his clipped, halting way, "is . . . is to own him."

An hour later, back at FBI headquarters, Lormel called his lead FBI agent in Dubai—the Hong Kong of the Arab world, a city whose longing, merchantile soul belongs to no country save that of desire.

He had bad news.

"Stand back on Wazir," Lormel told Tim, the lead agent.

"I don't understand," Tim responded, incredulous. "Why?"

Lormel was torn. It wasn't enough that he had to pass his highest-value target over to a rival agency. The handoff itself was classified.

"Sorry . . . I'm not at liberty to say. Just back off."

In late May, NSA had a gift for CIA, and Mike Hayden was on the phone to deliver it. They had as precious a dispatch as any since 9/11.

It was a communication from a designee of bin Laden. The al Qaeda chief had not used a cell phone or satellite phone since 1998. He was very careful. A ring of deputies, below the level of a Zawahiri or KSM, carried messages for him. The United States had determined who some of them were. They made calls, or sent e-mails, on bin Laden's behalf.

One such communication was passed to a mysterious character in the kingdom, who—on the sigint—went by several aliases. The most compelling of which was "Swift Sword." Two things were clear. Osama bin Laden seemed to be alive and well and providing guidance from some location in the tribal regions along the Pakistan-Afghanistan border; and Swift Sword was, indeed, al Qaeda's representative on the Arabian Peninsula. His hand seemed to be in several places at once in the kingdom, guiding several cells of angry opponents of the regime. The instructions from the top of al Qaeda: Turn your operational focus on the overthrow of the Saudi government.

The illegitimacy of the Saudi regime was a favorite subject for bin Laden. His dream was that it, along with regimes in Egypt, Jordan, and countries across the region, would be overthrown, and that he would rule a restored Muslim empire, a caliphate, stretching from Tehran to Cairo, from the Gulf to the Atlantic. But this communication was not about grand designs and distant dreams. It was an action plan for whom to kill and what targets to hit.

Specifically, kill members of the royal family, and destroy the oil fields.

The idea of sabotaging the Saudi oil fields—the world's largest oil reserve—strikes directly at the heart of the uneasy co-dependency of the Gulf's oil-producing countries and their avid customers in the developed world. Fifteen percent of U.S. oil comes from Saudi Arabia. The strategic import, and clarity, of bin Laden's dictate was immediately clear to U.S. policy makers. His goal was never the untenable idea of engaging in a lasting struggle with America. It was, rather, to prompt the United States to withdraw its support for various Arab regimes, led by Saudi Arabia, leaving them vulnerable to uprisings.

And there was something else that NSA was picking up: opinions by Saudi clerics, several of whom commanded respect from a wide array of followers, that weapons of mass destruction could be used against infidels or apostate Muslims, including the Saudi royals.

Tenet and Mowatt-Larssen informed Cheney in a briefing. Then they went over to see Prince Bandar.

The ambassador had recovered his footing since the heated days of fall, when he was appearing regularly on network television to express his outrage and sorrow. The Saudis and the U.S. government offered repeated public assurances that they were allies, good friends, who were working together in the "war on terror." The Crown Prince had bonded with Bush in Crawford; and U.S. policy makers were scrambling in the days and weeks after the meeting to respond to a few of the Saudis' demands. They applied pressure on Israel to allow Arafat to leave his compound. A siege by Israelis at the Church of the Nativity in Bethlehem was ended. More statements, such as that Sharon is a "man of peace" were not forthcoming. Abdullah had something, if not much, to take back to the Arab world.

Bandar greeted the delegation arriving at his palatial home in northern Virginia, Tenet and a small band of deputies.

They hugged. Tenet is a hugger. He and Bandar have passed countless hours together, trust building, a Tenet specialty. With his ever present deputy, Rihad Massoud, ready with his notepad, Bandar led them to a cluster of chairs in his library.

After brief cordialities, Tenet got down to business. He leaned forward. A concerned look crossed his wide mug. "Bad news," Tenet said. "Bin Laden has changed his focus. Now it's you. It's Saudi Arabia."

Bandar was grim. "Scotch?"

He got some. And they drank Johnnie Walker Blue Label as Tenet delivered the bad news. He described the intelligence—the contact from al Qaeda leadership with their representative in the kingdom. The royal family was now in the crosshairs. The oil fields were being sized up for attack.

"Can we see the cable?" Bandar asked.

"Can't," Tenet said. "But I'll tell you everything you need to know."

It was the start of a secret shift in relations between the United States and Saudi Arabia, getting the Saudis, so to speak, off the sidelines and on the field. Bush's odd meeting with Abdullah hadn't done it, nor had a stream of U.S. dignitaries arriving in Riyadh, exhorting the Saudis to allow the Americans to interview the families of the terrorists or, at least, to open accounts that might provide leads to terror financiers.

It was fear that moved the Saudis. Al Qaeda operations were poised to upset the country's delicate, and generally nonviolent, balance of fear and favor—of princes and clerics in a bond of piety and cash. The oil fields, the function of every equation, were targeted. The House of Saud was under direct attack. Violence had finally come to the kingdom.

Bandar was grim. He poured a second glass. "Where do we begin?"

* * *

The natural question, for top officials in every administration, is not exactly that famous Watergate query, but close: *What should the President know, and when should he know it?*

Presidents generally leave this problem to their senior staff. "Make sure I know what I need to know," they bark, often in frustration. After all, there is simply too much to know, and they will, at some point, need to sleep.

What was clear by the summer of 2002 was that George W. Bush would offer his own stamp on this equation, as he had with so many others, in facing the peculiarities of the "war on terror."

It is odd, first, for a significant portion of a massive government, with an annual budget of $2 trillion, to be committed to searching for a handful of men. We've done it a few times before, as when Woodrow Wilson sent the U.S. Army after Pancho Villa and his ragtag band. But the circumstances of this era, following 9/11, may mean we'll have to do it on a regular basis. Destructive weapons, obtainable by individuals, will do that. They make a small, ardent group of people as threatening as an invading army.

George W. Bush said as much in a speech in early June at the United States Military Academy at West Point, New York.

"For much of the last century," he said, "America's defense relied on the Cold War doctrines of deterrence and containment. In some cases, those strategies still apply. But new threats also require new thinking. Deterrence—the promise of massive retaliation against nations—means nothing against shadowy terrorist networks with no nation or citizens to defend. Containment is not possible when unbalanced dictators with weapons of mass destruction can deliver those weapons on missiles or secretly provide them to terrorist allies. We cannot defend America and our friends by hoping for the best. We cannot put our faith in the word of tyrants, who solemnly sign nonproliferation treaties, and then systematically break them. If we wait for threats to fully materialize, we will have waited too long," Bush intoned, to thunderous applause from cadets gathered on West Point's football field.

"Homeland defense and missile defense are part of stronger security, and they're essential priorities for America. Yet the "war on terror" will not be won on the defensive. We must take the battle to the enemy, disrupt his plans, and confront the worst threats before they emerge. In the world we have entered, the only path to safety is the path of action. And this nation will act. Our security will require the best intelligence to reveal threats hidden in caves and growing in laboratories. Our security will require modernizing domestic agencies such as the FBI, so they're prepared to act, and act quickly, against danger. Our security will require transforming the military you will lead—a military that must be ready to strike at a moment's notice in any dark corner of the world. And our security will require all Americans to be forward-looking and resolute, to be ready for preemptive action when necessary to defend our liberty and to defend our lives."

The carefully chosen word was "preemptive"—a parlance generally understood to be driven by evidence, by evidence of both means and desire, such as missiles in Cuba, a regime that had declared its hostility to the United States from 90 miles off Florida's coast. But many of those who heard the speech felt it danced close to a much broader concept—*prevention.* That meant preventing nations with an anti-U.S. posture from gaining destructive capability.

In public statements over the coming weeks and month, various administration officials pulled back from such a vast mandate; and they certainly wouldn't use the word. But, in fact, a prevention policy was a corollary of the even more sweeping Cheney Doctrine—where a one percent chance of catastrophe must be treated "as a certainty," where firm evidence, of either intent or capability, is too high a threshold; where the doctrine is, in essence, prevention based on suspicion.

In terms of the basic capabilities of even the world's most powerful nation, this is an enormous bite. What, for instance, does it cost—in terms of manpower and firepower and, maybe, in terms of blood and treasure—to chase a hundred "one percent" chances? How about a thousand of them? Or ten thousand?

And where does the President fit into such a day-to-day effort? The allocation of his time is not just a matter of personal preference: he represents all the people, and is elected to deal with all the most important issues, foreign and domestic.

Which is why senior managers at both the CIA and FBI often wondered if it was wise for a President to be so involved in the details of countless initiatives and investigations, many of which amounted to nothing.

Each morning, it is widely known, George W. Bush rises at 5:30, works out, brings his wife a cup of coffee, generally reads a religious text—the Bible or mini-sermons—and arrives at his desk by seven-thirty.

Almost immediately today, he saw Team Tenet, at 8 a.m. Next would be Team Mueller, which included Attorney General John Ashcroft and Tom Ridge.

"What do we know about Swift Sword?" he asked Tenet.

"Nothing more than yesterday," Tenet said, "but we're digging through Saudi sources" . . . "and sigint indicates" . . . and "I'm hoping to know more by tomorrow."

A question from the President is not just a question. Finding the answer can tie up wide swaths of the government, even if it may not be the most important question to those who are expert and engaged in the day-to-day fight. But, does the President wanting an answer make it the most important question?

"Well, in a way, it's like having a CIA case officer in training with absolute power," said one top CIA official. "It can cause a lot of havoc."

According to many people in law enforcement and intelligence who've briefed Bush, he's more interested, as one regular briefer put it, "in people who do things, the operators, rather than in people who just think things. Cheney is more interested in the latter, asking wider, more theoretical questions. The President is interested in how it's going on the ground."

And in the grit of the fight itself, Bush makes it personal. He'd ask about details of captures, "which of our men really did the job." He often wanted to meet them. He was fixated on how to get Zubaydah to tell us the truth—"Do some of these harsh methods really work?" he asked one briefer, and "How does bin Laden enforce loyalty?" of another.

Of course, in these engagements of men, mostly, fighting the good fight, there is bonhomie. "So if it turns out to be Zawahiri's head, I hope you'll bring it here," he said at one briefing, half in jest.

And, in this period, he was all over Mueller about Lackawanna.

"Look, are these guys dangerous or not?" Bush asked Mueller, in frustration, at one briefing. "Why isn't there a way we can find that out? A lot of the time it seems like we're just flying blind."

Bob Mueller always liked getting to the office first, 5:30 a.m., when he was a prosecutor. People noticed it—thought that was a little much, and went about their business.

But inside FBI's conformist culture, the habits of the chief get passed down like evidence files. People started coming in at five, a few at four-thirty.

It wasn't just the idea of the FBI man, or woman, subscribing to a code of conduct, and dress, and deportment, though there was plenty of that.

It was more, in this period, about effort. An "A" for effort was about all the FBI had going for it by the summer of 2002, much like a student who sits confused, class after class, but asks the teacher for extra work.

Nearly two thousand young men of Arab descent had been taken into custody in the United States since 9/11 and placed in various facilities, or deported. It was the classic process problem of garbage in, garbage out. The garbage in? Everyone, say, who'd shopped at a northern Virginia shop frequented by Mohammed Atta; a thick slice of Americans with a common name like Khan; and a dambreak of "suspicious activity" reports—sometimes a thousand a day—from a fearful, hair-trigger nation.

It was like it was for Eastern Europeans during the early 1920s— days of fear that the newly ascendant Bolsheviks would get a foothold on these shores—or the Japanese-Americans after Pearl Harbor; only now it was a time of presumed guilt for Arab-Americans. If a man was of Arab descent, any irregular or inexplicable behavior tripped an alarm. To wit: a car rented before 9/11 and then not promptly returned. Three men who *did* return a rented truck promptly but "seemed nervous." A man who told his employer he was a licensed pilot and wanted to save up to learn to fly commercial jets. Another who simply used an American Airlines credit card.

These are actual examples of men of Arab descent rounded up and thrown into jails in Brooklyn or New Jersey, or other facilities, in the nine months after the attacks. Many were caught with that most reliable snare, the credit card record, with address, phone number, age, and other pertinent data listed in subtext—an electronic identity, with data points more compelling and persuasive, in their mundane specificity, than any jumbled, sweaty, accented pleading in the holding cell. Omaha—supported by NSA dispatches—was like a power plant, sending a current through the entire criminal justice network, lighting paths for cops and prosecutors, shocking the system.

By the summer, it was clear that the ratio of arrest to prosecution would be more out of sync than at any time in the bureau's history. There would be virtually no prosecutions. As with so much else in the "war on terror," the deviation was downward. The default for FBI was the INS: if their behavior was suspicious, simply deport them.

With the first potential cell identified in Lackawanna, FBI was, again, on new terrain. Does the bureau sweep the men into custody, just to be safe—the principle that had guided their haphazard actions until then; or put them under tight surveillance to find out how

threatening they really are? The latter tack meant running a risk that—
if they were a genuine cell poised for violence—they could slip from
the FBI net and do grievous damage.

Mueller opted for the latter, and for full supervision from above.
That would be important if there were a mishap. And, as compared to
the thousands of quickly authorized, barely "papered" (or unpapered)
searches of the past nine months, FBI moved judiciously to the FISA
Court to get its surveillance warrants. The men, after all, were U.S.
citizens. This one, they'd do by the book.

By sunup on a sticky late-summer morning, the FBI headquarters
was starting to fill. It was a sea of blue suits, still a man's world, and
precise hair, with its own barbershop on the fourth floor.

The first call of the day usually came from the Buffalo FBI office;
there'd be another in midafternoon. Twenty-five counterterrorism
agents, and a CIA contingent, were crowded into what was once a
sleepy western New York State outpost.

For today, August 12, Mueller had summoned Ed Needham and
Dave Britten, the lead agents on the case, from Buffalo to his office in
Washington. Bush was pressing him for answers.

Needham and Britten hashed it out with Mueller in his conference
room. The problem: the President, so focused on this case, wanted answers and forward motion. Sometimes that doesn't happen in surveillance situations, no matter how much you want it to.

FBI agents were all but swarming over Lackawanna, a tight-knit
community that swiftly recognizes an outsider, any outsider. In this
case, residents were seeing agents in unmarked sedans everywhere.
One later told a local reporter that everyone knew they were from
Washington. How? Agents, sitting in their cars on stakeouts, were
reading *The Washington Post*.

The Lackawanna men "probably know we're there," Needham
told Mueller, "If you want them to relax, and maybe do what they'd
otherwise do, we should pull back a bit."

Mueller thought it over—all the key issues colliding. If the FBI is
about collecting intelligence, the move is to pull back: let the suspects

breathe, maybe even travel, see where they go. If the goal is prosecution, pick them up and start building a case. If there isn't enough for a case, but you're afraid about what they might do, just keep the pressure on—investigation as prevention.

"Just stay with them, stay close," Mueller told Needham. "We can't afford for them to slip away and do something."

That, of course, is where the President's relentless questions put a thumb on the scale. Reporting up, on every detail, creates risk aversion—the second-guessing and hair-trigger sensibilities, that constant review by one's superiors creates. It turns people of expertise, who run wide swaths of the government, into middle managers, concerned about delivering a ruinous report to the boss.

"But," as one senior intelligence official put it, "you don't want to be wrong and have people die—that's the nightmare. So you report everything upstairs."

Which means that information, both sound and less than sound, makes its way to the Oval Office just to be safe. The President rides up and down on the daily briefings, alerts, long-term initiatives, full of twists and turns. Through the summer, Bush was hopeful, as anyone would be, that the DNA testing of Zawahiri's head would pan out. Zawahiri had not, after all, been detected—no sigint, no off-hand reports he was even alive—in the ensuing months. One CIA analyst wondered aloud in a meeting as to whether the President's feeling that Zawahiri might be dead may be subtly "encouraging the President to think the job against al Qaeda was wrapping up—time to move to Iraq." The DNA, ultimately, didn't match—a bad day in the Oval. The skull that had carried such high hopes, from the President on down, was shipped to an FBI warehouse on Staten Island.

Near summer's end, several e-mails from Mukhtar al-Bakri, one of the Lackawanna men who had left Buffalo and traveled back to the Middle East, were collected in which he discussed an upcoming wedding. In the past, the word "wedding" had been used as code for an attack—and CIA analysts sounded alarms that traveled, quickly, to the White House. As with other alerts, there are hours of panic at the highest levels, briefings called, public warnings considered. The Justice Department huddles with the Pentagon to see whether the Lackawanna men should be immediately designated as "enemy combatants." The President is notified. In this environment, every crisis immediately becomes a crisis for the President—a case officer in training, putatively in charge of every case, everywhere. The commander in chief becomes a man riding a rollercoaster on Ritalin.

No one checked with the FBI office: They knew that al-Bakri was, in fact, preparing for his wedding.

On September 8, the *Sunday Times* of London published Yosri Fouda's interview with Khalid Sheikh Mohammed, and Al Jazeera began running stories on the disclosures, with Fouda's full documentary due to be aired on September 12.

Meanwhile, Pakistani police and CIA operatives closed in on the building. It had been under close surveillance for nearly a month. The timing was part of the arrangement between Tenet and the emir. To storm the apartment before Fouda's story came out would lead observers to believe that the CIA had been tipped off by the network. Now, the only charge could be that the coverage itself might have inadvertently helped the CIA know where the 9/11 hijackers were hiding.

At 3 a.m. on September 11, police officers kicked in the doors of several apartments. In one were the wife and children of KSM, who were taken into custody. The terrorist himself was nowhere to be found. In another apartment was bin al-Shibh with six other men. Here, the resistance was immediate and fierce, all reflex. One man threw a grenade at the police, which exploded; another was shot reaching for a bag that held grenades, among other weapons. As the police subdued three men, bin al-Shibh and two more started firing guns and throwing grenades. The authorities hadn't prepared for this resistance and they retreated with their prisoners and four wounded officers.

Over the next few hours, police fired bullets and tear-gas canisters at the apartment. Bin al-Shibh and his two remaining associates didn't move. The police, forced to go back in, were scared. Witnesses told *The New York Times* that the policemen said hushed prayers on their way back up the stairs.

The three remaining terrorists had retreated into a windowless kitchen. They fired a rifle at the police in the hallway, and when ordered to surrender only shouted, "Bastard!" One man broke and left the shelter of the kitchen; he was immediately shot dead.

Bin al-Shibh fought to the end. He grabbed at one officer's gun. As he was bound, he shouted at the police in Arabic: "You are going to hell!"

Later that day, a thousand miles to the southwest, Bahrainian police arrested Mukhtar al-Bakri on the day of his wedding.

The arrest was ordered by the President and Vice President, over some resistance by both FBI and CIA.

After being briefed for nearly four months on the situation in upstate New York, Bush gave the order as he was preparing for a September 12 address before the United Nations to make the case for war in Iraq. The day before, on September 10, he had ordered the terror alert level raised in the United States.

All of this may have been prompted by the equation: suspicion plus time equals arrest. In this instance, the wedding e-mail, plus another one Bakri sent to Lackawanna about the serving of "a big meal" (a phrase on a list of those that arouse CIA suspicions), may have tipped the balance toward immediate action. Or it may—as some in the FBI and CIA have since suggested—have been one of those moments when the President and Vice President exercised some of their vast, creative prerogatives in the "war on terror." Namely, to do what they want, when they want to, for whatever reason they decide.

★ ★ ★

The CIA was ordered to call the Bahrain police, who had picked up al-Bakri in the capital city of Manama, and the FBI sent over an interrogator—a man who happened to be the first Muslim FBI agent.

Bakri turned out to look more like a scared twenty-three-year-old than like a hardened jihadist, ready for martyrdom. He seemed to have stumbled into an al Qaeda training camp the previous year—then tried to back out by telling bin Laden that his parents were worried about him.

The next day, in Bahrain, he described to his interrogator how he had trained at al Farooq, the al Qaeda camp in Pakistan, along with six friends from Lackawanna. He described how they had met bin Laden, and how they learned to fire Kalashnikovs. He gave up their names: Jaber Elbaneh, thirty-six; Sahim Alwan, twenty-nine; Yahya Goba, twenty-five; Faysal Galab, twenty-six; Shafal Mosed, twenty-four; and Yasen Taheir, twenty-four.

They had been members in good standing of the area's Yemeni community. Galab was part owner of a local gas station. Taheir was "friendliest" in his high school class and was a varsity soccer captain. They all loved soccer and played in local leagues. On September 13 and 14, they would become objects of interdiction. Elbaneh was out of the country—he had never returned after leaving for his camp visit the year before. The other five, going about their business, were quickly arrested. Along with Bakri, already in custody, they would soon be known, far and wide, as the "Lackawanna Six."

In the days immediately following the UN speech—when the President had officially entered the fray to connect Iraq with the wider, ubiquitous threat of terrorism—the Lackawanna arrests made headlines and filled out the talking points for a variety of administration officials.

Ultimately, the FBI's four-month struggle to think clearly about this group—and to handle this first suspected terror cell in a sound and sensible way—was concluded with a single question from Bush. "Can you guarantee me that these guys won't do something?" the

President had asked Bob Mueller and his team as the 9/11 anniversary approached. The bureau's response, FBI counterterrorism chief Dale Watson told *The New York Times* a year later, was that "we are probably 99 percent sure that we can make sure that these guys don't do something—if they are planning to do something. The President's answer, Watson paraphrased, was that "under the rules that we were playing under at the time, that's not acceptable. So a conscious decision was made, 'Let's get 'em out of here.' "

The "rules" of which he speaks were, of course, developed by the Vice President. The FBI had just received a primer on the Cheney Doctrine.

There was an urgent call from Dubai for Dennis Lormel.

It was the last week of September. His assistant called him out of a meeting.

Tim, his lead agent from the UAE, was on the phone, sputtering, "Wazir's here—and he wants to meet with us!"

"Huh! You kidding me?"

Tim, talking fast, tried to lay out the key facts. Short version: The UAE's central bank had done its job—too well. They'd gone ahead on their own and frozen Wazir's assets. That was just the start. Wazir, seeing that his millions were frozen, called up the central bank, indignant. The head of the central bank told Wazir that he was under investigation by the FBI.

Cool customer that he was, Wazir expressed outrage. "Are there FBI agents in the country?" he asked the banker, who said, yes, right here in Dubai. "Well then, I'll meet with them, and explain everything," Wazir said. "I'm sure it's just a mistake."

The UAE bankers, proud of their catch, called the FBI team. Tim hung up in a panic and called Dennis.

"Got it," said Lormel to his deputy. "Just don't do anything."

He punched in the numbers for Langley.

"Wazir's in the Emirates," Dennis said.

"No, he's not," Nervous Phil said. "He's in Pakistan. We have him in Pakistan."

"Trust me, Phil. He's calling my guys. The central bank froze his accounts. He wants to meet with my guys to straighten it out."

"Oh shit."

Phil took a moment to regain his composure. Since midsummer, he'd been preparing one of the most daring initiatives yet tried by CIA. Wazir was to be at the center of it. Now he'd have to "go operational" in . . . in however long the FBI could delay the financial kingpin without making him suspicious.

"Tell your guys to not do anything!" Phil yelled. "Just delay. I'll tell you how long we need."

CIA needed to move quickly. The specific mishap: the UAE, bursting with cash, has one of the most sophisticated border check systems in the Arab world—all electronic, all centralized. This system, that both CIA and FBI relied on to know who came and went from the country, had gone down the previous week. Wazir had slipped into the UAE from Pakistan undetected.

But he wouldn't be slipping out. The next morning, a plump Emirates financier, in his white gown, vest, kufi cap, and fastidiously trimmed beard, left his palatial home in Dubai to travel downtown for his meeting with the FBI. In his driveway, he was greeted by a team of agents from the CIA. He went without a struggle.

Two things swiftly occurred: his accounts were immediately unfrozen, and he was taken to a facility in the Emirates for interrogation.

The expectation inside CIA was that this would be a successful debriefing. The secular Wazir wasn't a Wahabist. He was an opportunist. But in terms of the CIA's interrogation successes, Wazir proved no better than bin al-Shibh. They needed to know everything about his operation. He told them nothing.

Frustrated, a CIA team in Germany kidnapped Wazir's brother—his partner in a vast network of hawalas. He'll talk. He didn't. Days passed. Nothing.

Phil was expecting more but, in his usually fastidious way, he'd prepared for the worst, something that doesn't always happen at CIA.

Step two.

A CIA team in Karachi watched as two men closed Wazir's storefront bank in the bustling city. Each man, on his way home, was pulled into a passing car—a swift, almost invisible maneuver. They were brought to a CIA safe house in Karachi. The agents had to move fast. They only had one night to work. An offer was proferred. The duo could cooperate with CIA and be financially compensated. Both men refused. They, like Wazir and his brother, were rendered to a CIA "black site."

Step three.

The next morning, the storefront bank opened at the usual hour. Its new proprietors—CIA agents of Pakistani descent, specially trained by CIA over the preceding months, had their explanations ready. They were distant cousins of Wazir. They would be filling in for a while. The other men had to leave to meet with Pacha. Some sort of family illness.

And in an extraordinary act of high-risk Method acting, they began to receive customers.

Over the coming months, dozens of key captures in Pakistan and elsewhere would be made because the CIA had taken up residence inside al Qaeda's bank.

Secrecy isn't just a methodology. It's a way of viewing human interaction. When enough people, all together, live by its dictates, it can become a culture, ionizing the air. In the "war on terror," a war fought largely by small teams operating in secret and often with little oversight information, loops are everywhere. One loop breeds another. Who's in the know? Who's not?

The government of the United States was now, a year after 9/11, locked into an astonishing array of information loops. People sat in meetings, unable to say what they knew. They huddled in hallways, after meetings, and demurred that "I'm not at liberty to say," uncertain about the security clearances of old colleagues. Best be safe. Say as little as possible. Keep outside meddling—from policy types, or political appointees—to a minimum. The problem: this attitude is often the key to success inside the U.S. government.

On October 6, Dennis Lormel bumped into Bruce Gephardt, deputy director of the FBI. He'd be filling in for Mueller the next morning to do the presidential briefing on the Wazir operation. It wasn't an FBI operation, at least not anymore. But for almost a year, the FBI had tried to make a case against Wazir, using up resources and manpower. Now that it had been officially passed along to CIA, it became an active issue, ripe for a presidential briefing.

"Why haven't I heard about this?" Gephardt asked. "No one seems to have."

Lormel shrugged innocently. The Wednesday morning meetings in the Sit Room's workspace were confidential. For "invisibles" like Lormel—experts engaged in the battle all day, every day—the key to success was telling as few bigfoots, as few public people, or major players, as possible. Those in the top policy slots, or political appointees who attended portentous meetings of departmental deputies or principals and knew cabinet secretaries by their first names, were paid to meddle. Those people, in the eyes of many *invisibles,* should be told only what they need to know—a decision made, of course, by those who possess the secret. Gephardt didn't know—a full six months after the Wazir initiative had been launched—because, Lormel mused later, "Gephardt didn't fucking need to know."

CHAPTER FIVE

GOING OPERATIONAL

An extraordinary debate was catching fire inside the upper realms of the U.S. government in the summer and fall of 2002.

It was largely invisible to the public, and would remain so, but its effects would reverberate for years. It was over the definition, and uses, of an old, complex term: evidence.

"Evidence" is a word employed in many ways, but the first definition, in common usage, is always the same. Webster's, as usual, does it nicely, as "data upon which a conclusion or judgment may be based."

We had very little of it in the "war on terror."

There was, of course, a tight chain of evidence connecting the 9/11 hijackers to al Qaeda, and the organization to its host, the Taliban. Based on that, a war was fought in Afghanistan—a war based on a "conclusion or judgment" that was widely supported by the international community.

After that, actual evidence became increasingly scarce. A key feature of the Cheney Doctrine was to quietly liberate action from such accepted standards of proof, and it was effective.

Suspicion, both inside America and abroad, became the threshold for action.

The stress created by this, in a nation ruled by laws and not men, would build steadily, month by month, then across years, as U.S. citizens were arrested or wiretapped and immigrants rounded up and deported, a stress that created cracks in the nation's foundation of established principles. Whether or not there was a legal "papering" of such activities was almost a technical point: long-established rules of evidence, and their companion standard of "probable cause," were overrun. Not that embracing a reduced standard created demonstrable results. Lackawanna notwithstanding, after a year of frenetic activity by FBI—with backup from CIA and NSA—there was still no sign of any active al Qaeda cells in the United States. These extraordinary means of high technology and hunch, with all their costs, had borne no fruit.

On the foreign front, supposition was plentiful to fuel action. But there, as well, lessons about the perils of acting on little more than suspicion were drilled home through the summer and fall.

Zawahiri's head—which had brought such high hopes to the White House, and even flowed into analysis that it was time for the next stage of the "war on terror," namely, Iraq—had turned out to just be the skull of an unfortunate Afghan with a prayer scar. The problem of having to rely so heavily on thin, and often immaterial, facts is that the insubstantial takes on inappropriate weight. If the President suspects something—and pines, understandably, for it to be verified—that hope itself creates an effect on decision making *that may well bear out, and that would lead to this, or eventually mean that . . .* Whole constructs, built over valuable presidential hours, collapse into nothing.

Ramzi bin al-Shibh's capture brought a companion set of lessons, in this case about the true value, at day's end, of a mass of uncontextualized facts. The arrest was a victory, insofar as the slippery, talkative al Qaeda lieutenant would no longer be an agent of destruction. But, in the weeks after his arrest, it became clear that his interrogations might yield nothing. Everything was tried—from water-boarding, deprivation of various forms, and death threats, to rambling Koranic conversations—to no effect. The greatest value of the capture was in the phone numbers, hard drives, and assorted digitalia seized from the Karachi safe house. Much as in the case with Zubaydah, those hard bits of evidence were fed into Nervous Phil's models at CIA to further light up the worldwide matrix, create new leads and new suspects. Any bit would do. An address. An alias. A man who might know something, or someone—isolated nodes of data that would be fine, enough to create new lines of suspicion.

The gem, in this case, was a sign-in book. There was one in the Karachi apartment. Visitors signed in, and—in some sort of personnel accounting method used by al Qaeda—they also wrote down their passport numbers. The numbers on the passports were quickly passed to allied intelligence services around the globe . . . with a few key exceptions. Three names, and passport numbers, were routed to the offices of Tenet, Rice, and the Vice President for special handling. They were the names of bin Laden's two sons and his wife, all three carrying freshly minted Sudanese passports.

The passports had been issued in the months after 9/11, long after the President offered his edict that "you're either with us or with the terrorists," the edict that justified ousting the Taliban from power in Afghanistan. They were issued by officials in the Sudanese Embassy in Islamabad—one of Sudan's largest foreign offices, with a direct line to Khartoum.

These were compelling facts, but how high did even this discovery rise on the ladder of evidence—evidence that would lead to "conclusion or judgment"? How could the embassy have issued passports to bin Laden's wife and sons in early 2002 without Sudanese leaders knowing?

That was the President's question when Tenet presented this disclosure in mid-September after bin al-Shibh's capture. What does it mean? The Sudanese government, when confronted with these facts, registered surprise and said that officials must have been paid off—it would get to the bottom of it. They launched their own search for evidence. Sudan, at that point, was one of the "dark side" nations that had been cooperating with the United States. Did the discovery of the sign-in book provide a counterpoint to that ongoing cooperation, an indication that the Sudanese were playing both sides—helping bin Laden with one hand, the United States with the other—or worse? The discovery, indeed, generated a new burst of suspicion among U.S. officials about Sudanese intentions; the response from Khartoum was, in a show of good faith, to provide even more vigorous assistance on several CIA initiatives.

There was, after all, business to conduct. The Sudanese offered what we couldn't afford to refuse in the way of more facts, facts of modest use, facts—like the sign-in book itself—that did not lead to conclusions or judgment.

Essentially, the "war on terror" was being guided by little more than "the principle of actionable suspicion," as one former intelligence chief called it. "It was all happening in the shadows, so there was no debate about it. We were operating, frantically, in a largely evidence-free environment. But the whole concept was that not having hard evidence shouldn't hold you back. It was about action. Continuous action."

At same time—from midsummer into fall—a parallel, more public experiment in applying America's audacious new doctrine of action was under way.

The President's June speech at West Point on preemption tried to establish a new set of international rules, even though the key rule—that the United States would treat a "one percent chance" of a country passing WMDs to a terrorist as "a certainty" and be forced to act—was never spoken. Such a disclosure certainly would have provoked a widening debate over Iraq.

While the CIA and NSA were chasing terrorists, military planners, through the summer of 2002, were fine-tuning their plans for an invasion of Iraq. The issues of that invasion, per se, became a centerpiece of a tactical conflict. Cheney, Rumsfeld, and their support teams had been pushing for an invasion at any moment of America's choosing, and planning the particulars. Colin Powell, who was not in the President's inner circle, made his opposing stand in early August, managing to meet with Bush and express his concerns about the so-called "Pottery Barn" perils of Iraq—"You break it, you own it." A key point Powell made to Bush was that the United States couldn't manage a regime change, whatever the rationale, without international support; we'd need the resources, diverse skills, and legitimacy of the international community. It was a tactical discussion, more about the *hows* than the *whys*. Powell helped convince Bush that they would need to "make the case" for war with the international community to compel their assistance.

Brent Scowcroft, a member, like Powell, of the old guard of Republican pragmatists, weighed in the following week in the *Wall Street Journal.* Under the headline "Don't Attack Saddam," his August 15 column stated such an invasion would require that the United States pursue a "go it alone" strategy, and would "result in a serious degradation in international cooperation with us against terrorism. And make no mistake, we simply cannot win that war without enthusiastic international cooperation, especially on intelligence."

The day the column ran, the President was off on his annual summer vacation to Crawford. The next day, at an NSC meeting on a secure video line, he agreed to give a speech the following month at the UN.

First, though, Cheney, the administration's global architect, would set the framework for discussion. In a speech in Nashville, Tennessee, on August 26 before the Veterans of Foreign Wars, he talked broadly about the perils of equivocation. "The elected leaders of this country have a responsibility to consider all of the available options. And we are doing so," he said. "What we must not do in the face of a mortal threat is to give in to wishful thinking or willful blindness. We will not simply look away, hope for the best, and leave the matter for some future administration to resolve. As President Bush has said, 'time is not on our side.' Deliverable weapons of mass destruction in the hands of a terror network, or a murderous dictator, or the two working together constitutes as grave a threat as can be imagined. The risks of inaction are far greater than the risk of action."

This was Cheney talking forcefully about what he believed. "Preemption"—a case where the United States would preempt a discernible, imminent attack—would, in Cheney's view, be the rarest of exceptions. A country with destructive designs would, he felt, never telegraph the strike. Proof would be unattainable, certainly in "operational time." The operative concept was, in fact, "prevention"—using force against any country that has destructive intent, a geopolitical strategy based, in large measure, on supposition. Prevention, in its way, was simply a latest subchapter to the one percent doctrine, a public lexicon to, in this case, guide the actions of the lone superpower on the state-to-state terrain. While disagreeing with Powell that international support was tactically important—both he and Rumsfeld believed that, if need be, the United States could handle Iraq on its own and would be better off without the muddling influence of the international community— the Vice President now had to fashion his efforts around the President's decision to "make the case" for war before the United Nations.

He moved to redefine suspicions—the watery fuel driving the secret "war on terror"—as *evidence,* suitable to the rigors of international debate.

"The Iraqi regime has in fact been very busy enhancing its capabilities in the field of chemical and biological agents, and they continue to pursue the nuclear program they began so many years ago," he said in his speech.

He was on thin ice. Soon, others would follow.

Jami Miscik, deputy director in charge of the Directorate of Intelligence, recalled listening to the Vice President's speech. It received significant publicity due to the claims about Saddam and nuclear weapons—the first time those claims had been made with such certainty. Cheney hadn't first sent it to CIA, as the President did with his speeches. She quickly pulled up a copy of the text.

"He said that Saddam was building his nuclear program. Our reaction was, 'Where is he getting that stuff from? Does he have a source of information that we don't know about?' "

This confusion was the noisy, unwieldy cousin of the springtime's bewilderment about the overstating of the Zubaydah capture. That one, however, was more easily managed: knowledge of Zubaydah's limited role in al Qaeda, and apparent insanity, was closely held and deeply classified.

For the Vice President, under spotlights, to say such things about Hussein and nuclear weapons caused more widespread concern.

Alarms went off in several departments at CIA. The agency clearly was being cut out of the top-level very public decisions. Analysts immediately hustled to collect and review what was known inside CIA about Hussein and nuclear weapons. The Iraq division inside the DI was not an area of great strength. The CIA had few reliable humint assets inside Iraq; Saddam kept counsel with only a very tight circle. Though the CIA had been directed in a presidential order in February to start focusing on Iraq, the staff had discovered no hard evidence of weapons of mass destruction.

CIA analysts began asking more questions about areas that were mostly seen as nuisances, subordinate to the main goal of finding and stopping terrorists. They focused more intently on "Curveball"— code name for an Iraqi source of German intelligence officials, who was making detailed claims about Iraq's WMD programs. Reports were also filed with top CIA managers about a trip made to Niger in February 2002 by a former ambassador to Gabon, Joseph Wilson, to check on rumors—emanating from the Vice President's office—that Saddam had attempted to buy "yellowcake" from the country's French mines. It was a convoluted story about Nigerian documents sold to intelligence agents in Italy, which indicated Hussein was looking to buy the raw, porous uranium. Saddam already had a well-known yellowcake supply that was monitored by UN inspectors. Processing the material into an enriched state, suitable for weaponry,

was an arduous, almost untenable project. In any event, why would he
need more than the 500 tons he hadn't touched?

Heat was rising, meanwhile, throughout the administration. Cheney and Rumsfeld were battling Powell over what Bush would say before the UN. Beyond criticizing Hussein, and connecting the dictator
to the broader "war on terror," Powell was urging the President to ask
for a new UN resolution to support action against the Iraqi leader.
Cheney and Rumsfeld fiercely opposed the idea. For Cheney, even
"making a case" was foolish; asking permission was worse.

As they fought it out over the President's UN speech just days
away, Rice went on CNN and improvised. "The problem here is that
there will always be some uncertainty about how quickly he can acquire nuclear weapons," she said. "But we don't want the smoking
gun to be a mushroom cloud."

The statement sent off shock waves. Rice was criticized for fear-
mongering, for suggesting that there was evidence that Hussein might
have such a weapon. Arguments about proof, though, were missing
the point—Rice's roundabout argument was that the United States
should act whether or not it found a "smoking gun." She was showing
an edge of the actual U.S. policy: the severing of fact-based analysis
from forceful response; acting on any inkling was now appropriate—
to be safe, to be sure, to get an opponent before he can develop capability, so others know to not even start down that path.

Yet the debate was drifting, day by day, away from these deeper issues of the invisible U.S. playbook—a game plan built on an unspoken conclusion that "evidence" was an unreasonable threshold, that, at
day's end, didn't matter. Instead, the arguments roiled around the
proof of destructive weaponry, or the lack of it.

A few days later, Bush addressed the United Nations, listing
Saddam's sins and infractions, and asserting that if the UN didn't act,
it would become irrelevant as an institution. He had decided after
conversations with British prime minister Tony Blair and assorted
foreign leaders that he would ask for a new resolution. Yet that line—
the most important line, one that Cheney and others opposed—was

mysteriously missing from the text. Bush noticed the absence, and clumsily improvised this key line midway through his recitation.

And so, to gain international acceptance and assistance, the United States would now "make a case" for war based on verification that Saddam Hussein had weapons of mass destruction.

What was also clear, to anyone in the innermost circle around the President, was that it would be a faithless exercise; an exercise *for show*, considering that it was now a guiding principle of the U.S. government that suspicion was an adequate threshold for preventative action.

It is not clear whether Colin Powell would qualify as a member of the innermost circle to the extent that he would know this.

Tenet, of course, did—present, as he was, at Cheney's breakthrough moment nearly a year before. But now, as the standards of evidence abandoned by the U.S. government would be debated in international forums, the CIA director would have to stand on the fault line between the old world of evidence and a new day of action.

To be George Tenet in this period was to feel the perils of a lightning rod in a gathering storm.

A normal day would start with the presidential briefing, followed by congressional testimony, a meeting with Rice or Cheney, maybe an assortment of Senate leaders, the review of the drafts of upcoming presidential speeches and that day's NSA cables, more meetings "downtown" in the White House, lunch with Rumsfeld, then late-afternoon meetings back at Langley, anchored by the 5 p.m. intelligence gathering that had become one of the hottest tickets in Washington, with many agencies and the White House often sending representatives. On many days, sixty people would crowd Tenet's conference room, standing two deep along the walls.

And that's when he wasn't overseas—which he was about one of every three days, as maybe the only man in government who could poke Crown Prince Abdullah in the chest, slap Musharraf on the back, and consort with each man's intelligence chief without either leader being told an active verb more than he needed to know.

Something had to give—and it did. Little by little. The dilemma of Tenet's role was diabolical. Intelligence was the oxygen of the "war on terror," with CIA carrying burdens of collection, analysis, and operations beyond the capabilities of a seasoned, coordinated intelligence authority ten times its size. The agency, meanwhile, was neither seasoned in the complexities of fighting both terrorism and weapons proliferation, nor particularly well coordinated. Tenet, himself, was not much of a manager. He was good at scrambling, diving, and ducking, all day every day, a man who could cajole, hustle, and, when needed, turn up the volume, especially on the important issues of what to do, when, and why—and then shout, "What the hell's next?"

And the agency scrambled behind him, sometimes leaving loose ends hanging, laces untied.

Once the President had given his speech, and the mark of a new UN resolution was set, much of the U.S. government felt the pull of a fierce undertow toward war in Iraq. Scowcroft had predicted that an invasion would draw the foreign policy and intelligence communities away from the "war on terror"—but it was happening now, day by day, long before any troops were poised to attack.

This tension of competing priorities could be felt inside each building on the Langley campus. The agency's priority was still leading the "war on terror"'s *find them, stop them* effort—a mission that kept the Directorate of Intelligence racing to a staccato rhythm it had never before experienced. Its analysts were poised, day and night, to examine fast-breaking threat information, swiftly assess terrorist movements in parts of the world where the United States had thin intelligence assets, and place characters picked up by sigint and finint (thousands of them) in some workable context. Its focus, now, was that of a so-called "war fighting" agency. This change, which had come hours after the 9/11 attacks, was a shock for the DI, which traditionally had the largest portion of its resources applied to retrospective analysis, looking at events after they'd occurred, painting complex portraits, analytically, of various nations and regions of the world.

Oddly, it would be called upon to do more of the latter, a backward turn, in regard to Iraq. The challenge was carefully and swiftly to assess the eleven years since the end of the 1991 Gulf War in terms of Hussein's arsenal.

A ninety-page National Intelligence Estimate on Iraq and its weapons was delivered to the White House on October 1, blending—as do all NIE reports—analyses from the entire intelligence community. In this case, with such a highly charged subject and the "wartime" desires of the President familiar to the average American high school student, the NIE ended up being a giant pot of stew, with everything, from every shelf in the kitchen, thrown in. In its dense text and footnotes the NIE included a full range, from dissertations on Saddam's mobile weapons labs, to the way his aluminum tubes were ideal for uranium processing, to the statement, on page 24, that "Iraq also began vigorously trying to procure uranium ore and yellowcake." Each point also carried reasonable dissents.

Historically, a report of such import—pertaining to what was already known to be the core of an international "case of war"—would be carefully studied by a president, making a commander in chief accountable for both public statements and underlying analysis about the necessity of war.

But the Bush presidency had been quietly innovating new concepts in regard to presidential accountability—changes largely intuited and instituted by the Vice President.

Cheney, as far back as the Ford presidency, had experimented with the concept of keeping certain issues away from the chief executive—a reversal of equations that operated before the media age obligated presidents to spend so much time speaking under hot lights. Cheney's view, according to officeholders from several Republican administrations, is that presidents, in essence, needed a failsafe if they were publicly challenged with an importunate disclosure about the activities of the U.S. government. They needed to be able to say they had no knowledge of the incident, and not be caught in a lie. Lying is something presidents do at some peril. Trust, after all, is a precious element upon which rests a president's credibility, and, after a fashion, his power.

The thinking on this matter was, in many ways, a strategic response of Cheney and others to the Watergate scandal, in which Richard Nixon's taped statement about "stonewalling" investigations of the Watergate break-ins meant he couldn't then lie about what he knew. That was what placed him in violation of laws pertaining to obstruction of justice. He was accountable, and that doomed his presidency.

The thinking of several former Nixon administration officials, including Cheney, was not that the break-in and similar actions were the problem. The problem was that the President should have been "protected" from knowledge of such activities.

A president, in this model, can even say, in a general way, that he'd be happy if something were to occur—and have his subordinates execute such wishes—and still retain what, during the Reagan administration, was termed "plausible deniability." That was what Ronald Reagan essentially did by telling advisers that he wouldn't mind if they found a way to get around congressional bans on aid to the anti-Communist contra rebels in Nicaragua, but then, when later questioned in a videotaped deposition, saying that he hadn't "any inkling" of what they actually did.

For some presidents, like the first President Bush, this didn't work. He demanded to know everything pertinent in making decisions, so he wouldn't make mistakes. Presidents generally don't like being surprised, or ending up on a "need to know" basis. The idea of being inexplicitly briefed to water down accountability, or of using oft-reviled inefficiencies of government "process" to counteract the heightened transparency of the media age, is repugnant to them.

With this new George W. Bush presidency, however, Cheney was able to shape his protective strategy in a particularly proactive way. Keeping certain knowledge from Bush—much of it shrouded, as well, by classification—meant that the President, whose each word circles the globe, could advance various strategies by saying whatever was needed. He could essentially be "deniable" about his own statements.

Whether Cheney's innovations were tailored to match Bush's inclinations, or vice versa, is almost immaterial. It was a firm fit. Under this strategic model, reading the entire NIE would be problematic for Bush: it could hem in the President's rhetoric, a key weapon in the march to war. He would know too much.

If somehow the contents of the NIE were revealed, the White House could say that the report was too cumbersome and that Bush had only read the one-page NIE summary. However, the summary itself presented two problems: first, its statement that although "most agencies judge" that the aluminum tubes were "related to a uranium enrichment effort," the Energy Department's intelligence branch and the State Department's Bureau of Intelligence and Research "believe that the tubes more likely are intended for conventional weapons"; second, the fact that it didn't mention the yellowcake at all. That was not among the "key findings" distilled into the summary—too flimsy to make the cut. Yet with the CIA putting up resistance to affirming charges of Mohammed Atta's meeting with the Iraqis in Prague, the aluminum tubes *and* the yellowcake were now the most prominent points in the "case."

On that last score, CIA had already alerted the British—in mid-September—that MI6's similar claims about the yellowcake had been investigated by U.S. intelligence and shown to be suspect.

Also in September, Tenet told both Bush and Cheney that the State and Energy Departments felt the aluminum tubes were most likely for rocket construction—and that some CIA analysts agreed.

Each one of these acts of analysis and briefing put CIA at odds with the White House. In the view of Cheney's office and the Pentagon's civilian leadership, the major impediment to war—now that Bush had decided to make a public "case"—was turning out to be CIA. It was a classic of organizational dysfunction. While CIA's operational arm knew it would often act on little more than supposition, the Directorate of Intelligence couldn't quite fathom that it was expected to do the same. There were clues aplenty about the lack of a so-called "policy process" throughout the administration. Already, by fall of 2002, others across the government—from economic analysts at Treasury to global warming experts at the Environmental Protection Agency to child welfare experts at Health and Human Services—were realizing that their jobs were not to help shape policy, but to affirm it.

"We understood that the government was more ideologically driven and that analysts were being ignored all over, including the teams at State and even some at Defense," said one official from the DI. "It's just we thought that such a thing wouldn't apply when we were going to war—that it was a different standard than, say, budget policy or tax cuts. Our job is to tell the President what's true, so he can make sound decisions when lives are at stake. It's what we do. To ignore that is to say you don't need a CIA."

In matters concerning the run-up to war, that is what the White House *was* saying. This left Tenet in a bind of colliding loyalties—to the President, who could have fired him after 9/11 but didn't; and to his analysts, whom he was institutionally and emotionally committed to defend.

On October 5, Tenet sat at his desk, a rare occurrence, reading a draft of the President's upcoming speech slated for two days hence in Cincinnati, and carrying the claim that Saddam Hussein's "regime has been caught attempting to purchase" uranium in Niger.

The CIA immediately fired off a memo to Deputy National Security Adviser Stephen Hadley and presidential speechwriter Mike Gerson that the statement was wrong. Another letter the next day—this one also addressed to Rice—repeated that the evidence on Niger was weak and that any such purchase, in any event, would not have been particularly significant since Saddam already had a large yellowcake supply that he could not process into anything usable.

That wasn't quite enough to reassure Tenet that the line would be excised. He knew the underlying philosophy at work: that evidence, loosely defined, was summoned at the convenience of action. In this case, to convince the world community what it needed to hear. He called Hadley late on October 6, the day before the speech. The question, Tenet understood, was not whether the Niger charge was true or false, it was whether the President's claim, springing, as it did, from classified materials, could be proven wrong.

Hadley resisted. This was a key claim in their case for war. Tenet knew how to pose the response, to put it in political terms: "Steve," he said, "you really don't want the President to be the fact-witness on this. Trust me."

The line went. And that was just one battle.

Two weeks later, Tenet slipped into the large hearing room in the Hart Senate Office Building. It was standing room only; the marquee, televised hearings of the Joint House and Senate Select Intelligence Committees on 9/11—the so-called "JIC Hearings." Co-chaired by Bob Graham, Florida's veteran Democratic senator, and Porter Goss, a Republican congressman from Florida who'd once been a CIA case officer, the hearings were a sharp-edged affair. Graham, nearing the end of his Senate career and preparing a presidential run, was testy, feeling as though he was being misled by some of the witnesses, as they had misled the country. Goss, meanwhile, was holding forth as though he'd just finished a stint as DCI.

Today was a big day: Tenet, Lieutenant General Mike Hayden, head of the NSA, and Bob Mueller were all due for the hearing table.

Tenet had already logged countless hours under the hot lights of Capitol Hill. His face had come to represent the intelligence community—all fifteen separate agencies—and the disastrous failure of not having known what America needed to know, in time.

He'd worked for three days on his speech. It would be, he told a colleague, "my manifesto."

After Tenet's swearing in, Graham said he was "going to ask if our panelists could summarize their statements into approximately 10 minutes so that we will maximize the time for questions . . ."

"Mr. Chairman, thank you. I'm not going to be able to get this done in 10 minutes," Tenet responded. "I will try and be as fast as I can, but we have a lot we have to say, and we'll be as quickly—quick as we can, and I thank you for your indulgence in that regard . . ." And in he dove.

"On September 11th, nearly three thousand innocent lives were taken in brutal acts of terror. For the men and women of American intelligence, the grief we feel, the grief we share with so many others, is only deepened by the knowledge of how hard we tried, without success, to prevent this attack. . . ."

His Queens accent and no-nonsense demeanor—like one of those CSI police chiefs—works well on television, a gift, considering the presumption of intelligence community incompetence. He runs through the long arc leading up to 9/11, the mistakes that were made and how now "the process" has been corrected.

Graham interrupts him at ten minutes.

And again ten minutes later, as Tenet is describing how CIA officers "did not recognize the implications of the information about al-Hazmi and Mihdhar they had in their files. During August of . . ."

SEN. GRAHAM: Mr. Tenet, 21 minutes now.

MR. TENET: Well, sir, I just have to say I have been waiting a year. I have got about another 20 minutes. I think I want to put this in the record. It's important. It's contextual, it's factual, and I would like to proceed!

Senator Orrin Hatch, the Utah Republican, jumped to Tenet's aid. "Mr. Chairman, I would like to hear the whole story."

Senator Dianne Feinstein, the California Democrat, added: "I would, too."

Cheers went up at CIA, where people had gathered to watch the hearings. Fifteen miles away there was cheering in an auditorium at FBI, too.

Not at any time in recent memory had there been as burning a need to assign blame—to find the odd comfort of identifying those at fault and dispensing with them. Congress was in on it; the White House, too, in its way. CIA and FBI were in the crosshairs.

Graham settled back and Tenet, wanting to hoot, powered to the end of his carefully written speech. After that, and fifteen minutes of questions, there was a break. Tenet felt elated. He'd said his piece; showed that CIA, despite its mistakes, was up to the task at hand.

He stood up, as the room bustled and stretched for a short recess, and gathered his notes next to the table mic.

A woman approached him. Middle-aged lady. Nondescript. Brown hair. He bent toward her, instinctively, as though he might know her.

She stopped, up close, and looked at him with watery eyes.

"You killed my husband."

The first weekend of November 2002 was a moment of dawning satisfaction for George W. Bush.

He had been whistle-stopping the country on behalf of Republican candidates for a month, an effort that seemed to be paying off. The Saturday before that Tuesday's midterm election, tracking polls by Republican pollster Matthew Dowd showed a Republican surge. The tradition of a first-term President's party losing seats in the midterm election—a tradition that is remarkably consistent—would be reversed.

Amid the noise and haste of the political season, one simple—and for Americans very personal—calculus seemed to carry the day: we had not been attacked again.

If success, in its cleanest form, is a case of results exceeding expectations, there was a widespread sigh of relief, or thanks, that the anticipation of more mayhem on American soil had not been met.

What did the reasonably informed American know? That Richard Reid, the British shoe bomber, was stopped by heroic flight attendants and passengers; that the *Wall Street Journal*'s Danny Pearl, handsome and earnest, had met a grisly end, showing the barbarism of our enemies. That enemies were lurking among us—such as Jose Padilla and the Lackawanna cell, whose alleged treacheries were widely trumpeted, though underlying evidence was thin. Color-coded security alerts were fodder for late-night comedians, but showed, if nothing else, a kind of sweaty, doing-whatever-we-can effort, the ardor of a government facing genuine danger and fussing over what the public really needed to know. Isn't the spreading of fear a sort of defeat? Is it better to know what's afoot, or not to know? These questions hung, unanswered.

Overseas, meanwhile, the threat was seen as real and present as ever, if diffuse and intangible. Though bin Laden's presence, and activity, remained the stuff of speculation, al-Zawahiri had reappeared on a day in early October when U.S. Marines were attacked in Kuwait. He was seen on Al Jazeera, assuring future attacks on the United States, its economy, and its allies. "I promise you," he said, "that the Islamic youth are preparing for you what will fill your hearts with horror."

But in America, nothing, or nothing yet. And if this provided some wary comfort to the wider public, it offered little solace to those involved in the fight. The lack of another U.S. attack, they assumed, might be due to a host of strategic decisions by al Qaeda: namely, the idea that the fear created by 9/11 would carry, like an echo, until it was supplanted by another attack—an attack whose scale would act, anew, as a gauge of al Qaeda's capability and intent. Al Qaeda wouldn't want to act unless it could top the World Trade Center and the Pentagon with something even more devastating, creating an upward arc of rising and terrible expectation as to what, then, would follow. That fearful expectation, multiplied by time passing, would last until the next attack, and so forth. It's a "special event" strategy. The goal is to show that a war against terrorists is endless and futile and escalating, nudging Americans toward the realization that they could live happily without the United States supporting corrupt Mideast regimes, or having its soldiers on the Arabian Peninsula.

People will do all sorts of things to make fear stop—so creating fear is a goal of the terrorist.

But fear is also central to the American arsenal.

On the morning of November 3, while the President was gazing at poll numbers predicting a midterm sweep, George Tenet was drinking coffee at CIA after pulling an all-nighter.

He'd need to be alert for hours still.

A cluster of sigint operators, including those working with NSA and the U.S. surveillance satellites, were huddled with CIA operatives at the Counter-Terrorist Center with Tenet.

Flashing before them on a wide screen was a grainy, gray-washed video of a jeep traveling through a barren stretch of Yemen's Ma'rib desert. In the vehicle, according to Yemeni security forces and U.S. sigint, was Qaed Salim Sinan al-Harethi, known as "Abu Ali," one of the suspected al Qaeda planners of the attack on the USS *Cole*. With Harethi were six companions—all believed to be al Qaeda members, and now visible in the lens of a U.S. Predator drone, launched from the nearby, postage-stamp country of Djibouti. As the jeep drove through an isolated section of highway, one of the passengers chatted on the phone to an al Qaeda soldier who happened to be in U.S. custody. Of course, the jeep's passenger didn't know that. He thought the man was nearby, trying to locate the moving jeep for a rendezvous. "We're over," he said. "Can't you see us? We're right over here."

It was fourteen months, almost to the day, since Tenet had sat in an NSC meeting on counterterrorism on September 4, 2001, and told the group that "It is important for us discuss whether we want the DCI to fire a weapon like this. I'm not saying I'm for it or against it, just that it changes the nature of what the DCI does. It crosses a line we haven't crossed." The group had adjourned that day without making a decision.

After 9/11, no meeting was needed to discuss the matter further. Everyone did everything they were capable of, hoping something would work.

The armed Predator certainly worked. Tenet gave the order and a Hellfire missile screamed forth from the drone, eviscerating the jeep. Seven men, including Harethi, died. Among the dead, the CIA soon found out, was Kamal Derwish, the inspirational friend and guide to

the Lackawanna men, one of the world's most-sought-after men—
sought largely because he could clarify whether the "Lackawanna six"
were truly an al Qaeda cell, bent on destruction, or a half-dozen confused friends from Buffalo who had got in way over their heads. The
consensus—despite tough talk and press releases from Washington—
had settled, already, on the latter. The only potential counterpoint was
now a charred corpse in the Yemeni desert.

The act troubled Tenet but elated the President, especially in how it
created shock for al Qaeda, according to follow-up sigint dispatches,
and awe among leaders of key Arab nations.

"We're talking to them in a way they can understand," Bush said to
a senior adviser, a line he often repeated. "Capability like this changes
the game."

Briefing Bush each morning in gory detail—enabling him to "go
operational"—was now part of CIA procedure. Tenet brought a variety of briefers; some Bush seemed to respond to more than others.
Most presidents, in their morning intelligence briefings, sit with analysts. The details of an operation are described, then the analyst works
through the architecture of what it means to a state, a region, U.S.
strategy, and Bush certainly saw plenty of analysts. But he likes operators, the people, virtually all men, involved in the struggle, the face-to-
face and hand-to-hand.

Briefers, all the way to principals and department heads, feel Bush's
itch, his impatience, and pick up his cadence. They all start talking like
operators, no matter what's being reported. These are men who, on
balance, never experienced the bracing effects—humbling, uplifting,
oddly settling—of military action. The few who have, like Powell, and
his deputy Rich Armitage, smooth over these disparities—piquant at a
time of war—by joining in the tough talk that they know, from experience, is hollow at its core.

Bonhomie swirls, led by the chief, animating the room and, in
some cases, the action that flows from it.

Just pick a day in this period. After Tenet and his team finished one morning, Bruce Gephardt, deputy director of FBI, entered, filling in for Mueller, who was on the road.

It was a morning, and previous evening, of high alert at the bureau.

Gephardt went through it, piece by piece, FBI-precise and thorough. A report had come to the bureau about a group of men of "Middle-Eastern descent" in Kansas. They were looking to pay cash, Gephardt told Bush and the half dozen assembled for the briefing, "cash for a large storage facility." A big one, costing a few hundred thousand.

Gephardt ran through everything the FBI knew, which was not enough. The men weren't farmers, but they were looking for something as big as a silo. The men were suspicious. And they were at large.

Bush was laser-sharp, glasses on the end of his nose, pad on his lap, as everyone in the room started to imagine scenarios—dots connecting, fear building.

Intelligence operatives and criminal investigators tend to take a deep breath at a moment like this, after a thousand days filled with varied alerts, blind leads, things they at first missed that made all the difference. What don't I know? What do I think I know, without having really checked? What is the array of things this might be, rather than only the most fearsome one?

"Middle-Easterners in Kansas," Bush says. "We've got to get on this, immediately."

Of course, it would occupy the President's thoughts that day, and a current of high voltage, directly from the Oval, raced through the FBI and law enforcement crowd.

The next morning Gephardt's back. Bush is all over him.

"What have you got for me, Bruce?" And Gephardt, a former head of the FBI's San Francisco office, "talked it" like a man with a gun on his hip.

"Mr. President, the FBI has Kansas surrounded!"

"That's what I like to hear," Bush all but shouts. And, indeed, he does.

Flea market operators. It took a few days to find them. Men of Middle-Eastern descent—there are actually quite a few in Kansas—were planning to run flea markets. They needed something large to store all the stuff—the handmade jewelry, old flannel shirts, dinette sets, and Frank Sinatra records. A cash business.

There have been lots of these sorts of episodes—reports of a domestic threat that throws the government—from the "going operational" President on down—into a frenzy. And there'd be more to come from FBI. None of them turned out to be anything but misplaced suspicion gone operational.

The meeting on December 13 in the Cabinet Room had chewed up the lives of a battalion of high-level schedulers for months.

Try to bring the top two dozen officials in the U.S. government together for two hours in the middle of a weekday.

The idea was an end-of-year review of the state of the "war on terror," an opportunity to set upcoming strategies, a brown bag lunch that would stretch well into the afternoon.

General John Gordon, a longtime Air Force general, former number two at CIA, and now the President's counterterrorism czar on the National Security Council, presided.

Or rather, Bush did. Or was supposed to. Or Cheney, maybe, who was there as well. People gave reports on aspects of "the war," and, no doubt, progress had been made. Afghanistan, and the smashing of al Qaeda's sanctuary; the rounding up of the Pakistani nuclear scientists, and their supporters in Pakistan; the capture of a few significant operatives, though they weren't giving up much under brutal interrogation; the closing in, it seemed, on anthrax purveyors linked to terrorists. The Karachi sting operation and the CIA's vast worldwide matrix, supported by NSA and various financial institutions, were churning nicely, lighting up the battlefield. But Zawahiri and bin Laden were alive—the latter having released an audiotape calling

Bush "a modern-day Pharaoh" a few weeks before. There was an up-and-coming player named Zarqawi—we'd been tracking him through 2002—who'd set up a biological and chemical weapons labs in an outlaw region of Iraq, a no-man's-land, beyond Hussein's control. He was, it seemed, behind several biochemical attacks in Europe, including a scare involving ricin, the toxic paste made from castor beans, in Britain the previous summer.

Bush just listened, eating his sandwich. Back in the spring of 2001, Tenet and Richard Clarke had descended on him in one of the morning presidential briefs—a way to use Tenet's daily slot to get around casual resistance to sounding an alert about al Qaeda by Rice and her NSC process. They had alerted Bush that day to the global threat and the multipronged capacities of their opponent. Bush, according to Clarke, couldn't attach to much that was thrown at him, the array of Arab names and countries he knew little about. He said he didn't want to be "swatting flies," and wondered if there wasn't some way to destroy al Qaeda in a swift blow.

Now, in the Cabinet Room, the flies buzzed all around, as they'd been doing for more than a year, too many to swat.

He turned, distractedly, toward Kenneth Dam, deputy Treasury secretary, an old Republican hand who'd served Nixon and Reagan.

"Ken, where are we on terror finances?"

Dam shuffled some papers. "Mr. President, the majority of the funders for al Qaeda are Saudis."

This was the lead of a one-page memo that Dam had passed around at the start of the meeting—a memo listing the fifteen or so top funders for al Qaeda, almost all of them Saudis.

Bush looked at Dam, perplexed, as though he either hadn't read the handout in front of him, or was somehow surprised—though this was all but common knowledge.

"How do we know this?" he asked.

Dam paused. "It's in a piece of paper I just handed out, which was compiled from the agency," he said, and then turned to McLaughlin, in the chair beside him. The deputy director nodded, yes—CIA was the source.

Bush smiled, chewing on this morsel of due diligence. But, when it was soon digested, his mind drifted elsewhere. There was no sweeping strategy for the "war on terror," no sensible metrics to determine progress, no clear idea of how to fight, much less win, the so-called "hearts and minds" struggle. It was a day-to-day grind, with slow progress, victories that turned to defeats than back, "dark side" alliances with perilous regimes that now acted like friends, old European friends acting, these days, like foes, and alerts in the United States—one after another, keeping him wound tight—that amounted, time and again, to absolutely nothing.

"That's enough for today," he said a few minutes later, surprising the group.

The meeting ended after an hour. There was nothing else to talk about.

Except Iraq.

The driving concept was one of continuous, disruptive pressure. The homeland was unprotectable. America's enemies had constantly to be in a reactive mode, so they never had a chance to stop and think and plot their next initiative. The *find then, stop them* "war on terror," despite its modest successes—despite the government's painful run up a learning curve to understand how to actually fight this new kind of war—wasn't enough pressure, enough to change the behavior of potential competitors and enemies.

Iraq, in a way, was the default. A default to action.

Selling the invasion, to command international support, would be the subject of this morning's meeting in the Oval Office.

It was December 21. Christmas was coming, with the assorted parties and official festivities for the President to preside over.

But before all that, before the year ended, Bush wanted to hear a first solid crack at "making the case," at the pitch.

McLaughlin and Tenet entered the Oval. Everyone exchanged pleasantries, and best wishes for the coming holiday.

The President had brought a gang on this Saturday morning: Rice, chief of staff Andrew Card, the Vice President.

McLaughlin—the CIA veteran, quiet and deliberative, judicious, well read, a former Army officer and professional magician—broke out a series of flip charts.

An analyst for thirty years, McLaughlin knew the pressure that the administration's words and planned actions put on this presentation. He had read everything he could, and did a dry run first with NSC principals. The hard evidence, the facts that had been verified, were old, dating from the era of regular UN inspections between 1991 and 1998—the year Saddam threw the inspectors out. Since then, the information was sketchy, almost impossible to check. And, as McLaughlin often lectured his analysts, intelligence is no good if it can't, in some way, be verified.

Over the next half-hour McLaughlin presented a wide array of probables, and possibles—some with a dense array of facts—about the presence of WMD in Iraq.

There was a chart of an unmanned aerial vehicle, a UAV, that was picked up by U.S. satellite surveillance flying in circles for about 500 kilometers—much farther than the 150-kilometer limit on such an item set by the UN. It might or might not be equipped to carry a weapon, but the distance capability alone was a violation.

There was an intercepted radio conversation in which two soldiers discussed removing the words "nerve agents" from something, maybe a manual, or future communications.

There was an account from a human source—al-Libi, the Libyan al Qaeda trainer who had been identified by Musa Kousa and captured a few months after 9/11—about Saddam providing training to al Qaeda in biological and chemical weapons, an allegation some in CIA already doubted that al-Libi would recant a year later.

"Nice try," Bush said, according to a soon to be celebrated account given to Bob Woodward. "I don't think this is quite—it's not something that Joe Public would understand or would gain a lot of confidence from."

Bush then turned to Tenet and said, "I've been told all this intelligence about having WMD and this is the best we've got?"

Tenet, according to Woodward's account, then rose, threw up his arms in the air, and said, "It's a slam dunk case!"

The account of the meeting, which ended with Bush telling Tenet to "make sure no one stretches to make our case," was provided to Woodward by White House officials not long before the reporter's final, December 11, 2003, interview with Bush for *Plan of Attack,* due out the following April.

The President, who was extensively briefed before his sit-downs with Woodward, then told the veteran reporter, emphatically, that Tenet's reassurance "was very important."

Indeed, it was. In fact, it provided a firewall for the President on the most serious charge history might level at him: taking the country to war under false pretenses. It was Tenet's fault. The SLAM DUNK sign would forever hang from around Tenet's thick neck and be in the first sentence of his obituary.

Tenet and McLaughlin don't remember the meeting very well. Tenet, though outnumbered by what the President and other advisers claim they heard, doesn't actually remember ever saying "slam dunk." Doesn't dispute it. Just doesn't remember it. McLaughlin said he never remembered Tenet saying "slam dunk" either. He doesn't recall Tenet ever, in any context, jumping up and waving his arms. He and Tenet have both told close friends that it was a marketing meeting, not about the actual research, but about presentation. This may be a fine point of distinction, but when so much weight is placed on two words, context is important. The President's question, McLaughlin recalled, was "whether we could craft a better pitch than this—a PR meeting— it certainly wasn't about the nature of the evidence."

There's one other thing McLaughlin remembers clearly. Driving back to Langley from this Oval Office meeting, as from several others

Tenet and McLaughlin attended with the President's close confidants present, McLaughlin said something he'd said several times: "George, sometimes I think we need to be very careful about what we say in that room."

Tenet disagreed. "No, what we say in there won't come back to haunt us. It's what we write down. That's the permanent record. That's what'll count."

Relentless pressure is a strategy. Usually quite successful. It was employed both in the "war on terror" against al Qaeda, and by the White House against the CIA.

Apply force to the weakest area—your opponent will start to look for ways to relieve the discomfort. There was a presumption, widely held, that Saddam had weaponry. There was, as well, a surety inside CIA—also widely held—that the President would eventually get his way and there would be an invasion. "We started to worry about what our troops might face," said a senior CIA official in the DI overseeing Iraq. "That was part of what drove this forward. We were looking to figure out what Saddam might have so our troops would be ready for anything he threw at them. It had a better-safe-than-sorry quality. It affected what ended up in the assessments. And every time we offered another thing that Saddam might possibly have in his arsenal, you could feel the gratitude from the top."

The DI's "war fighting" role was now activated on behalf of the Iraq campaign. Libby and Hadley, meanwhile, continued to push, and push hard, on the analysts, asking the same question Tenet was often asked in high-level meetings. Aren't these potential threats precisely why an invasion is necessary? Is there even the slimmest possibility—a one percent chance—that uranium was bought in Niger, that the aluminum tubes were usable in uranium centrifuges, or that Mohammed Atta managed to meet with an Iraqi, any Iraqi, in Prague?

The thing to watch out for with a program of relentless pressure is the blowback.

On Friday afternoon, January 10, Jami Miscik, the head of the DI walked down the hall on the seventh floor shaking with rage.

John Moseman, Tenet's chief of staff, saw her as she passed his office.

"You okay?"

"No. I'm not okay. I'm definitely not *okay!*"

A moment later, she'd made it to Tenet's suite.

She barely could get out the words. Stephen Hadley, Condi's second, had called from the office of "Scooter" Libby, Cheney's chief of staff.

They wanted her down at Libby's office in the White House by 5 p.m. At issue was the last in an endless series of draft reports about the connection between Saddam Hussein and al Qaeda. How many drafts? Miscik couldn't remember. The pressure from the White House—and from the various intelligence divisions under the Vice President and the Secretary of Defense—had started a week after 9/11.

Cheney's office claimed to have sources. And Rumsfeld's, too. They kept throwing them at Miscik and CIA. The same information, five different ways. They'd omit that a key piece had been discounted, that the source had recanted. *Sorry, our mistake.* Then it would reappear, again, in a memo the next week. The CIA held firm: the meeting in Prague between Atta and the Iraqi agent didn't occur.

Miscik was no fool. She understood what was going on. It wasn't about what was true, or verifiable. It was about a defensible position, or at least one that would hold up until the troops were marching through Baghdad, welcomed as liberators.

A few days before, when she had sent the final draft over to Libby and Hadley, she told them, emphatically, *This is it.* There would be no more drafts, no more meetings where her analysts sat across from Hadley, or Feith, or the guys in Feith's office, while the opposing team tried to slip something by them. The report was not what they wanted. She knew that. No evidence meant no evidence.

"I'm not going back there, again, George," Miscik said. "If I have to go back to hear their crap and rewrite this goddamn report . . . I'm resigning, right now."

She fought back tears of rage.

Tenet picked up the phone to call Hadley.

"She is not coming over," he shouted into the phone. "We are not rewriting this fucking report one more time. It is fucking over. Do you hear me! And don't you ever fucking treat my people this way again. Ever!"

They did not rewrite the report.

And that's why, three weeks later, in making the case for war in his State of the Union address, George W. Bush was not able to say what he'd long hoped to say at such a moment: that there was a pre-9/11 connection between al Qaeda and Saddam.

One down. But two salient points—wobbly, but still standing—on the heart-stopping issue of nuclear weapons remained in the text: "The British Government has learned that Saddam Hussein recently sought significant quantities of uranium from Africa. Our intelligence sources tell us that he has attempted to purchase high-strength aluminum tubes suitable for nuclear weapons production."

Both statements were crafted to carry the clarion ring of proof, and both were known, by people inside the CIA and the White House, to fall far short of that standard.

CHAPTER SIX

CAUSE FOR ALARM

The King Fahd Causeway, connecting the countries of Saudi Arabia and Bahrain, is seen by many Saudis—both religious and not—as an illicit passage.

It is steel and cement as metaphor—tied, on one shoreline, to a truce, struck between the Saudi ruling family and religious traditionalists in the kingdom. The Sauds get virtually limitless wealth, a healthy chunk of which they share with their dour clerical partners and their Wahabist accountants. In exchange, they receive a stamp of religious approval, as the true protectors of the Holy Sites of Mecca and Medina, as well as an understanding that 25,000 or so members of the royal family can do, more or less, anything they please, while the country's 26 million citizens live under strict religious laws, mandating traditional dress, shrouding of women, prohibitions against the consumption of alcohol or premarital sex. Adultery carries a death sentence.

For such indulgences, and countless others, you cross the bridge to the island principality of Bahrain—a country of almost 700,000, with high-rise hotels, a playboy king, a base for the U.S. Fifth Fleet, and significant cashflow from its role as a discreet "service provider" for Saudi Arabia.

The lives of Saudis, and Bahrainis, are thoroughly framed by this arrangement, and its attendant hypocrisies. And both suffer the presence of its by-product: groups of stealthy, violent religious purists, graced with many opportunities to feel self-righteous.

One such group was traveling across the King Fahd Bridge toward Bahrain on February 13, 2003, when they were picked up by Bahraini police.

The United States, specifically the CIA, was behind the arrest. That is common at this point in this part of the world. We have intelligence, especially sigint, they don't have; they have proximity we can't match. In this case, the NSA had picked up calls and e-mails from a cluster of Bahrainis that were troubling—boastful talk of what should be done to infidels, and some problem phrases, such as picking up "honey pots." "Honey" is often terrorist code for destructive items.

By early 2003, leaders in Saudi Arabia and Bahrain were wondering about the appropriate response to their violent, long-bearded malcontents. In past years, they had consigned homegrown terrorists to the unwritten fine print of their bargain with fundamentalist imams. If there were problematic actors, the Wahabist clerics would take care of them—*take care of their own*—a service for which the religious men might command some added compensation in petrodollars.

Both governments, however, also valued their relationships with the United States, which said forcefully after 9/11 that this status quo was no longer acceptable. The subsequent crackdowns—especially in Saudi Arabia, with its more serious internal, and exported, threat—tended to be fitful and unenthusiastic. Arrests were judiciously reported to the Americans and, once credit was collected, suspects would soon return to the streets.

So, over the past year, the United States had been asking for more: namely, some direct involvement after a capture. Get us involved, was the message from CIA. Let us check out who you've got; we can help you decide whether they're important.

That is what the CIA teams in the region did in the days after this arrest. The Bahraini group consisted of five men: two gunrunners of a traditional criminal stripe, and three men with strong jihadist credentials. All were put through the basics of law enforcement procedure that are not necessarily common in their part of the world. Their belongings—cars, cell phones, wallets—were held in a secure place, used to glean further leads, and their apartments were searched.

One of the jihadists, Bassam Bokhowa, an educated fiftyish professional, with computer skills, had visited an apartment in Saudi Arabia. And there, a joint Saudi-U.S. Counter-Terrorist unit, formed after the meeting with Bandar in his study, found a computer. The contents were dumped onto a separate hard drive, which was sent to the United States for imaging—a way to suck out digitalia, encrypted or not.

That's where they found it: plans for construction of a device called a mubtakkar. It is a fearful thing, and quite real.

Precisely, the mubtakkar is a delivery system for a widely available combination of chemicals—sodium cyanide, which is used as rat poison and metal cleanser, and hydrogen, which is everywhere. The combination of the two creates hydrogen cyanide, a colorless, highly volatile liquid that is soluble and stable in water. It has a faint odor, like peach kernels or bitter almonds. When it is turned into gas and inhaled, it is lethal. For years, figuring out how to deliver this combination of chemicals as a gas has been something of a holy grail for terrorists.

Ramzi Yousef attempted to release the gas into the ventilation system of the World Trade Center prior to his bombing in 1993, and couldn't quite manage it. The famous chemical attack by Aum Shinrikyo on the Tokyo subway in March 1995—the release of sarin gas that killed twelve people and sent nearly a thousand to area hospitals—was followed, two months later, by an attempted cyanide gas attack. A small fire, set in a Tokyo restroom that ventilated onto a subway platform, was designed to disperse the gas and was extinguished by alert subway guards.

Terrorism experts inside many governments have been on the lookout for a solution to these engineering hurdles. Now, the CIA had found it. The word means "invention" in Arabic, "the initiative" in Farsi. The device is a bit of both. It's a canister with two interior containers: sodium cyanide is in one; a hydrogen product, like hydrochloric acid, in the other; and a fuse breaks the seal between them. The fuse can be activated remotely—as bombs are triggered by cell phones—breaking the seal, creating the gas, which is then released. Hydrogen cyanide gas is a blood agent, which means it poisons cells in a way that stops the cell from using oxygen in the blood. Exposure leads to dizziness, nausea, weakness, loss of consciousness, and convulsions. Breathing stops and death follows. (The antidote for blood agents is amyl nitrite. Since blood agents are carried only through the respiratory system, a gas mask is the only protection needed.)

In a confined environment, such as an office building's ventilation system, or a subway car, hydrogen cyanide would cause many deaths. The most chilling illustration of what happens in a closed space comes from a twentieth-century monstrosity. The Nazis used a form of hydrogen cyanide called Zyklon B in the gas chambers of their concentration camps.

When the plans were discovered on Bokhowa's hard drive, Rolf Mowatt-Larssen and his counterpart analyst, Leon, who headed the CBRN (chemical, biological, radiological, nuclear) division for terrorist groups (there's a different, long-standing division for creation of such weapons by states), went into something just shy of a panic. Leon instantly pulled together a team to make a model of the device that he could eventually test.

At 5 p.m. in Tenet's conference room in early March, Leon waited until everyone was seated. He pulled from a bag a cylinder, about the size of a paint can, with two Mason jars in it. He placed it in the center of the large mahogany conference table, sat back down in his chair. People had heard various things about the recent discovery of a delivery system.

But seeing it was something else.

"Oh shit," Tenet whispered after a moment.

McLaughlin sat forward in his chair—thinking of how easily it might be transported in a backpack, a suitcase, a shopping bag, and how innocuous it looked.

The room fell silent.

"The man's got to see this," Tenet said, and called the White House to clear a few extra CIA briefers for the next morning's presidential briefing.

The White House in early March was a place of frenzy and expectation. The ultimate threshold in "making the case" had finally been crossed, care of Colin Powell. Having been marginalized in the White House decision-making process through two years of battle with Cheney and Rumsfeld, Powell, on February 4, was at last placed in a role of enormous value to Bush: making the WMD "case for war" to the world. It was, in all, an ugly turn for Powell, his hard-won credibility on the line—and only a few days to prepare the most important speech of his life. When he settled at CIA to review the WMD intelligence in late January, he was like a minister dropping by the home of a couple of parishioners at the end of their long bad marriage—and trying to sort things out.

The sixty-two-page dossier of "findings" for the speech sent over by Scooter Libby to CIA was a chance for the White House to revive every allegation, including many that had already been slapped down by the agency. John McLaughlin, one of those who sat at the United Nations with Powell on behalf of CIA, said later that half the White House offering was thrown out immediately. Now, with the speech approaching, he, Powell, and others raced through a frantic attempt at due diligence. It was like the whole long battle between CIA and the White House on issues of evidence condensed into forty-eight hours. What came out was a hash of allegations and props and slides. Powell, sensing danger, demanded that Tenet sit behind him. And he did. They'd go down together. But, ultimately, it was Powell who'd take the fall. Just a month after his presentation, questions were already simmering among the analytical teams at State and CIA about some of Powell's UN assertions. That would grow, and eventually Powell confronted Libby. The White House lawyer, Cheney's Cheney, demurred, telling Powell his presentation was not meant to be an explanation, a balanced disquisition, so much as "an argument a lawyer might give in a courtroom." Of course, without the benefit of opposing counsel.

But inside the White House, the Powell presentation was viewed as a rousing success. The UN General Assembly offered its vote of confidence, and the U.S. Army was gathering in the Gulf, 150,000 strong.

Finally, the Defense Department and America's powerful military would make its contribution—bringing a land war to the heart of the Arab world, being an agent of regime change, disarmament, promotion of democracy, support of the old world order . . . the list went on.

But rationales mattered less and less. The status quo would soon change from anxious peace to state of war.

Meanwhile, the original and essential battle—*find them, stop them*—was ratcheting up.

Tenet entered the Oval Office first, to prebrief Bush for four or five minutes. This was common practice: a short confidential primer from Tenet, so Bush could be authoritative and updated when others arrived.

The CIA briefers were summoned from the waiting area. One of them placed the mubtakkar on a low table in the sitting area.

Bush looked at it. Cheney and the others were seated. The President picked it up—felt its weight.

"Thing's a nightmare," he said quietly, almost to himself, and put it down.

A CIA briefer went through a dissertation on the device, the technical problems it solved, its probable uses, and the long road of trial and error leading to this moment.

But the device bent laws of physics in this chamber atop the world. Everyone just sat in the Oval Office, looking at it—thinking about the era and its challenges, and saying nothing.

★ ★ ★

An invention like this doesn't spring from necessity, solely. People across the planet, half of whom still live on less than a dollar a day, have always had profound needs, desperate energy, inventive vigor. What's changed is how easily available, downloadable information—and instantly buyable products in an ever more diversified world economy—nourish necessity's many offspring. This, of course, is largely for the best; people, the world over, are more able than ever to harness ingenuity to solve their own problems. But then, there's the mubtakkar. Blending readily attainable products in a deadly combination, it is among the darkest translations of the word "invention."

After the Oval Office briefing, Bush ordered alerts sent through the U.S. government. Tenet held meetings with the intelligence chiefs. Rolf and Leon showed the device to the relevant people in law enforcement and other intelligence services. The word had to be spread. The device was unstoppable—for people walking onto subway cars, railroad trains, or through crowded, enclosed areas of any kind. Selective awareness, under intense standards of secrecy, seemed to be the only response.

In the world of terrorist weaponry, this was the equivalent of splitting the atom. Obtain a few widely available chemicals, and you could construct it with a trip to Home Depot and then kill everyone in the store.

It was time for Dan Coleman to go home.

And that wasn't because he was exhausted, which he was. Or because there was nothing left for him to do as FBI's special emissary without portfolio to CIA and elsewhere, as someone who knew what bits of information would actually be important in the battle against al Qaeda. On that score, there was still plenty to do.

No, he decided one night in mid-February that he had to get home—immediately!—because of his tooth.

Or the lack of a tooth. It had been pulled, a wisdom tooth, on February 13, and he wasn't healing. A "dry socket" is what the dentist called it, when he went back a few days after the extraction. The gap in his gums wouldn't fuse and scab, the way it usually works. So it had to be packed with gauze, while the rest of his body was packed with Percocet.

But now, five days later, on Friday night, as the digital clock screamed 2 a.m., the drugs were turning against him. He was in some sort of narcotic, pain-addled swirl, pacing the one-bedroom rental—a madman in briefs.

Then it came, a mystical, saving revelation: He had to get home, and back to his old dentist in New Jersey. He'd know what to do.

The roads were clear in the middle of the night—no one in either direction at 4 a.m. on the Jersey Turnpike. So Coleman could drive in the only way that brought him a modicum of relief: head out the window, mouth open.

What followed was three weeks of dental hell. Getting the tooth packed every other day. Trying out new painkillers. Ranting around the house, driving Maureen insane.

"Can you go back in, do anything?" she asked one morning.

"Thure, there plenty I kud thu," he said, through the gauze. "Thertainly."

Having been in Washington for a year and a half meant that he didn't have a whole lot to return to in New York. He didn't really work there anymore.

But he drove the black Olds from Jersey through the Holland Tunnel to the enormous nondescript FBI Building in southern Manhattan and into the underground garage. His parking spot was gone. No spots, anywhere. The guy who introduced bin Laden to America—thirty years with the bureau, and he's doing quarters at a meter.

The office had changed. Offices do, quickly, with so much happening. But it was nice to be back. Coleman was a hero up here. John O'Neill, the FBI's obstreperous al Qaeda hunter, was dead. But Dan was still around.

And, drug-addled, the big guy walked right into a brewing storm.

Joe Billy, the head of the FBI's New York office, was on the horns of a dilemma and wondering what to do. The CIA New York station had called. Someone was coming to town from overseas. A bad guy from England. CIA would send over the "need to know" information—guy's name, arrival flight, photo. FBI's job was to follow him. Period.

There had been similar directives of late from CIA. Someone's coming, tail him. Easy to say, hard to do. Once a suspect gets to America, it's much more difficult to stick with him than the CIA, or others across the government, understand. In fact, over the past eighteen months FBI had lost a few.

Joe Billy argued with the CIA's station chief, a woman. "Look, you say here's some basic information—stick by him. It's not that simple," he told her. "At the very least, we need a lot more before we say yes. Who is he? What have you got on him?"

CIA was generally the "originator" of actionable information. Often, it actually came from NSA, through to the CIA, though the agency would rather not admit that. The FBI, in any event, was far downstream—there, it seemed, at CIA's convenience. It was a frustrating position for Billy. FBI wasn't just a hound dog: here's the scent, stay with him. They were being asked to do a tough, high-risk surveillance job—of a type they'd tried before with uneven results—and they needed to be brought into the control room. "Need to know" needed to be replaced by full disclosure.

That was the FBI's position: it was an ultimatum. The CIA station chief hung up and called CTC, whose orders she, in fact, was following. A CTC manager, a fierce spiky-haired woman, blew up. This was the breaking down of established walls between the agency and the bureau. What other departments in the government are told about key intelligence was the decision of the "originator." But FBI wasn't budging. After heated consultations with other bosses in Langley, the file on the British suspect was sent to FBI's New York Office.

And directly to Dan Coleman. He and one of Joe Billy's deputies went through the file. There were several NSA cables of phone calls and e-mails.

It was a file that revealed the nature of the NSA's expansion of power under Bush. The suspect was a British citizen. He was in touch with American citizens. There were also e-mails between American citizens. All of it was in a package, cable after cable, no warrants of any kind.

One of the Americans was Ahmed Omar Abu Ali—a northern Virginia resident, just twenty-one, who was the valedictorian of the Islamic Saudi Academy in Alexandria, Virginia. Ali, who had already traveled abroad to various Arab countries and then returned to Virginia, was of interest to the United States. He was smart. He was a leader. He was bent on action. Other cables involved Islamic radicals from Brooklyn, including other U.S. citizens, who communicated with Ali.

The name of the British citizen was Mohammed Sidique Khan.

Khan, Ali, and others exchanged e-mails discussing Khan's upcoming trip to the United States and plans for various violent activities. They included a desire to "blow up synagogues on the East Coast." Other records showed that Khan had been to the United States at least three times in the past two years, meeting with fellow radicals.

Dan read the cables, intently. "This is a very dangerous character," he told colleagues at FBI. "We and the Brits should be all over this guy. But we have to do it right. Unless we have some coordinated effort between us and CIA to handle him—arrest him on some charge that'll stick, or work close, coordinated surveillance on him and all the people he's in contact with over here when he comes—we just can't take the risk. Let's say he goes and blows up a temple in Washington. You going to explain to the President that we knew what he was going to do and we let him into the country anyway?"

What happened next speaks volumes about the "war on terror," and the perils of a war being fought by competing bureaucracies. Coleman is a case agent, a guy who has spent countless hours, face-to-face, with violent Islamic radicals. He knows many varieties of them, knows their habits, inclinations, profiles—and knows one when he sees one. Guys like Coleman, with this level of firsthand experience, usually don't get to be bosses in a bureaucracy. They don't suffer fools well. They know right answers because they've earned their insights the hard way, hour by hour, day and night. Of course, all that subtly undercuts the authority of any bureaucratic boss, who has to manage to stay in charge—and justify his or her elevated salary, position, and power—even though they generally haven't been on the harrowing front lines, or at least not lately. The response, by the boss, is to fight battles on behalf of his or her troops against the bosses of other departments and their white-collar armies.

Discussing these matters of process, the way large organizations function, causes heads to nod. But in a battle so reliant on who knows what, and what they decide to do inside vast bureaucracies, process matters. Bad process, poor communication, institutional self-protection, isn't merely fodder for some report that will never be read. It causes deaths.

Dan Coleman's assessment was passed, hurriedly, to Joe Billy, who called back the CIA New York station. Billy's focus was on the interdepartmental conflict. He echoed Dan's concern, but didn't say much about swiftly launching an ambitious, joint FBI-CIA effort to track the Brit. The discussion was about who'd ultimately be responsible for Khan, and who would take the fall if he did anything. "We'd be wide open on this one," he told the CIA's New York chief. If Khan managed to do some damage, "everyone—including Langley—will blame FBI. It ain't gonna happen."

They had to make a decision. Khan, according to the sigint, was due to fly to the United States the following afternoon. After a few more calls between FBI and CIA—tense exchanges that went all the way to top bosses in Washington—Khan was put on a no-fly list. Essentially, inaction. A default.

The next day, he arrived at Heathrow for his flight to the United States. At the ticket counter, he was informed that the United States had a problem with him. He was on a no-fly list. He wouldn't be going anywhere. Befuddled, and alerted for the first time that he was known to U.S. authorities, Khan quietly returned to his home in Leeds. He knew, now, that he'd have to keep an especially low profile, not do anything that would arouse suspicion, and not talk on phones or send e-mails that might be traceable. All of this was very valuable information to a young man bent on destruction.

U.S. intelligence and law enforcement officials—and British officials, who were told of Khan's plans and the default decision to put him on a no-fly list—might have selected from a wide array of options. Arrest Khan upon his arrival at Kennedy Airport. Follow him intensively, with a multidepartmental effort, encompassing FBI, CIA, and NSA, that would involve—as one CIA official described it—a sophisticated surveillance and "brush bys." That meant agents from CIA and FBI in disguise would squeeze onto a subway next to Khan, or into a nearby booth at some diner, a swirl of costumed bodies augmented by round-the-clock electronic surveillance. Wherever he went, he'd be passed, hand to hand. He might have then lit up avenues to various American counterparts—jihadists in the United States with destructive intent.

Instead, Mohammed Sidique Khan returned to his job as a schoolteacher in Leeds, worked intently with three young Muslim men he recruited. On July 7, 2005, he masterminded a series of terrorist attacks in London subways that killed 56, injured 700, and brought England to its knees.

The phone in John McLaughlin's bedroom rang at midnight.

For the average citizen, a midnight call means trouble. Illness of a family member, or worse. A neighbor's house on fire. An emergency, sufficient to shatter sleep.

For McLaughlin, twenty-nine years with CIA, it's no more unusual than a call to the office as he slips out for lunch, or is running late for a meeting. A nuisance. That's all.

He picked up.

"Son of bitch—we got him!" It was Tenet.

McLaughlin whooped.

"Sometimes, it's good to be lucky," he cheered.

The past two days had been about seizing opportunity.

The search for Khalid Sheikh Mohammed had been intense since the near miss the previous September, when bin al-Shibh and KSM's family were rounded up.

In the ensuing six months, the CIA, in partnership with the Pakistani security forces, rounded up nearly two hundred al Qaeda soldiers or supporters. Many of the breaks came from the sting operation at the Wazir money store.

The undercover agents working the sting provided reams of actionable intelligence. The challenge was to foil plots without revealing that the storefront hawala was owned by CIA. E-mails from Wazir were fabricated. The agents, facilitating transactions, could often tell where operations were due to start, and by whom. They could also detect who, precisely, was funding al Qaeda operations. As the financiers were taken down, one after another, money for operations, or basic supplies for the far-flung al Qaeda network, started to dry up.

But no KSM. Many times since the previous summer—after the emir of Qatar had revealed the location of KSM and bin al-Shibh—notices had been posted about a reward for assistance that led to the capture of the 9/11 mastermind. Whether it was KSM, bin Laden, or Zawahiri, the CIA, in fact, had received no response to any of the proffers. The closest they got was the head that wasn't Zawahiri's.

At the end of February 2003, that changed. The CIA got what various officials in Langley called a "walk-in." He was a man who was moving through the al Qaeda ranks, moving in and out of various operations in the area of Islamabad, Pakistan's capital, and Rawalpindi, an old Silk Road trading post that is now a city of 3 million.

He contacted CIA, which has one of its largest stations—with nearly fifty agents—in Islamabad.

That night, he was due to meet various al Qaeda operatives in the area and a high-ranking official in the organization. There was talk of the reward. A system for the man to signal an agent was arranged.

It was nearly midnight when the man called. He'd been sitting next to KSM at dinner, and in a car with two other men and KSM as they snaked through a fashionable neighborhood of Rawalpindi, looking for the safe house where the al Qaeda chief would spend the night. They found it. Dropped KSM off.

Then, the contact was called in. CIA agents burst forth, picked up the informant, and spent the next several hours driving furiously through the labyrinthine neighborhood, as the informant tried to pick up landmarks he'd noted. Just before dawn, the house was located. CIA agents assembled along with Pakistani security forces. The house turned out to be that of an al Qaeda sympathizer.

The key was to capture KSM alive. The team entering the house woke KSM, who grabbed a gun. Shots were fired, hitting a Pakistani agent in the foot, but KSM was subdued, dragged out, and photographed—a photo of a bedraggled, overweight man, in an undershirt, with a three-day growth, that, hours later, was circling the globe.

Tenet flew out to Islamabad a few days later. He met in a Pakistani government office with the team who had raided the house. There were fifteen of them in a conference room, led by their tough leader— a fit, agile man, about five foot seven—who said he and the others were honored to meet Tenet. Tenet said it was he who was honored, that they were kindred in historic struggle, and there were tears and hugs. Then the leader gave Tenet a gun, KSM's rifle, which had been seized in the raid. Tenet, a conference-table warrior, held it in his hand like a rare violin—thanked them all for the gift—and slipped out. He turned to an aide at his side. "Jesus, would you do something with this?"

Tenet also had another meeting on the trip, one with more than ceremonial import. It was with the informant. In that encounter, there were also expressions of gratitude. Tenet asked why the man had done what he did. The man said that he had problems with what happened on 9/11, that killing innocent people was a violation of the code of the

Koran. Then he asked Tenet, "Do you think the President knows what I did?"

"He knows," Tenet said. "I told him."

That question may have been part curiosity, part insurance policy.

In the battle against al Qaeda, this man was the CIA's first major experiment in payoff and relocation. If the President knew, the informant might suppose that his deal, an extraordinary deal, would always stay in force, intact. At least, he'd know where to appeal.

The informant is now living in America, somewhere in America, with $25 million in the bank, and benefits, such as cradle-to-grave insurance and private school tuition for his children, and his relatives, and their children. He, and his extended family, will be under protection for the rest of their lives. "I know it seems like a lot of money," said a CIA official who worked the case. "But in terms of countless millions committed to finding a few people—with KSM high on the list—the math works. This guy got him for us. He's a hero. You want to replicate him times a hundred."

Bahraini police found a phone number in Bassam Bokhowa's records that led to an address in Saudi Arabia. Three men were arrested in Riyadh. They were part of a diffuse community of radical Islamic activists in the kingdom, but not much more was known about them than that they were directly connected to the Bahrainis. The Saudi trio was connected to another trio of jihadists in the kingdom. They were arrested as well.

All of these actions were handled under the supervision and encouragement of the CIA, which had large stations in both countries.

This investigation was now a priority. Finding the mubtakkar designs in Bokhowa's computer had assured that.

But getting action from the Saudis, even now, nine months after Tenet had delivered his warnings to Prince Bandar, was anything but easy. Interrogations commenced. CIA operatives could only stand on the sidelines. The questions posed to the prisoners—both the Bahraini group and the two sets of captives in Saudi Arabia—were pointed. Yet compared to what was happening to Zubaydah or bin al-Shibh at "black sites," these interrogations were polite, respectful. The captives were all religious men. Day after day, they praised Allah and talked about their bonds of religious commitment to one another. This is a problem, said one CIA operative on the case. "Some of these guys are looked at almost like clergy. It's hard to interrogate clergy."

Bokhowa was especially savvy. He was too old to be a courier; more an analyst than an operator. He had highly placed friends in the country's community of Islamic activists.

If there was a wider plot here, it remained out of sight.

The Bahraini trio and the two Saudi trios were clearly tied to one another, but where they fit in a broader array of the region's jihadists was unclear. They did not seem to be tightly connected to several other Saudi cells that were being tracked by the U.S.-Saudi intelligence teams. Nor did they seem connected to the mysterious Swift Sword, who had appeared numerous times on cables picked up by the NSA, and seemed to be running matters on the peninsula.

The President, at each morning's PDB, would ask Tenet, "What've you got on the mubtakkar?"

Tenet would reply, "Not much more, but we're doing anything we can to pin down who these guys are."

In the middle of March, as the invasion of Iraq directed the energies and focus of the administration, CIA chiefs huddled in Langley. They simply had no context for either the trio in Bahrain or the ones in Saudi Arabia.

The White House and CIA pressed officials in both countries with a single message. We're on the case. *Just don't let these men go free.*

On the morning of March 19, Dennis Lormel led a delegation over to CIA. With him were Western Union executives, the CIA station chief from Chicago, a handful of others. This journey "down the river" was to make a pass—to make Western Union's informational riches available to the wide, clandestine world.

The most effective coordination of resources, manpower, and ingenuity in the U.S. government had been in the financial realm. Lormel was a central player, along with Treasury's David Aufhauser, the consensus-building coordinator of the "financial war," and Nervous Phil from CIA.

The key to success was *not* doing only what the President had first recommended—namely, trying to "starve the terrorists" by cutting off funds. There was modest progress on that front: countless meetings between officials from CIA, Treasury, State, NSC, and the Saudis had borne results. The kingdom's decision in late 2002 to stem the tide of terrorist-bound contributions from mosques by forcing clerical accountants to audit how daily contributions were being allocated was also helpful. It was harder for al Qaeda to pay bills and fund some operations. Financial need, the thinking went, would push them toward time-consuming criminal activities, where they might make revealing mistakes and get caught by law enforcement.

Deep beneath this surface, however, there was a fluid, secret experiment under way in how to manage the conflict between interdiction and intelligence. Day by day, U.S. officials grew to appreciate that they *wanted* cash to flow—manageably, modestly flow—so they'd have something to follow. On an intelligence-scarce landscape, *money was intelligence.*

First Data, in a way, was a first step. The massive data sweeps, loosely targeted, implicated the privacy of tens of thousands of Americans to find the odd bit of worthwhile intelligence, or a splinter of evidence worthy of its day in court. The national security letters, the flurry of subpoenas, and the vast number of searches conducted with thin papering threatened Fourth Amendment protections against "unreasonable search and seizure" like floodwaters against a levee. The FISA Court's criticism of the FBI for being sloppy in its reporting as to why prosecution and intelligence needed to be blended in seventy-five cases is laughable to people with the highest security clearances inside FBI or CIA or Justice. Seventy-five cases? A bucketful from a roiling ocean. Countless Americans will now live with their names, financial and personal profiles—an electronic identity—held in FBI computers and various "war on terror" databases. The information does not get purged. They want to hold on to it, just in case, for future reference.

Western Union had been the most efficient part of that effort. As compared with credit-card-charge rendering of activity, wire transfer information bespeaks a different kind of communication. Wire transfer information found at Zubaydah's apartment, and the Karachi safe house of KSM and bin al-Shibh, had provided key links for investigators with both senders and receivers. Requests for Western Union assistance started to come to FBI from "down the river" at CIA. Western Union was asked for historical data on clients in more and more areas of interest.

Of course, in a high-anxiety information war, there is always a desire for more. Lormel and his partners at FBI pushed deeper. What about real-time information—transactions as they occur? And photos? Western Union had pinpoint cameras in some of its offices. Just as someone making an ATM transaction is photographed, so, often, is the sender of a wire transfer, and the recipient, though they often don't know it. Could the company expand its use of the pinpoint cameras?

The further such initiatives progressed, the more Lormel talked to Nervous Phil, and the more he realized that his prized relationship—the FBI's valued secret partner—would have to be passed to CIA.

At least, that was the idea. When it was proffered in early 2003, Western Union and its parent company executives at First Data were nervous. FBI, that was one thing. The evidentiary traditions of the bureau, its law enforcement orientation, provided a thin blanket of comfort.

CIA, the company fretted, was about secrets and, lately, worse.

So Lormel thought it might be worthwhile to meet with a "deal closer." He set up a meeting with Tenet.

The DCI, at this point, was a celebrity—one of the recognizable, unelected faces, along with Rumsfeld, Rice, and Powell—in the "war on terror." This had immediate effect in first encounters, and Tenet—with such a natural capacity for persuasion and willed intimacy—knew it.

The Western Union executives, settling in Tenet's office after traversing the Langley campus, were wide-eyed. There were telling imbalances in this encounter, between the private and public realms, that executives from telecom companies have also felt in their sit-downs with NSA. The first premise, suggested but never spoken: *You folks are doing very well for yourselves . . . while I do well for other people.* One set of men (and, it is, at this point, mostly men) sit in their off-the-rack suits and coffee-stained ties—though, hell, they were the smartest in their class, if you remember—while across the table is the reflection of a different path, a set of pleased men in hand-tailored Savile Row, or Zegna, or Armani, who once thought winning corporate competitions would be a measure of toughness or triumph—like an Olympic medal—but discovered otherwise. Increasingly, it seems to measure the confluence of luck and artful deception.

Unlike some public officials, say at Treasury, but increasingly like those in the military brass, Tenet could add in a shot of machismo to the brew. Though George was schooled in bureaucratic battle, his actions were ever more those of a warrior: pulling the trigger on Predator strikes, capturing the enemy, acting more like a general than a collector of secrets.

The Western Union executives, Lormel, the CIA men, traded barbs and small talk as they got comfortable on a cluster of couches and chairs. The office is filled with an array of inspirational fare—from a large American flag, with burn marks, pulled from the World Trade Center's rubble and framed on Tenet's wall to a red helmet of the Oklahoma Sooners, signed by Coach Bob Stoops. One of the executives admired the helmet. "A great guy," Tenet said, "a winner."

And then they talked. Lormel talked a bit about what a good friend Western Union had been since 9/11. Nervous Phil talked a bit about what might be done going forward. Western Union had twelve thousand offices across the globe, thirteen hundred in Pakistan alone. There was no country more important in battling the terrorists.

Everyone nodded, a show of consensus, until one of the Western Union executives had something to say.

He looked at Tenet. "Here's my concern," he said. "If it seems that Western Union is a global front for the CIA, we'll go out of business."

Tenet leaned forward in his chair and dropped the ace.

"I know we're asking a lot," he said. "But this country is in a fight for its survival. What I'm asking is that you and your company be patriots."

After that, it was all about logistics.

At one point, an executive asked Tenet, "Do you think we'll be invading Iraq?"

Tenet laughed. "It's a slam dunk."

That evening, the President of the United States—in a blue suit and baby-blue tie—addressed the nation from the Oval Office.

"My fellow citizens, at this hour American and coalition forces are in the early stages of military operations to disarm Iraq, to free its people and to defend the world from grave danger . . . on my orders, coalition forces have begun striking selected targets of military importance to undermine Saddam Hussein's ability to wage war. These are opening stages of what will be a broad and concerted campaign."

The war in Iraq had begun, ending a chapter in America's complex reaction to 9/11, and starting a new one. From the first days after 9/11, the issue was how regime change in Iraq could be integrated into the broad, yet somewhat unrelated, mission of the "war on terror"—to find terrorists with the commitment and reach to hurt the United States, and to stop them.

The many attempts to create a seamless weave would be reviewed, and assessed, by Americans and people worldwide: To bring democracy to the troubled Arab world and extinguish a potential safe haven where terrorism could grow—even though England, Pakistan, and countless other countries, from democracies to dictatorships, were havens for terrorists. To show that no leader could consistently flout international law and UN mandates and survive (though, of course, many leaders did). To remove massively destructive weapons from the hands of a dictator, though many dictatorships—from North Korea to Iran to Pakistan—had much more destructive arsenals than Hussein was rumored to possess.

Ultimately, it was none of those things, and a little of each—a default, like so much of the way we'd tried to define something as diffuse and unwieldy as a "war on terror."

Yet this default deduction was driven by certainties that the administration embraced, though rarely discussed in public. One was the realization that—as Rumsfeld wrote to the President and NSC principals in January 2001—"the post–Cold War liberalization of trade in advanced technology goods and services has made it possible for the poorest nations on earth to rapidly acquire the most destructive military technology ever devised, including nuclear, chemical and biological weapons and their means of delivery. We cannot prevent them from doing so."

That futility was driven home to the President in countless briefings after 9/11. The Kandahar campfire, the anthrax labs in Afghanistan and elsewhere, and now, the mubtakkar—a portable disaster, easy to assemble.

Those hard facts matched badly with another area of futility: a realization that the American mainland is indefensible. Despite necessary and regular public assurances to the contrary, there was no senior official in the government who doubted it. When pressed, the closest anyone would come to speaking such a dispiriting truth would be to say, as Tom Ridge did at a congressional hearing, "We can set up hurdles to make their job tougher, but we can't stop them."

All of this slippage, this cascade of hard truths and poor options, did manage to settle into a response, of sorts, by the night of March 19—a response that flowed naturally from the measure of each man: Cheney and Bush.

Part of the default of this presidency is that Cheney is the global thinker of the pair. Usually, presidents fill this role, as Nixon did, or Reagan—who could talk Soviet history and affairs for days on end—or Clinton, or Kennedy, or Johnson. Bush has sweeping ideas, some born of strong personal or religious beliefs, like bringing freedom to the world, or spreading democracy, or ending terror. Those are hopes—grand ones, common to the urges of many people—but not policies, or hard assessments of a nation and its place in the world.

That part is Cheney's job. This fact, clear from the start and ever more so after the 9/11 attacks, gave pause to leaders in various realms of the administration and Congress. Included among them were officials at CIA, which had the advantage, and disadvantage, of being institutionally constructed to serve the commander in chief as a disinterested honest broker—with no function other than collection and analysis, and guided solely by evidence. This President, driven by ideas that are born, as he often says, of "instinct," doesn't have much need for that service; and Cheney, doing what is usually the President's job, is somewhat miscast to receive it.

As the country drove toward war in the early months of 2003, this role reversal revealed itself in a jest. At this point, Cheney's nickname inside CIA was "Edgar." As in Bergen. The President would, by implication, be in the Charlie McCarthy role. This isn't fair, but it is at least half true.

The Iraq war was launched, in large measure, from the left brain of the Vice President. The prospect of Saddam having destructive weapons and giving them to a terrorist is, in fact, "a low-probability, high-impact event" that, despite the paucity of hard evidence of weaponry or al Qaeda links, would certainly meet a one percent probability threshold. So, the doctrine states, it must be treated "as a certainty" in "our reaction." The minions fussing over evidence, or the lack thereof, in the lead-up to the war were missing the point. As

Rumsfeld told NATO leaders a year before, you'll never get "absolute proof" in such matters. The President, in unfurling his June 2002 doctrine of preemption at West Point, was disingenuous in suggesting that proof of an emerging threat would be needed to trigger action. No one in the inner circle believed that. "Making a case for war" fell under public relations, under marketing, not R&D, a disorienting, dispiriting notion that CIA analysts, and for that matter Colin Powell, recoiled from, looking away. Whether or not Tenet engaged in similar bouts of denial, it was clear he was conflicted, easy to roll with a foot on each crossbeam. "Justification, legitimacy," Cheney would say, were a part of Old World thinking.

The "different way" of Cheney's doctrine was an audacious challenge to international legalities. Where once a discernible act of aggression against America or its national interest was the threshold for a U.S. military response, now even proof of a threat is too constraining a standard.

America was, in sum, ready to act, with hard evidence or not, to thwart any possible challenge. Thus, the job of every country, just to be safe, is to avoid at all costs even an implication that it is not aligned with the interests of the United States. Saddam, felt by Wolfowitz, Feith, and company to be an easy mark, was simply a demonstration model to show the new resolve of the United States and its postmodern rules of international behavior. That's the way you change behavior. The way you do it, any behavioral scientist will tell you, is to enforce the desired behavior, over and over, no matter what the subject does. Then the desired behavior becomes ingrained, reflexive, impulse.

This is the way you buy time in a futile struggle—whether stopping the unstoppable spread of destructive weapons or keeping terrorists, with or without state sponsors, off our shores. You can't fight them all. You have to change the way everyone thinks, everywhere.

And the way you do that is through action—continuous, forceful, unrelenting. That's the "game changer," and where George W. Bush's character fits so neatly with this global experiment in behaviorism.

You need a certain type of leader to run this protocol.

Among the many stories about how well George W. Bush was suited for such a task, one story, never publicly disclosed, is particularly resonant. It comes from his days as a member of Harvard Business School's class of 1975, the time when he first started to emerge into his fullness as an adult. At HBS, Bush—according to interviews with a dozen classmates—was short on academic skill, but long on bravado and cornball charisma. He distinguished himself in intramural sports and became de facto captain of his class's winning basketball team, which played against a winning team from the class below, the class of 1976. The game was tight. The other team's captain, Gary Engle—a mirror image of Bush, athletic, same size, headlong, crafty, mild attention deficit disorder—went up for a shot. Bush slugged him—an elbow to the mouth, knocking him to the parquet. "What the hell are you doing?" Engle remembers saying. "What, you want to get into a fistfight and both of us end up in the fucking emergency room?" Bush just smiled.

Moments later, at the other end of the court, Engle went up high for a rebound and felt someone chop his legs out from under him. Bush again. Engle jumped up and threw the ball in Bush's face. The two went at it until two teams of future business leaders leapt on their captains, pulling them apart. Engle, angry and vexed by what had happened, began wondering why the hell Bush would have done what he did. He lost his composure, and his team lost its leader.

A few years later, Engle, who was fast making a fortune in Florida real estate, bumped into Jeb Bush. It was 1980, and the young Bush was working with Armando Codina, a Miami businessman who was the chairman of George H. W. Bush's Florida campaign for the Republican presidential nomination. Engle, a Republican contributor, had thought from time to time about his game against George. Nothing like that had happened to him before or since. This was his chance to get a little insight about it. He told the story. Jeb kind of laughed, Engle recalled. "In Texas, they call guys like George 'a hard case.' It wasn't easy being his brother, either. He truly enjoys getting people to knuckle under."

Cheney came up with the doctrine, but George W. Bush intuitively understood how to carry it forward. A sudden blow for no reason is better than one for a good reason. Makes your opponent second-guess themselves. That's when they make mistakes.

It's a dangerous world. The opposing team has some natural advantages. If you feared them, you had to figure out a way to make them fear you—to knock them off their game.

Two days after his speech to the nation, with U.S. troops racing toward Baghdad, George W. Bush gathered up personal effects for a trip to Crawford. He was meeting Japanese prime minister Junichiro Koizumi. Japan was one of the few major countries to voice support for the coalition of the willing, if a bit reluctantly. They'd eventually send 600 troops and a few hundred million dollars.

He needed to help Koizumi understand what the United States— and the civilized world—was facing, and why they had to do something dramatic, maybe irrational, even willful, to change the behavior of America's enemies, make them second-guess themselves, knock 'em off their game.

Why was this so necessary? He packed up the mubtakkar. That would sure as hell show Koizumi what we're up against. *Just look at it.*

It has been generally acknowledged that the United States does not have any significant human sources—or, in intelligese, humint assets—inside al Qaeda.

That is not true.

It was, in fact, not true by early 2003. There was a source from within Pakistan who was tied tightly into al Qaeda management.

Call him Ali.

Ali was, not surprisingly, a complex character. He believed that bin Laden might have made a mistake in attacking America. This was not an uncommon sentiment among senior officials in the organization. It is, in fact, periodically a point of internal debate, according to sigint picked up in this period. Bin Laden's initial calculation was that either

America wouldn't respond to the attacks, or that its response would mean a new army, the U.S. Army, would soon be sinking in an Afghan quagmire. That, of course, did not occur. U.S. forces—despite the mishap of letting bin Laden, Zawahiri, and most of the organization's management escape—had managed to overthrow the Taliban and flush al Qaeda from its refuge. The group was now dispersed. A few of its leaders and many foot soldiers were captured or dead. As with any organization, time passed and second-guessing began.

That provided an opening. The disgruntlement was enough to begin working a few potential informants. It was an operation of relationship building that reflected—despite Cofer Black's admonition—traditional European spycraft. Build common bonds. Show sympathy to the sources' concerns. Develop trust. While al Qaeda recruits were ready for martyrdom, that was something its more senior officials seemed to have little taste for. As one CIA manager said, "masterminds are too valuable for martyrdom." Whatever Ali's motivations, his reports—over the preceding six months—had been almost always correct, including information that led to several captures.

Now, in late March 2003, the CIA was in a jam. The Saudis were complaining that they couldn't hold prisoners without some evidence of wrongdoing. The trio directly connected to the Bahrainis, they could only hold for a few more weeks. Three men from one of the two Saudi trios, they also released. They had nothing on them.

It was time to call on Ali.

His handler contacted him through an elaborate set of signals, and a meeting was set up. CIA operatives mentioned to him the names of the captives in Saudi Arabia and Bahrain, and the existence of the mubtakkar designs.

Ali said he might be able to help. He told his CIA handlers that a Saudi radical had visited Zawahiri in January 2003. The man ran the Arabian Peninsula for al Qaeda, and one of his aliases was "Swift Sword." Ali said the man's name was Yusef al-Ayeri.

Finally, the United States had a name for Swift Sword, who was both elusive and ubiquitous, appearing frequently on sigint.

This brought elation—a mystery solved, a case cracked—and then screams of pain. Al-Ayeri was in the Saudi group that had been released. They had had him. The Saudis let him go.

But what Ali would next tell his American handlers would shape American policy and launch years of debate inside the White House.

He said that al-Ayeri had come to tell Zawahiri of a plot that was well under way in the United States. It was a hydrogen cyanide attack planned for the New York City subways. The cell members had traveled to New York City through North Africa in the fall and had thoroughly cased the locations for the attacks.

The device would be the mubtakkar. There would be several placed in subway cars and other strategic locations and activated remotely.

This was well past conception and early planning. The group was operational.

They were forty-five days from zero hour.

Then Ali told his handlers something that left intelligence officials speechless and vexed. *Zawahiri had called off the attacks.* Ali did not know the precise explanation why. He just knew Zawahiri had called them off.

Ali then offered insights into the emerging structure of Islamic terrorist networks. The Saudi group in the United States was only loosely managed by al-Ayeri or al Qaeda. They were part of a wider array of self-activated cells across Europe and the Gulf, linked by an ideology of radicalism and violence, and by affection for bin Laden. They were affiliates, not tightly tied to a broader al Qaeda structure, but still attentive to the wishes of bin Laden or Zawahiri. Al-Ayeri passed Zawahiri's message to the American terror cell. They backed off.

Over the next days, teams of CIA briefers, analysts, and operatives were in the Oval Office. The President and the Vice President sat in the two wing chairs, each with his back to the fireplace.

"We need to figure this out," Bush said, "as long as it takes. We need to get our arms around this thing."

First, a nightmare delivery system—portable, easy to construct, deadly.

And now, *this*—evidence of a truly operational attack on American soil, the first since 9/11. Mubtakkars in the New York subways? As the questions rose and swirled, in the back of each person's mind ran disaster scenarios, continuous play, of panic underground in New York.

The Vice President was intense. "The question is why would Zawahiri have called them off? What does it indicate about al Qaeda's strategy?"

Bush cut him off. He was more interested in Ali.

"Why is this guy cooperating with us? That I don't understand."

The CIA analysts attempted answers—each question was aptly characteristic of the questioner, and their relationship to one another. Cheney tends to search for the broad ideological arc, a coherent system of thought that frames intent and action. Bush, from the opposite direction, seeks a way to make sweeping, often complex matters intensely personal. Connects them to his gut, his instinct, for swift decision. Who are my opponents? What's their nature, their character? What do we do about them?

And around they went. Many of the questions were simply unanswerable.

Bush became focused on the players. Now that the United States finally knew the identity of Swift Sword, how did he fit? CIA analysts explained a triangle of relationships—and that al-Ayeri had been captured and then released: "the Saudis didn't know what they had." But, having al-Ayeri's identity confirmed helped CIA establish links between al Qaeda's Saudi chief and the Saudi group that was still in custody. The U.S. cell, whereabouts unknown, was linked to them both.

Bush, in tactical mode, pressed them. "Who came to New York?" and "Are they still here, somewhere?"

The answer from the CIA briefers: "We don't know."

As Bush dug deeper, Cheney moved to reframe the discussion. Did Zawahiri call off the attack because the United States was putting too much pressure on the al Qaeda organization? "Or is it because he didn't feel this was sufficient for a 'second wave'?" Cheney asked. "Is that's why he called it off? Because it wasn't enough?"

The destruction tape—still running, unexpressed, in everyone's head—turned toward calculation. Ten subway cars at rush hour—two hundred people in a car—another thousand trampled in the underground in rush-hour panic as the gas spreads through the station. As many dead as 9/11, with a WMD attack, spreading a devastating, airborne fear?

Not enough of a second wave?

"I mean, this is bad enough. What does calling this off say about what else they're planning?" Bush blurted out. His eyes were wide, fist clenched.

"What could be the bigger operation Zawahiri didn't want to mess up?"

CHAPTER SEVEN

CONVERSATIONS WITH DICTATORS

What did it mean that Moammar Gadhafi's men were making overtures about disarmament in March—a time when U.S. troops were massing in the Persian Gulf to invade a rogue state?

Did it show that the behavioral experiment was working, that an outlaw state was ready to bend to America's new rules and new order?

Or was it a matter of scheduling; that, after many years, the time had simply come round for Libya's next, and maybe final, step toward its return to the community of nations?

What was clear: Gadhafi's intelligence chief, Musa Kousa, contacted the British government. His son, Seif al-Islam, made a call, too. The first contacts came a few weeks before the Iraq invasion was announced on March 19. The message reached Tony Blair: Gadhafi himself was ready to talk to representatives of the United States and Britain.

Blair called Bush.

Bush told Tenet at a morning briefing.

And Tenet asked for a day or two to digest the disclosure and pull together a game plan. Gadhafi himself? That was encouraging.

Though not particularly surprising.

Disarmament had been the goal of a long, patient conversation, dating back to secret negotiations between the United States and Libya in 1992 over the Lockerbie crash, to Bandar's proffer to Tenet and McLaughlin in 1998 in Jiddah, to Ben Bonk's liaison with Musa Kousa on intelligence issues in the months after 9/11. Bonk and Kousa's conversations, productive though they were, were running on a separate track from another crucial dialogue: a final settlement with the Lockerbie families. That had to be completed first, U.S. and British diplomats agreed, and taken off the table before negotiations about Libya's disarmament could commence in earnest. "It needed to be one step completed, before the next could begin," said a senior State Department official involved in the talks. "You didn't want these families and their compensation to be mixed with the dismantling of chemical weapons facilities." That first step was all but completed, quietly, in May 2002. Not that it would appease the families, or lessen the anger and grief that had driven the sanctions against Libya for nearly fifteen years. It was money, though. Each family of a Lockerbie victim would receive $10 million, for a total Libyan payout of $2.7 billion.

Tenet brought the President's disclosure about a possible next step back to Langley, and the agency scrambled. The "war on terror" was "an intensely personal endeavor," Tenet had said at the previous fall's Joint Intelligence Committee hearings—stressing that relationships, in this battle, were almost as important as traditional alliances between nations and armies in a conventional war. Who knows whom? Who has built a foundation of trust? Ben Bonk left CTC in January 2002 to head up the CIA's Mideast division for the Directorate of Intelligence, and a key connector to the Libyans and Musa Kousa, was—as they say in bureaucratese—"repurposed." Through 2002, CIA wasn't talking much to the Libyans.

That was about to change. Tenet quickly returned to the Oval Office with a man to handle the job. His name was Steve Kappes—a respected operator with twenty-two years of experience in the clandestine service, a college football lineman and former Marine, with a ramrod-straight carriage, soft voice, and gift for terse, verbal precision. He was, at that point, associate deputy director for operations—number two in the DO—and being groomed to take Jim Pavitt's job.

Bush, Cheney, Tenet, and Kappes talked over the coming days about some of the complexities of a disarmament negotiation with the Libyan leader. Everyone saw opportunities, but also perils. Dealing with Gadhafi would be challenging. He had absolute power in Libya and could shape a situation, and the people under him, in any way he liked. His assurances, if he made any, might be difficult to collect on.

Cheney, in particular, voiced skepticism. He was thinking of the broad, unspoken U.S. strategy of altering the behavior of sovereign states through the use of U.S. force. Gadhafi "had behaved badly for a long time," Cheney said, and "you don't want to reward bad behavior" with an agreement or a suggestion of absolution.

Bush, meanwhile, saw Gadhafi's offer as proof that Iraq was a game changer. He was told it wasn't clear causation. Iraq may have been a modest contributing factor, but if the United States hadn't long insisted that the financial settlement be completed before getting to disarmament, Gadhafi might have made this move years ago. Bush nodded along. All that would be immaterial. The particulars, in an area that was classified, and the surface timing of Gadhafi's overture would speak volumes, whatever the underlying reality. The key, he said, was "to make sure we get some deliverable from this process." Then, an announcement could be made that the new Pax Americana was working, with Libya as proof. That, alone, would shape behavior. It wasn't just a matter of presentation. Perception management was the goal.

Elated at the prospect of Libya's acquiescence, Bush focused on the personalities. He immediately liked Kappes, who seemed like a man who was not easily impressed or easily swayed. Those would be important qualities, both Bush and Tenet figured, if Kappes were to sit with loquacious, megalomaniacal Gadhafi.

Also, Kappes was clearly a man who could keep a secret.

So Bush gave him one. No one at State or Defense, not even Rumsfeld or Powell, should know about this major initiative. No one.

"Policy process" is one of those flat, bland terms that hide some of the most vivid concepts of self-governance.

A first principle is that while final decisions, and accountability, rest with the President, the job is, on so many days, more than any one individual can aptly handle. These so-called "dilemmas of scale" have, in the past few decades, placed acute burdens on the process of analyzing and deliberating over issues in order to present them, wholly and completely, for the President's decision. The guardians of this process are often presidents themselves. The burdens of leadership, with so many decisions over such a wide array of foreign and domestic concerns, impel presidents to be mindful of what is occurring beneath their office. Are they hearing all points of view; are the key facts known, or knowable? Are they receiving a concentrated distillate of choices and consequences? The force that fiercely drives them on this score is fear of making errors—*avoidable errors.*

There is nowhere that this anxiety is more pronounced than in the foreign arena. While domestic concerns, despite their import, have a fluid, controllable, and often politicized quality, the conduct of America abroad—a realm that falls most firmly under the current definitions of executive power—carries added weight. Errors, here, could mean the difference between life and death on a vast scale.

That's why, at the start of the administration, many of those in the foreign policy establishment were befuddled by the way the traditional policy process—of policy shops in various departments creating reports and then revising them as issues worked their way up from committees of assistant secretaries to deputies and finally to principals of the National Security Council—seemed to be viewed as more perilous than productive.

Powell and his longtime friend and partner Deputy Secretary of

State Richard Armitage often complained to Bush, Cheney, and Rice that the policy process was broken; that to not fix it would cause peril; that the President would be denied the balanced counsel he needed and deserved.

Little was done. And the blame, in Powell's eyes, was often directed at Rice, for not doing her job—one that Powell knew intimately—or Cheney, for creating a captive dialogue on foreign policy under his own purview.

But, by the spring of 2003, it was becoming clear that the way policy was, or wasn't, vetted inside the White House was an extension of George W. Bush's leadership style. A president, it is often said, gets the White House he wants, and deserves.

For George W. Bush, there had been an evolution on such matters—from the early, pre-9/11 President, who had little grasp of foreign affairs and made few major decisions in that realm; to the post-9/11 President, who met America's foreign challenges with decisiveness born of a brand of preternatural, faith-based, self-generated certainty. The policy process, in fact, never changed much. Issues argued, often vociferously, at the level of deputies and principals rarely seemed to go upstream in their fullest form to the President's desk; and, if they did, it was often after Bush seemed to have already made up his mind based on what was so often cited as his "instinct" or "gut." Later, after Armitage and Powell left office, Armitage—in his blunt manner—put it succinctly: "There was never any policy process to break, by Condi or anyone else. There was never one from the start. Bush didn't want one, for whatever reason. One was never started."

Of the many reasons the President moved in this direction, the most telling may stem from George Bush's belief in his own certainty and, especially after 9/11, his need to protect the capacity to will such certainty in the face of daunting complexity. His view of right and wrong, and of righteous actions—such as attacking evil or spreading "God's gift" of democracy—were undercut by the kind of traditional, shades-of-gray analysis that has been a staple of most presidents' diets. This President's traditional day began with Bible reading at dawn, a workout, breakfast, and the briefings of foreign and domestic threats, led by Tenet and Mueller, respectively. The hard, complex analysis, in this model, would often be a thin offering, passed through the filters of Cheney or Rice, or not presented at all.

This was a new twist for Cheney's long-standing ideas of "protecting" presidents from certain information—and placed unique weight on the Vice President, the quintessential number two, to have to act presidentially for key assessments in the foreign realm.

But, at the same time, this granted certain unique advantages to Bush. With fewer people privy to actual decisions, tighter confidentiality could be preserved, reducing leaks. Swift decisions—either preempting detailed deliberation or ignoring it—could move immediately to implementation, speeding the pace of execution and emphasizing the *hows* rather than the more complex *whys*.

What Bush knew before, or during, a key decision remained largely a mystery. Only a tiny group—Cheney, Rice, Card, Rove, Tenet, Rumsfeld—could break this seal. For the next circle of those with firsthand knowledge of the President's words or thoughts—say Mueller or Wolfowitz, McLaughlin or Feith—the warning was delivered early and clearly: nothing said in the presence of the President should ever be heard again, by anyone. Infractions were punishable by permanent exile.

This tightly managed arrangement created gaps in several areas. Cabinet-level officials, like Paul O'Neill at Treasury or Colin Powell or EPA commissioner Christine Todd Whitman, would complain that they "didn't know the mind of the President," making it difficult for them to carry out his mandates. They'd say they needed to know the underlying rationale—whether there was a clear rationale—if they were to effectively defend policies. But voicing desire for a more traditional, transparent policy process—actively presided over by the President—prompted accusations of disloyalty. Beneath the cabinet officials, leading experts in various areas, knowing their services were not valued by the chief executive, began to leave the government in 2003 and onward.

Sober due diligence, with an eye for the way previous administrations have thought through a standard array of challenges facing the United States, creates, in fact, a kind of check on executive power and prerogative. Though the "permanent government" has been widely reviled by politicians of all stripes, the long, consistent, year-to-year arc of major policy debates keeps the American ship of state from veering more than a few degrees in any direction—something of value when a sudden turn by the world's sole superpower can roil the globe.

But, here again, is a distinction between the current administration and its predecessors—the embrace of "constructive instability." That's the term used by various senior officials in regard to Iraq—a term with roots in pre-9/11 ideas among neoconservatives about the need for a new, muscular, unbounded American posture; and outgrowths that swiftly took shape after the attacks made everything prior to 9/11 easily relegated to dusty history. The past—along with old-style deliberations based on cause and effect or on agreed-upon precedents—didn't much matter; nor did those with knowledge of prevailing policy studies, of agreements between nations, or of long-standing arrangements defining the global landscape.

What mattered, by default, was the President's "instinct" to guide America across the fresh, post-9/11 terrain—a style of leadership that could be rendered within tiny, confidential circles.

America, unbound, was duly led by a President, unbound.

And free from conventional snares of accountability. Without proof that deliberations in crowded rooms were ever heard, directly, by the President, he could then be free to creatively craft the "narratives" of various initiatives once they were completed.

Such creative opportunities would distinguish the two major experiments in disarmament that now stood, side by side. One, rumbling toward Baghdad, took a year of painful, fractious, intramural deliberation—a debate finally reined in by dubious assertions backed up by force, loyalty, and message control. It involved 150,000 men and women of the U.S. armed forces, a guardedly hopeful American nation, the inhabitants of Iraq, and the trepidations of much of the rest of the world.

The other involved enough people to crowd into the Oval Office and leave a few spare seats.

Though Libyan negotiations had been proceeding for nearly a decade, the finish would be Bush's—and Bush's alone—to make of what he wished, whatever he needed it to be.

"We keep this completely off the grid," Bush said, as Kappes prepared for a trip to Tripoli. "No one knows."

After a year and a half of frantic searching—of analysts and operatives, thinkers and doers, working round the clock in America and abroad—a top al Qaeda manager, a true boss, was finally in U.S. custody . . . and ready for interrogation.

Khalid Sheikh Mohammed was the prize, the goal, and the theoretical model, even in absentia, for the justification of "extraordinary measures."

Desperate measures may be a more accurate term, and ever more desperate considering the failure of interrogation with the other two major figures who had been captured.

Now, as CIA received daily reports about what was being done to KSM and how little intelligence was harvested, debates broke out on the seventh floor in Langley.

At one 5 p.m. meeting in April, Buzzy Krongard raised the issue of "what have we learned to this point, and what might we do differently?" What had they learned? "There was a grudging professional admiration for how hard these guys were," Krongard recalled later. "They were real soldiers. They went through hell, and gave up very, very little."

This was especially true for the most valued captive, shy of KSM: Ramzi bin al-Shibh. In the six months since his capture, he'd received death threats, water-boarding, hot and cold treatments, sleeplessness, noise, and more death threats. Nothing worked. Several CIA managers suggested that they threaten him with disinformation: if Ramzi didn't start cooperating, they'd send out word that bin al-Shibh had been completely flipped, was now working enthusiastically with the United States, had received cash and comfort, and was actively turning in his associates. The CIA would create documentation of his assistance—crediting him with intelligence gained by other means— possibly spurring a violent reaction by al Qaeda and its supporters against bin al-Shibh's family and friends. Ultimately, the agency decided against this strategy, which was essentially threatening the captive's family to force him to talk.

While bin al-Shibh managed to convince his interrogators that he knew less than they thought he did, there were no such demurrals with KSM. He knew everything, including the whereabouts of bin Laden and Zawahiri, and the status of many active operations.

In the first few weeks of intense interrogative pressure, the most effective method is sleeplessness. After a few days of no sleep, a person will say almost anything for relief. KSM, half delirious, described several plots that were in the talking stages, including the potential hijacking of other airliners in an attack on Los Angeles in 2002. There were other plots he mentioned that had never passed the stage of talk. And, at one point, he said, "There's a man in London named al-Hindi." That was it. All parts of the intelligence community and every U.S. ally in the intelligence war, starting with Britain, were alerted about someone "named al-Hindi." Not much had been given in that one sentence. No one picked up any leads.

But, as the days of stony silence passed, with interrogators sending thin daily reports to Langley, the pressure built. Many days, Bush would ask Tenet, "What are we getting from KSM?" in the morning briefing. Tenet would have to answer, Not much of anything. Then, the next day, the same question.

This is how, time and again, boundaries are stretched. The President, or Vice President, repeatedly expresses a desire, or need, to a senior official. It's clear that neither elected official wants to know too much about the *hows*. They just want it done, accomplished, to do something—as the President often said to top aides—"you didn't think you were capable of."

With such prodding, the United States would slip into the darkest of ethical abysses.

KSM's two children, a seven-year-old boy and a nine-year-old girl, were also in U.S. custody, picked up when the Karachi safe house had been raided the previous September. From Langley, a message was passed to the interrogators at a secret detention center in Thailand, where KSM was being held: do whatever's necessary.

According to several former CIA officials, interrogators told KSM his children would be hurt if he didn't cooperate. The response, said one CIA manager with knowledge of the incident: "He basically said, so, fine, they'll join Allah in a better place."

The traditional models of debriefing, used by both FBI and CIA, involved the building of a relationship, no matter how long and arduous a process. It's the need for some human contact, some basic comfort, rather than simply the bottomless human fear, which ultimately triumphs. The captive's previous life starts to fade and is slowly replaced by one constructed, often ingeniously, by his captors. This method, which the FBI still recommends, was canceled out by what they did to KSM. That's the gamble. Once you do something as horrific as threaten someone's children, and it doesn't work—there's nowhere else to go.

Avi Dichter, head of Shin Bet, the Israeli intelligence service, was an agent of change, an important cameo player in America's "war on terror." On the afternoon of September 11, it was Dichter who was on the phone to his close friend Tenet, saying, "We are ready to do anything we can to help America, George. It is as though we ourselves have been hit."

During his many trips to America since then, Dichter often dropped by the FBI, to see what new techniques were being tried. On one such trip, he chatted with Lormel. Dennis told Dichter there were "untapped, real-time capabilities" the government could harness at Western Union. He described how it might work.

Back in early April, two weeks after Western Union officials met with Tenet, Dichter happened to be on the phone to the FBI from Tel Aviv. "So," he asked Lormel, "you think we might try what you said you could do through Western Union?"

Shin Bet, Dichter said, had information that a wire transfer would be coming from Lebanon into Israel. They had a good idea of who the sender might be. It was the receiver, of course, who was the prize.

And a surprisingly elusive prize. The tactical brilliance of suicide bombing is that there is no barrier to entry, or qualifications that are easily identifiable, or much in the way of prerequisites beyond desire. In an era of cheap technology and ubiquitous, fast-firing global images, the sense of participation felt by anyone sitting before a television has generated a dark window of interactivity. Don't just watch the news, *be the news.* Be an actor in history's drama; audition for immortality. Suicide bombing—whether by an anarchist in nineteenth-century Budapest or a young man with a backpack in Tel Aviv—has old roots, but an astonishing, recent growth curve. In 2003, the RAND Corporation noted that, of the five hundred or so suicide bombings recorded in the past thirty years, three quarters had occurred since 2000. The "Intifada" uprisings, which were started in 2000 in the Palestinian territories by groups like the al-Aqsa Martyrs' Brigade, Hamas, and Palestinian Islamic Jihad (PIJ), helped drive that total, but were also a field for innovation of the technique.

Where once young men with generally identifiable characteristics were to be feared, women, old men, and even children had started to enter the fray in the past few years. Some terrorists dressed as hip young Israelis, others as Orthodox Jews. In early 2002, activity began to rise, and the choices of targets stretched far beyond the nightmarish tradition of the downtown bus. They hit off-the-grid locales, like small markets and bookstores; the bombs were now so small and powerful—sewn into clothing or worn in easily concealed belts—that a bomber could walk the streets looking for a crowded area. By March

2002, the situation had grown into a crisis. That month, 119 the Israel were killed, the equivalent of 5,000 deaths in America, and the Israeli Defense Forces launched a program called "Operation Defensive Shield."

It was an aggressive military operation, with curfews and restrictions on movement in the territories, augmented by improved intelligence efforts, all directed toward preempting suicide bombing. The strategy showed steady results, producing nine months of reduced bombings, until January 2003, when PIJ claimed responsibility, along with the al-Aqsa Brigade, for a double suicide bombing in Tel Aviv. The bombings killed twenty-three people and wounded more than a hundred. Shin Bet got to work. It knew it needed to deepen its intelligence capabilities if it was to manage preemption. Intelligence, much as it was with America's struggle, would be the key.

When Dichter picked up the phone to Lormel, Dennis told him that his timing was ideal. Dichter said that the prospect of secretly identifying the "receiver" of operational cash in real time—without the receiver suspecting it—could be a breathtaking leap. The receiver could be followed to a safe house, where handlers and "commanders" tend to congregate. Just as the CIA's initial electronic surveillance of Zubaydah's safe house in Faisalabad yielded clues about contacts across the region, identification of a hideout in the territories would do the same for the Israelis.

Dichter gave the United States a piece of intelligence to begin the process: the name of a supporter of Palestinian Islamic Jihad who was expected to wire money from Lebanon to a point somewhere in Israel. Early in April, Western Union's offices in Lebanon received the expected order. The Terrorism Section of the Department of Justice, on twenty-four-hour call, kicked into gear. In an arrangement with the U.S. Federal Court for the Eastern District of Virginia, based in Alexandria, they issued an instantaneous subpoena. It allowed Western Union—a U.S.-based company—to notify FBI and CIA about which location the money was being wired to, and who was picking it up. All of it occurred in minutes. Israeli intelligence officers were

hailed. They raced, silently, to the right Western Union office in He-
bron, and then followed the PIJ courier to his safe house in the West
Bank. From there, electronic surveillance equipment swiftly tracked
communications to other cells in the Palestinian territories.

Two further wire transfers were targeted in early May. And, each
time, the golden disclosure was handed by the U.S. government to Israeli forces, altering the balance of power in a low-grade war.

While these gears turned invisibly, publicly it was apparent that
what Israel called "targeted killings" of terrorist leaders in Gaza and
the West Bank were escalating. Israel seemed to know with heightened
precision where the leaders of the insurgency were hiding.

On April 8, a "targeted" strike killed Hamas's military commander,
Sa'id Arabid, in the Gaza Strip along with six others. On May 1 Israeli
troops invaded a Hamas stronghold in Gaza while trying to arrest
Yousef Abu Hein, a senior Hamas bombmaker. Fourteen Palestinians,
including Abu Hein and several other terrorist leaders, were killed.

It went on through the spring, as more leaders were killed. Reactions from the Palestinians, including riots and demonstrations, grew
fiercer by the week. The violence was, if anything, intensifying.

Two years before, at the first NSC meeting of his presidency, Bush
had said his focus would be on Iraq, and that the United States should
withdraw from the Israeli-Palestinian conflict, which he saw as hope-
lessly mired in minutiae and distrust. Powell, at the time, said that a
U.S. pullout would unleash Sharon and brutalize the Palestinians.
Bush's response: "Sometimes a show of force by one side can really
clarify things."

This was the spring when experiments in the use of force to "clarify things" were conducted across the world's most troubled region:
from the Nile to the Ganges.

On April 9, after a lightning charge, U.S. forces overwhelmed the
Iraqi army, and the statue of Saddam Hussein crashed to the ground in
Baghdad. Much like Afghan forces a year before, the armed opposition to the U.S. presence fell back and dug in for an insurgency—a
more sensible tactic than head-on collision with a superior force.

In Israel, the wire transfer snare was repeated, and the Israelis increasingly found themselves inside the control room of the terrorists.

The game had changed.

While the world's many eyes were trained on Iraq, and vivid images—satisfying, certainly, to the West—of U.S. tanks settled along Baghdad streets, the CIA's analysts and operators were sending urgent messages to the Saudis: something was coming.

The kingdom, with a subpar system of telephone landlines, is the land of the cell phone. And not cell phones that were being judiciously discarded and replaced, a technique of the more skilled jihadist operative. Saudis love their "mobiles." That love meant that the sigint was strong.

And deafening. The United States started to discover proof of thousands of militants, sympathetic to al Qaeda and maybe bent on violence, operating inside Saudi Arabia. Since the warning delivered to Prince Bandar the summer before, cooperation between the CIA and Saudi intelligence had broadened. There was still a kernel of distrust—the United States would not show the Saudis its sigint cables—and actionable intelligence it passed along often vanished when it reached the salons of the royal family, whose interests were often inscrutably complex.

Tenet called Prince Mohammed bin Nayef, who runs the country's interior department for his father—the imperious, religious Prince Nayef bin Abdul Aziz, the country's chief of interior and intelligence matters. Operators of the Mideast desk at NSC made calls to midrung Saudi officials. Bob Jordan, the U.S. ambassador, was asked by the State Department and White House to talk directly to contacts in Riyadh. The United States didn't know the time or the place—but al Qaeda's Saudi army was gathering.

There was another, companion message. A message of pressing U.S. interest: find al-Ayeri.

Since the Americans had identified the elusive "Swift Sword" in early March as Yusef al-Ayeri not long after he had been released by the Saudis, the status of the al Qaeda operative had risen swiftly.

A name will do that. It helps fix identity. First, it was discovered that this al-Ayeri was behind a Web site, al-Nida, that U.S. investigators had long felt carried some of the most specialized analysis and coded directives about al Qaeda's motives and plans. He was also the anonymous author of two extraordinary pieces of writing—short books, really, that had recently moved through cyberspace, about al Qaeda's underlying strategies. *The Future of Iraq and the Arabian Peninsula After the Fall of Baghdad,* written as the United States prepared its attack, said that an American invasion of Iraq would be the best possible outcome for al Qaeda, stoking extremism throughout the Persian Gulf and South Asia, and achieving precisely the radicalizing quagmire that bin Laden had hoped would occur in Afghanistan. A second book, *Crusaders' War,* outlined a tactical model for fighting the American forces in Iraq, including "assassination and poisoning the enemy's food and drink," remotely triggered explosives, suicide bombings, and lightning strike ambushes. It was the playbook.

Once it became clear that the writer wasn't some enthusiast looking to curry favor with al Qaeda but the organization's chief for the Arabian Peninsula, the writings took on predictive import. Al-Ayeri was conducting a kind of cyberspace conversation with bin Laden and Zawahiri.

And more specific conversations, as well. Tucked inside the sigint chatter in April of possible upcoming attacks inside the kingdom was evidence of a tense dialogue between al-Ayeri and another, less senior operative in the Gulf, Ali Abd al-Rahman al-Faqasi al-Ghamdi, over whether the Saudi al Qaeda operation had enough men, weapons, and organization to truly challenge and overthrow the Saudi regime. Al-Ayeri said no, it was too soon, the organization had not yet matured, while al-Ghamdi strongly recommended pushing forward. Zawahiri, who managed the discourse, sided with al-Ghamdi.

Speaking through intermediaries, whose communications were picked up on sigint, Zawahiri said now was the time to attack the

Saudi regime. The doctor cited the Bush administration's recent decision to pull U.S. troops out of the kingdom—something the Saudis hoped would quell domestic unrest prompted by the oft-cited American presence. Al Qaeda's goal had always been to extinguish U.S. support for the region's "corrupt and apostate" regimes. Zawahiri thought attacks would prompt Americans in the kingdom to follow the U.S. military to the country's borders, helping to sever the key U.S.-Saudi linkages. Bin Laden, he said, agreed with this assessment.

Indeed, on May 1, the United States—heeding its own sigint chatter, even if the Saudis were not—ordered all nonessential U.S. citizens to leave Saudi Arabia. On May 6, the first inkling of trouble surfaced: a gun battle between well-armed terrorists in Riyadh and Saudi security forces. The Saudi government issued a most wanted list—citing nineteen insurgents, including al-Ayeri and al-Ghamdi, and adding photographs.

Six days later, on May 12, explosions ripped through an apartment complex on the outskirts of Riyadh, killing 35—including 9 Americans—and injuring 309. War broke out in the streets of Riyadh, as Saudi forces clashed with well-armed al Qaeda soldiers. Finally, the front pages of the country's state-controlled newspapers showed burning buildings and Muslims fighting Muslims. Statements from the nation's clerics all echoed the same line—one that they had hesitated, previously, to voice: killing Saudi citizens is not the way of Islam.

Events were being monitored by the hour inside CIA. "Owning Iraq," a country in confusion, with its oil wells shut down, was one matter. The overthrow of Saudi Arabia—the true nexus of oil and Allah, exporter of 25 percent of the world's exported petroleum and, by some U.S. estimates, nearly all of the world's most far-reaching terrorism—was entirely another. At a 5 p.m. meeting in mid-May, CIA's top management huddled. Tenet, that morning, had been grilled by Cheney about the status of CIA's investigation of the reputed mubtakkar cell in the United States.

"What do we know?" Cheney pressed CIA operatives. "This could be another 9/11. This one we can't miss."

Tenet's response was dispiriting. He told Bush and Cheney that interrogations of both the Bahrainian trio and the Saudi trio had, thus far, yielded nothing. The Saudi trio had recently been let go. They had been held for nearly three months. There was no hard evidence against them, save a connection to the Bahrainians. The Saudis let them free, though Saudi intelligence said it was keeping track of their whereabouts. Short of Zawahiri, the only person who could potentially identify the U.S. mubtakkar cell was al-Ayeri. Cheney was grim. The priorities were clear, he intoned. Al-Ayeri—writing shrewd assessments of Iraq's future, going head-to-head with Zawahiri, managing al Qaeda affairs in Saudi Arabia, and, possibly, guiding the only operational WMD attack in America—might be the most important active member of al Qaeda. He must be found. As things heated up in the kingdom, calls from the White House and the CIA to the top of the Saudi hierarchy were urgent and clear: make sure al-Ayeri is captured, *alive.*

On May 31, a carful of young men ran a Saudi roadblock near Mecca. As they passed, the driver threw a grenade at the guards. Saudi security forces gave chase and cornered the men in a building. A standoff took shape. The Saudis called in reinforcements. Overwhelming force was applied to the situation. All the terrorists were killed, including a man easily identified from pictures plastered across the kingdom: Yusef al-Ayeri.

In the breast pocket of the bullet-riddled body was a letter from Osama bin Laden. It was an affectionate, personal letter, six months old, congratulating the young man on his good work, and on a successful celebration of Eid al-Fitr, the feast at the end of Ramadan. The letter was now covered in al-Ayeri's blood.

The Saudis put out no press reports in the days following the gunfight. It took several days before they notified the United States. They never bothered to collect al-Ayeri's personal effects—his cell phone, his address book, the registry of his car, or trace such clues back to an apartment that might be searched.

The news hit hard at CIA. It soon became a metaphor, a Chinese box displaying the dilemmas of the "war on terror." The Saudis—like the Pakistanis, the Yemenis, the Sudanese, and so many "dark side" states allied with the United States in the battle—had a way of often disappointing America. Beneath the warm handshakes and affectionate words, there was always that kernel of distrust. Were our interests truly aligned? What were they telling us; what were they withholding? All were ruled by dictators, who, necessarily, view power and their own self-preservation in ways that differ from a democracy.

We, of course, had told the Saudis about the mubtakkar discovery, and about the report of an operational Saudi cell with chemical weapons in America. We hadn't told them exactly how we knew. We never told them about Ali, the al Qaeda inside source in Pakistan, who fingered al-Ayeri. We couldn't because, deep down, we don't trust our friends from Riyadh. As they do not trust us.

But in the urgent days of May, the CIA let on that al-Ayeri might know about the mubtakkar cell—and that he might be the only one. In postmortems that roiled through Langley, that last part was seen, maybe, as a misstep.

Nine-eleven, with fifteen of the nineteen hijackers from the kingdom, created the greatest fissure in the long, dime-a-dance waltz between Saudi Arabia and America. The effect of a second disaster—with chemical weapons and a clear link to Saudi Arabia—would be unfathomable.

"It was a bad day. We wondered, was it an accident that they killed him, or not? The Saudis just shrugged. They said their people got a little overzealous," said one of the top CIA operatives who was fixated on al-Ayeri, hoping he might lead investigators along a Saudi trail to the WMD attack cell in America. "The bottom line: the missing link was dead and his personal effects, which can be pretty important, were gone. Like so much else when you're dealing with these countries, you're never sure—was it an issue of will or capability? Just try to sort those two things out."

Tenet brought the bad news to Bush and Cheney at the next morning briefing.

Bush was angry. At the very least, he told Tenet, tersely, someone should be sent to Riyadh to get the Saudis to rearrest the trio that had recently been released.

A few days later, Mowatt-Larssen entered the chambers of Prince Nayef bin Sultan, at the Royal Palace in Riyadh.

He knew not to expect much. Meetings with Nayef were often short and nonproductive.

Mowatt-Larssen dispensed with pleasantries.

"With al-Ayeri dead, we want you to rearrest the others and hold them for as long as possible," he said, referring to the other trio.

Nayef nodded. "Fine."

"But," he added, "we cannot hold people indefinitely when there is no hard evidence against them and no charges."

After a few more minutes of the lecture—about how important due process and civil rights are to the Saudis—Nayef said they would rearrest the men, but could hold them only for a few more months. "We're doing this because you are asking us. But if you have any evidence against them, you better show it."

The meeting lasted five minutes.

Mowatt-Larssen smiled, a tight, tense smile, then thanked the Prince for his extremely valuable time and cooperation.

It was becoming clear by June 2003 that there were no weapons of mass destruction to be found in Iraq. U.S. teams had been roving the now-occupied country for more than two months. And nothing. Claims from the National Intelligence Estimate, and Powell's UN address, were turning to sand.

It was around this time that a friend of George Tenet heard rumors. Someone was being fitted to replace him. A few tidbits were passed to John Moseman, Tenet's trusty chief of staff.

Tenet, busy elsewhere, shrugged it off. A chestnut around CIA is that oft-cited rule about intelligence: if it can't be confirmed, it's worthless.

So Moseman looked for confirmation. The CIA, after all, had contacts everywhere. After a bit of digging, he found out it was true. Jim Langdon, a longtime Bush friend, contributor, and "pioneer"—a designation given to those who raise $100,000 or more for the Republican campaign—was telling partners at Akin, Gump, Strauss, Hauser & Feld, the powerhouse Washington firm, to start planning for his absence.

Langdon had a distinctive pedigree, though not in intelligence matters. His father was a member of the Texas Railroad Commission, a commission created in 1891 to oversee railroads but that soon regulated production of oil and natural gas in the state, strongly influencing price and supply throughout the United States. Langdon got undergraduate and law degrees from the University of Texas and moved to a job at Akin, Gump, specializing in oil, gas, and energy-related issues. He spent the next thirty years handling everything from pipeline construction to representing U.S. energy conglomerates to lobbying for the governments of oil-producing nations around the world—from Latin America to Russia to the Persian Gulf—and eventually headed up the firm's energy practice.

He and his wife, Sandy, became close friends of George and Laura Bush. Langdon was a key fundraiser in the 2000 campaign and helped run the Energy Department transition team, a group that soon became a legend in Washington for holding meetings for the town's energy lobbyists to submit their "wish lists" for U.S. energy policy. Some of these engagements hardened into investigations over how lobbyists may have improperly influenced the Vice President's Energy Task Force in the spring of 2001, and a response from Cheney—ultimately successful—that records of those meetings be kept secret.

By early 2001, however, Langdon was given a new post, as one of sixteen members of the Foreign Intelligence Advisory Board—the board, then headed by Scowcroft and little used by Bush, that has advised presidents on intelligence matters since the 1950s.

Moseman looked for the right time to deliver the troubling news to

Tenet. Late one afternoon, he entered George's office and closed the door. "It's Langdon," Moseman said. "And he's telling people that he's all cleared for your job, that he's finished with all of his security checks."

Tenet just sat for a moment, listening, as Moseman laid out the particulars. To replace him with Langdon—an energy lawyer and lobbyist, whose official foreign policy and intelligence experience was sitting on a board Bush almost never consulted—was an affront. What he was, clearly, was a Bush friend, loyalist, and supporter; and an expert on the needs of big oil, for however much that might guide the complex dance of an intelligence chief with a host of foreign nations. Is that what the President really wanted for this job, as important a job as any, in Tenet's view, in fighting a defining struggle for the country's future?

Tenet shook his head.

"If the President wants to replace me, I suppose he's gonna replace me," he said to Moseman, with a tone of resignation. Tenet thought about a few people who would be happy. Cheney, probably—he, and his men, had put Tenet through hell over the past few years. They were probably behind the move, Tenet figured. His wife would be elated; she never thought he should have stayed on as CIA director when Bush made the offer in 2000. She told him and friends that she didn't trust the Bush crowd, she thought they'd chew George up and discard him. And then there was their son, now a junior in high school. He was in the fifth grade when Tenet became director. "Wouldn't be the worst thing, I guess," Tenet said, after a moment. "I could spend more time with Stephanie and my son. God, that would be nice."

John Moseman's phone rang on the afternoon of June 4. It was an extension he knew well—home of his old friend from the Senate. Before he came to CIA in 1996, Moseman, like Tenet, was a Capitol Hill man—eleven years as chief of staff and legislative director for Alaska's

Republican senator Frank Murkowski and also as minority staff director for the Senate Select Committee on Intelligence (SSIC).

The current counsel from the SSIC—now chaired by Senator Pat Roberts, the Kansas Republican—was on the phone.

The committee had finished one investigation, about events leading up to the 9/11 attacks. Earlier that day, Roberts had announced a new inquiry: Iraq WMD. It was now clear that there weren't any WMD in Iraq. Roberts, and the committee's ranking minority member, Senator Jay Rockefeller, the West Virginia Democrat, were intent on finding out where the failure had occurred.

"Anything you need—as fast as we can pull it together," Moseman said. "We want you to see everything and, trust me, there's a lot to see."

The CIA, unbidden, had already started its own internal probe into what went wrong. Jami Miscik was heading it, with a group of senior analysts pulled together by Tenet.

Over the next two weeks, dozens of boxes, filled with annotated files, were shipped to the Hill. "We were enthusiastic about it," Moseman said. "The feeling was, give them everything, instantly."

It took a few weeks, before the first call came back. It was a Senate investigator.

He was mentioning a classified sigint cable. "John, it doesn't actually say what you guys said it said."

"Sure, it does," Moseman replied. "Let me go get it." He did. And called back. "You're right," Moseman said. "It doesn't say what we claimed it said. Yeah, that's a problem."

Moseman recalled hanging up the phone and feeling his "stomach drop."

"That was the moment that I first knew that there was a problem. That something had gone wrong with the analysis, that, in some cases, we were looking for what we needed to see—what we, and everyone else, knew that the White House wanted us to see—and not always what was really there."

★ ★ ★

The phone rang in a darkened room in the Sun Valley Lodge, nestled in the Idaho hills.

Tenet sat up in the blackness. *What time is it?*

It was the middle of the night.

He grabbed the receiver. Heard a woman's voice.

"George?"

"Condi . . . what's up?"

It was Rice calling from Africa. She said she was sorry to call so late, but they had to talk *immediately.*

Tenet was spending the week at the "summer camp" for media moguls, corporate chiefs, and assorted notables presented each year by Allen & Company, the New York–based investment bank. He was scheduled to give a speech on U.S. intelligence later on this very day— Friday, July 11—as the capstone to a week of recreation, hobnobbing, and panel discussions on big issues.

But the world was fast encroaching. A column written by Joseph Wilson, the former ambassador to Gabon, was just published on Sunday, July 6, in *The New York Times.* Wilson had been sent by the CIA, at the behest of Cheney, in February 2002, to investigate claims that Hussein was attempting to buy "yellowcake" uranium from the African nation of Niger in order to support a nuclear weapons building program. He unleashed a storm with his 1,452 words, which started, "Did the Bush administration manipulate intelligence about Saddam Hussein's weapons programs to justify an invasion of Iraq? Based on my experience with the administration in the months leading up to the war, I have little choice but to conclude that some of the intelligence related to Iraq's nuclear weapons program was twisted to exaggerate the Iraqi threat."

Since March, when the International Atomic Energy Agency filed a report showing that the documents underlying the yellowcake claims—by both the British and the Americans—were forgeries, the administration had been working hard to dodge the issue, moving from denial to acceptance and stagey surprise. Their goal was to avoid admitting that it might have known the Niger assertion was hollow long before Bush relied on it in making the case for war in his January State of the Union address.

That was all but impossible after Wilson's column. Now the issue was finding someone to blame. As the President and his entourage whistle-stopped Africa—talking about water, AIDS, and terrorism from Senegal to South Africa, Nigeria to Botswana—the press corps traveling with them had become emboldened. The President, when questioned about Niger, stated that, still, "removing Saddam Hussein was a good idea," but would go no further. Elaboration about Wilson and Niger would be Condi's job.

Which was why she was on the phone with Tenet. She needed to be sure that they were, as they say, "on the same page."

Tenet took a moment to wake up, and then ran through the chronology with Rice. He reviewed, broadly, what had happened the previous fall, when he and McLaughlin had briefed members of both congressional intelligence committees that there were doubts about the yellowcake intelligence and CIA opposition to plans by the British—who had more confidence in it—to make the story public. October's classified, ninety-page National Intelligence Estimate did not mention the yellowcake among its key findings, and carried caveats from the State Department that cast doubt on the assertion. And, also in the fall, Tenet had expressed his concerns to Hadley that the President shouldn't be a "fact witness" on the yellowcake in the Cincinnati speech, concerns that were included in a memo copied to Rice. They talked briefly about flurries of faxes between NSC and CIA on the day before the State of the Union in January, and that it was difficult for CIA to get a handle on all that NSC was proffering, fax by fax, on deadline. In other words, there was, in this case, a trail of paper, a few clear recollections, and visible actions.

Tenet's rendition of the key, probably discoverable, evidence in the matter might incline someone like Rice—who, along with the President, bears some culpability in this matter—to acknowledge what she knew and when she knew it.

A few hours after they hung up, Rice made statements during a press briefing aboard Air Force One on July 11, as the plane arced from Botswana to Uganda.

A key exchange soon circled the globe:

QUESTION: "Dr. Rice, there are a lot of reports, apparently overnight, that CIA people had informed the NSC well before the State of the Union that they had trouble [with] the reference in the speech. Can you tell us specifically what your office had heard, what you had passed along to the President on that?"

RICE: "The CIA cleared the speech. We have a clearance process that sends speeches out to relevant agencies—in our case, the NSC, it's usually State, Defense, the CIA, sometimes the Treasury. The CIA cleared the speech in its entirety."

And on she went.

"Now, the sentence in question comes from the notion the Iraqis were seeking yellowcake. And, remember, it says, 'seeking yellowcake in Africa' there in the National Intelligence Estimate. The National Intelligence Estimate is the document that the Director of Central Intelligence publishes as the collective view of the intelligence agencies about the status of any particular issue.

"That was relied on to, like many other things in the National Intelligence Estimate, relied on to write the President's speech. The CIA cleared on it. There was even some discussion on that specific sentence, so that it reflected better what the CIA thought. And the speech was cleared.

"Now, I can tell you, if the CIA, the Director of Central Intelligence, had said, take this out of the speech, it would have been gone, without question. What we've said, subsequently, is, knowing what we now know, that some of the Niger documents were apparently forged, we wouldn't have put this in the President's speech—but that's knowing what we know now."

While the conventional response is to surmise Rice said what she said *in spite* of Tenet's predawn briefing, it is probably more apt to say she singly blamed CIA *because* of what Tenet told her. He had a strong case of shared culpability to make; her job was to preempt the emergence of that case with overwhelming force.

Meanwhile, through the morning hours, Tenet was on the phone with his team back at Langley, as they constructed their own statement to release—a statement that they ran by Karl Rove and other aides at the White House. "The CIA approved the President's State of the Union address before it was delivered . . . I am responsible for the approval process in my Agency . . . the President had every reason to believe that the text presented to him was sound. These sixteen words should never have been included in the text written for the President."

Tenet's statement went on to discuss some of the complexities of the Niger claims, including the loss of faith in the Brits' certainty on the matter. That would be lost in the ensuing news cycles.

But Tenet assuming blame—while Rice fiercely leveled accusations—was more than Tenet's protective minions at CIA could bear. They took matters into their own hands. Over the next week, CIA leakers noted the particulars of the Cincinnati incident. The White House was forced to sacrifice Hadley as bearing some blame—he had, after all, received written objections to an almost identical set of words in the speech he and Tenet fenced over.

Hubris is, in its way, a loss of context. Those with hubristic clarity of their rightness view even small setbacks as a profound affront, an attack on one's gilded identity. Opposing points of view shrink to invisibility. Hadley taking a hit was seen inside the White House as insubordination, evidence that CIA—with all that potentially destructive information in its vaults—might be turning against the President. From this point forward, the agency was on probation; with any future offenses—in Rove's often used parlance—to be "duly noted."

Yet, there was quite a bit more to reveal about the sixteen words, and what really had happened in January.

On the Tuesday of the speech, there was a last-minute deadline hustle, as the NSC faxed disparate pages of the final text carrying the Niger charge to a CIA analyst named Alan Foley. It was a flurry of pages, sent on deadline. At that hurried moment, Bob Joseph, an assistant NSC adviser, brokered the fudge—"the British Government has learned"—with Foley.

That afternoon, Tenet was involved with what he considered the day's most significant controversy—a prospective announcement in the State of the Union text about the creation of something called the Terrorist Threat Integration Center, or TTIC. The concept and announcement of the center were hastily thrown together by the White House in the weeks before the speech, a response to congressional investigations criticizing the FBI's ability to handle domestic threats and to recent calls by legislators for a domestic intelligence bureau, like Britain's MI5. As usual, there were West Wing expectations that many members of the intelligence community would oppose the idea, so there was virtually no notice of the initiative, much less meaningful interdepartmental discussion or analysis about what such a center ought to look like. It was sprung late and inserted into the text. A preemptive strike at prospective naysayers. But as word leaked out on Monday, Tenet, as the leader of the intelligence community, was swamped with concerned calls. Is the TTIC really needed? In creating a daily threat matrix, would it be duplicative of what CIA, or Homeland Security, was doing? Would CIA get to pick the new center's director? Would it draw key talent away from other agencies?

Tenet pleaded with Card to take it out of the speech. It wasn't thought through, the DCI said. It could add a whole layer of new bureaucracy, when the goal should be flattening out the structure, reducing the number of layers. Card refused. "The President wants it in the speech," he told Tenet, "it's in the speech."

So, while Tenet fought—and McLaughlin, meanwhile, was arguing with Libby about a prospective line in the speech about a pre-9/11 link between Saddam and al Qaeda—Rice's NSC faxed pages to Foley.

As a member of the innermost circle, who, in this period, happened to spend more time with George W. Bush than did his wife—Dr. Rice worked with the President, hour by hour, preparing this speech, one of the most important he would give in office. Between the actions of Bob Joseph, one of Rice's top deputies, and Hadley, who'd been in a similar conundrum over Niger in a speech three months before, Tenet knew it was not plausible that Rice, and probably the President, didn't know exactly what was happening.

And while this is extraordinary, considering Rice's public statements from Africa, it still doesn't solve, fully, the riddle of Tenet's behavior. From the moment of her airborne African press conference, he could barely speak Rice's name. But why wouldn't he, himself, reveal her, knowing what he knew? The check on his actions may have been his relationship with Bush—the deep, invisible issue, always, for those close to any President.

George W. Bush, with his demonstrative firmness, his willed, unflinching certainty, shows vulnerability and confusion only to those in a very small, secretive circle, just a handful of people. He is very good at some things that presidents are prized for, and startlingly deficient in others. No one in his innermost circle trusts that those imbalances would be well received by a knowledgeable public, especially at a time of crisis. So they are protective of him—astonishingly so—and forgiving. That goes for Cheney, Rove, Rice, Card, Rumsfeld, and Tenet, the trusted half dozen. In fact, it may be the only impulse they all share. This desire to support a President in need, at a time of peril, is what kept Tenet from attacking Rice—hurting her would hurt the President—while impelling him to overlook what, in many cases, was obvious to others.

As the calls and faxes had flown in these weeks between Africa and Sun Valley, Langley and Pennsylvania Avenue, Tenet continued to search for a way to absolve Bush of any involvement. He'd say, several times, to aides and close associates that "this is being driven by Condi" and that "this isn't the President."

Time and again, the same response would come back: "Jesus, George. She works for him."

* * *

Juxtapositions are sometimes revealing, sometimes not.

Here's a case where they are illuminating.

While the White House was expending significant energy during the summer of 2003 to duck the charge that its "case" about Iraq's WMD was knowingly false—an effort that included identifying Joe Wilson's wife, Valerie Plame, as a CIA agent, and burning up fax machines trying to manage what George Tenet might or might not say in public—demands of the real "war on terror" began to overwhelm the inessential, the political, the self-defensive.

What was building—from mid- to late summer was what Tenet would begin to call "a perfect storm."

Start with a theory—a framework for expectation—that was soundly rooted in the recent past. It was thus: al Qaeda does what it does for reasons and it appreciates the value of synergy, of how several, nearly simultaneous actions combine to carry forward larger goals—chaos, fear, and the persuasive efficacy of a seemingly global campaign.

The model for this was, of course, 9/11. The assassination of Ahmed Shah Massoud, the charismatic rebel leader of Afghanistan's Northern Alliance—and America's key ally in the country—occurred two days before the Trade Center buildings and Pentagon were attacked. Al Qaeda expected that the United States would attack Afghanistan, and, preemptively, killed the man who could shape and lead that effort. Coordinated events bespeak global strategy.

Small glimpses the United States managed through sigint and the rare humint—such as Ali, the inside source—broadly confirmed this theory. Assassination attempts against Musharraf in April and September of 2002 corresponded with "threat spikes," where CIA and NSA had clues to other possible attacks around the globe that would have coincided with the hoped-for demise of Musharraf and the havoc it would produce in Pakistan.

The specific issue of so-called "coinciding events," however, now involved Saudi Arabia. The springtime of noisy gun battles in the kingdom and the headlines they produced were publicly cited as what spurred the Saudi leadership finally to become deadly serious about the threat posed by indigenous terrorists.

But there was more to it—much more. It was, in fact, in a file that Tenet carried to Riyadh in the summer. It was, at this point, many years into the relationship of Tenet and Abdullah. The DCI had spent more time with the Saudi ruler than had virtually anyone else in the U.S. government—countless hours over tea, making requests, explaining the latest insights and information, listening as Abdullah talked about the challenges of ruling a kingdom of contradictions. That meant Tenet had earned an intimacy that allowed him to do something no one else in the U.S. government could: poke Abdullah in the chest.

"They are coming to kill you," Tenet told Abdullah, gently poking the older man. "You." And then he opened the dossier with the particulars of a sophisticated plan by Saudi radicals to kill the Crown Prince. Abdullah was ashen. Message delivered. For the next few months, Saudi cooperation flowed unfettered.

That was the first part—a major assassination attempt to happen in the late summer; and, maybe, on the anniversary of 9/11. What else, CIA wondered, was al Qaeda planning for the auspicious moment of Abdullah's death?

For part two, go east.

On August 11, twenty members of a Thai antiterrorism task force kicked down the door of an apartment in Ayutthaya, a city thirty miles north of Bangkok. Inside, wearing a T-shirt and jeans, sunglasses under a baseball cap, was Riduan Isamuddin, also known as Hambali, the leader of Jemaah Islamiyah. JI is the affiliate of al Qaeda in Southeast Asia—though some call it a peer—an organization with goals to unify the large Muslim populations of countries from Indonesia— with nearly 220 million Muslims in a population of 250 million—to Malaysia and the Philippines under a caliphate of theocratic rule.

Hambali, who first met bin Laden while, side by side, they fought the Soviets in the 1980s, had been sought by the CIA and police in the region since 9/11 and hunted with increasing ardor since an October 2002 nightclub bombing in Bali, organized by Hambali, killed 202.

The CIA sent Hambali to Jordan for interrogation. Of all the various U.S. partners in the "war on terror," the Jordanians were some of the most successful interrogators in terms of getting information that proved credible.

The United States—essentially the consumer of the intelligence—directed the affair. Hambali was long thought to be tightly connected to the biological operations by al Qaeda. Yazid Sufaat, a Hambali associate who had a degree in chemistry and laboratory science from the California State University in Sacramento, was picked up by Malaysian police in December 2001 on a trip from Afghanistan. The Malaysians—who have mixed feelings about cooperating with the United States—granted the U.S. access to Sufaat in late 2002. That questioning, and intelligence gathered in the ensuing months, helped the Jordanians focus Hambali's interrogation.

One disclosure was particularly alarming: al Qaeda had, in fact, produced high-grade anthrax. Hambali, during interrogation, revealed its whereabouts in Afghanistan. The CIA soon descended on a house in Kandahar and discovered a small, extremely potent sample of the biological agent.

Ever since the terse anthrax meeting with Cheney and Rice in December 2001, CIA and FBI had been focused on determining whether al Qaeda was involved in the anthrax letter attacks in 2001 and whether they could produce a lethal version that could be weaponized. The answer to the first question was no; to the second, "probably not." Though the CIA had found remnants of a biological weapons facility—and blueprints for attempted production of anthrax—isolating a strain of virulent anthrax and reproducing it was viewed as beyond al Qaeda's capabilities.

No more. The anthrax found in Kandahar was extremely virulent. What's more, it was produced, according to the intelligence, in the months before 9/11. And it could be easily reproduced to create a quantity that could be readily weaponized.

Alarm bells rang in Washington. Al Qaeda, indeed, had the capability to produce a weapon of massive destructiveness, a weapon that would create widespread fear.

The next puzzle piece was tucked, inconspicuously, inside a computer. The computer was picked up in late August in Pakistan in a sweep by ISI of apartments that were once safe houses for al Qaeda operatives.

On the hard drive were pictures of a very precise, very professional casing effort in New York City.

Grand Central Terminal, and its cavernous vault, from many angles.

Banks.

Hotel lobbies.

The headquarters of famous Manhattan-based companies, with pictures that included everything from heating, ventilation, and air-conditioning systems to locks on security doors.

Many of the sites photographed represented closed spaces, each ideal, in different ways, for mubtakkar attacks or, now, an anthrax attack.

A "perfect storm?" Not yet.

But there was also Zarqawi, just coming into his own as leader of the insurgency in Iraq, who started to make public statements about the need to win the battle for Iraq by hitting at the source—the American mainland.

And, as August drew to a close, Hambali was still talking. He told interrogators of a specific JI plan. It included planes flying from Indonesia to the United States that might contain explosives.

Tenet, watching each part fall into place through the summer, finally blew the whistle as fall approached. He told Bush of his concerns and requested a special meeting in the Situation Room. The President agreed.

So, in early September, a few days before the 9/11 anniversary, the top officials of the U.S. government—all of the NSC principals and all of the deputies—crowded into the Sit Room.

The President, rested and tan from his August vacation, took his seat at the head of the table and welcomed the group. Cheney, because the entire leadership of the U.S. government was gathered in this single room, was—for security purposes—on video from a secure location. Everyone else was there: Ashcroft, Ridge, Mueller, from the domestic front; Powell and Armitage; Rumsfeld, who brought along General Richard Myers.

Tenet and McLaughlin grabbed Mowatt-Larssen at the last minute to "set the table," so to speak. He was particularly good at describing the "connective tissue of threats" theory, how the CIA viewed the linkage of events. Mowatt-Larssen briefly did that a few minutes into the meeting and then talked about his understanding of the purpose of this gathering: to pull together the leaders of the various branches "to think about action, about what we do domestically at a moment of gathering threat."

John Brennan, now head of the newly formed TTIC, the Terrorist Threat Integration Center, gave the threat report—listing all the particulars, from Abdullah's assassination plan to the newly discovered anthrax to Hambali's disclosure about incoming flights from Indonesia to casing photos of New York.

Then Bush turned to Mueller.

"Bob, what does FBI have on any of these threats? What's the domestic picture look like?"

Mueller paused. He'd been briefed by CIA about what the agency would be presenting. This was part of a protocol that had been established in early 2002, when Mueller found himself following Tenet—and his wide array of CIA threat offerings—to brief Bush and Cheney and having very little to say about what FBI was finding.

Mueller said that CIA's theory, its view of al Qaeda having the capability to strike the United States at "a time and method of its choosing," didn't seem right to him; he didn't buy it.

"Time out," Bush barked, waving a hand and stopping the proceeding. "Okay, Rolf, go over it again, this time in more detail. Let's figure this out."

Which is what Mowatt-Larssen did, now getting into specifics about why and how a foreign event—such as the assassination of Musharraf or Abdullah—would create a host of strategic synergies for al Qaeda. Then he began to list names—names and profiles of al Qaeda supporters, and possible sleeper cell candidates, who CIA suspected were currently in the United States.

Name by name, Mueller was being buried.

If they don't commit a crime, Mueller said, these individuals would "be difficult to identify and isolate."

Cheney then weighed in from the video screen, saying that was the "same mentality" that allows a terrorist like Mohammed Atta, who did nothing to draw attention to himself, to lie in wait inside the United States "until the moment he's activated."

The Vice President pressed on. "Bob, do we have anything domestically on any of these CIA reports?"

"Up to this point," Mueller said after a moment, "we haven't been able to find anything to add, domestically, to these perceived threats."

"Nothing?" Bush asked.

"Nothing really to add, Mr. President."

The room was quiet.

"That's just not good enough," Cheney said from the video screen. "We're hearing this too much from FBI."

Bush stepped in, to stop a pile-on.

"It was horrible," said one key player in the Sit Room that day. "But this is the way it is with FBI. They're not an intelligence service, but they're asked to act as one. And they often have very little to offer."

Bush redirected. "We got too much talk, not enough action."

From the video screen came the one percent doctrine. Many of those in the room had heard it—or various renditions of it—but now it was offered, as such, by its creator, the man driving much of U.S. foreign policy. Cheney went through it—the "nature of a high-impact, low-probability event," and how "even without hard evidence we need to act as if these threats are a certainty. We have no choice. So, where are we now and what can be done?"

In this case, it was one of the reactive, rather than proactive, applications of the doctrine, and the conversation shifted to homeland security.

Bush went around the room—chair by chair—asking what was being done or could be done. The conversation moved to "pressure points"—chemical plants and nuclear plants and the power grid. "How protected are we, really?" Bush asked.

Tom Ridge spoke up. The picture was not encouraging. The nuclear plants were best protected, and alerts had already been passed. Chemical plants, even those near cities, remained exposed.

Bush turned to the TSA chief. What was happening with flights from Indonesia? he asked. It had been decided a few days before that they wouldn't be grounded. "How can we guarantee we're safe, here?" Bush asked.

The TSA chief started to go through a dissertation of how many agents were deployed, and where, and procedures for specific kinds of threats.

Bush cut him off, angrily.

"I don't want to hear any more about policy and procedures," the President said. "I want to know exactly what they are doing in Indonesia to check bags!"

That was the tone of it—for the next hour—from both Bush and Cheney. What about protection of the airports? What about Grand Central Terminal and the buildings in the casing photos? Are we ready for another anthrax attack? Then back to the planes. The information from Hambali was imperfect. It could be interpreted as a bomb, with a timer, in the cargo bay. It could be another 9/11-style hijacking.

"Don't worry, if this gets out of control and they're flying over the Rose Bowl, I'll shoot them down," Rumsfeld volunteered, in a burst of machismo.

Bush looked hard at him.

"Don, your son or daughter is on that plane," he said. "That's the criteria we'll use as to whether to shoot down that plane."

Rumsfeld nodded, mutely.

And, as the meeting progressed, others would do the same. So many questions, so few answers. So many threats, and a country that was largely undefendable.

"I think this is a good exercise," Rumsfeld said after a bit, attempting a recovery. "To really get a sense of what our capabilities are when an attack may be imminent."

Yes, "our capabilities" were quite clear.

Even with the "threat matrix" on flashing red, America's ability to prevent a possible attack was only slightly better than it had been on September 10, 2001.

Everyone left the Situation Room tamping down panic.

A few days later, Mowatt-Larssen and Leon traveled to New York City. They stopped by the FBI's New York office. They held a meeting in the conference room of Ray Kelly, the commissioner of the New York Police Department. Then they visited groups of security chiefs of the major New York companies, many of whom are former FBI, or NYPD, or CIA. Everyone was sworn to secrecy. The mubtakkar was explained to them, as was the new anthrax threat, so they'd know where to look *and* what to look for.

A few dozen people left those meetings and alerted others—police officers or security guards—but only in the most general way. Be on alert, but in a quiet, inconspicuous way. Look for anything suspicious, or anyone, or, possibly, for a canister—or paint can—left unattended.

And then, these few dozen went home, usually to their wives, or, in a few cases, husbands, and hugged them. What do you say? It's classified. You're supposed to say nothing.

How was work, today, honey?

Just fine. Like any day.

But, of course, it wasn't like any day.

This few dozen felt, as the days passed, a central dilemma of this era, and the so-called "war on terror."

Is it better to know? Or not to know?

What does knowing get you? Fear. Isn't that what the terrorists want?

Does that fear begin to settle, in the quotidian passage of pedestrian time, into a resigned awareness and, maybe, vigilance?

One thing is indisputable.

A small, select group of New Yorkers knew that, all other things being equal, they, and their loved ones, should avoid Grand Central Terminal.

CHAPTER EIGHT

WAGES OF FEAR

The nuclear proliferation debate in the past several decades has been a classic case of unasked questions in crowded rooms. The central question has been studiously avoided: why, exactly, should some countries have the bomb, but not others?

The post–World War II period was characterized, of course, by a threat of mutually assured destruction that kept two great alliances, NATO and the Warsaw Pact, in a fitful deadlock. The nuclear weapon was as much strategic theory as actual warhead, the thing to have and never use; a check on nationalist or regional ambitions, a peacekeeper. At least for those who sat smugly in the nuclear club. They made grand, self-righteous pronouncements about the perils of the nuclear weapon, while sitting on enormous stockpiles and working ardently to prevent anyone else from getting one. This was, in large measure, effective, a matter of power enforcing its prerogatives. The nonnuclear countries sometimes groused that it wasn't entirely clear that the spread of similar weapons would do much beyond create added "MAD" standoffs, and, maybe, a hesitation about the use of conventional forces, and that they had, at least in theory, as much right to this sort of defensive weapon—a weapon of self-protection, they'd say—as the more privileged nations. And, make no mistake, it was an issue of haves and have-nots, especially with Israel in the club—like its brethren in the developed West—while no Arab nation had gained entry.

Pakistan would change that. It went into a panic after India conducted an underground nuclear explosion, about equivalent to the power of the Hiroshima blast, in 1974. A decade later, Pakistan proved to be the most compelling advertisement for nuclear upward mobility. It acted unilaterally, built what it needed, and then rose to challenge its archrival. For those wanting to purchase a similar modern history, the 1980s provided a "gray" marketplace and it was just a matter of knowing where to look. Despite the Nuclear Non-Proliferation Treaty, enacted in 1970, individual companies—including A. Q. Khan's, and several less publicized firms in Western Europe—were doing a bustling trade, secretly introducing have-not regimes to the nuclear genie, a step-by-step process that often involved building a "cascade" of hundreds of uranium-enriching centrifuges. The customers' expectation was it would take years, cost hundreds of millions, and be well worth it. In the late 1970s, Iraq first tried its hand—an experiment that was snuffed when an Israeli airstrike destroyed its Osirak reactor. By the early 1990s, Iran and North Korea were regular customers of Khan, who brought Pakistani generals, scientists, engineers, and members of the intelligence services into his ever more remunerative global operations.

Khan also had a network of associates and suppliers from Germany, England, Holland, Turkey, and Switzerland, who provided key components and specialized machinery for his clients.

One of them was Friedrich Tinner, a Swiss mechanical engineer who had been dealing with A. Q. Khan since the 1980s. He prepared certain centrifuge components for Khan, including safety valves, and he acted as a sort of buyer for the Pakistani, arranging for several companies in Europe to send the needed items to handlers in Dubai where they'd then be sent along the supply chain to Khan's operation.

Tinner grew prosperous, and, eventually, he brought his sons into business. Marco Tinner, the elder son, officially owned the Traco Company, a Swiss firm that found, outfitted, and sold the sophisticated machinery—high-speed lathes, band saws, and tool grinders—to the Khan network. However, it was the younger son, Urs Tinner—in his late twenties in the mid-1990s—who soon was the Tinner operation's pride and joy. Trained as a nuclear engineer, Urs was responsible for the importation and installation of the machines across the globe. He was scientifically skilled, and fastidious, and ambitious. He knew where each part went and, thereby, the progress of various programs that Khan had seeded and supplied.

Khan and his associates had been under intense surveillance for years by the CIA and MI6—a tight mesh that included sigint and financial tracking. But in the late 1990s, CIA agents, working undercover among the European vendors of specialized centrifuge machinery, managed to isolate, co-opt, and flip Urs.

It was a great victory of spycraft. In the world of intelligence gathering, nothing matches the power of the well-placed mole. It was as though the CIA had found night-vision goggles. Now it wasn't just the obvious that they'd spot; they could see everything, from dusk to dawn.

But getting what they hoped for raised a thorny question: what to do with this precious knowledge in the dysfunctional world of disarmament and proliferation, a world in which Khan's network continued to flourish. He became stupendously wealthy and even advertised his services, as did, at one point, Pakistan's Ministry of Commerce, taking out a full-page ad in 2000 in an English-language newspaper touting the nuclear weapons components and assembly expertise that the country offered.

Of course, the United States knew far more than the ad copy, and more each passing day. But—very much like our dilemma over not telling the Saudis how, exactly, we learned of the U.S. mubtakkar cell—we didn't trust Musharraf enough to tell him that we had a golden insider. In fact, confronting Musharraf with the most pertinent information about Khan's activities might expose Tinner; we could lose our inside window. The conflict of knowing versus acting, intelligence versus interdiction—which would become so acute after 9/11—left the CIA and various policy makers playing a game of Twenty Questions with Musharraf.

Finally, in 2000, the Americans attempted an intervention, of sorts. They confronted the Pakistani leader with photographs showing Khan's trade in centrifuge parts—evidence that would not spoil the CIA's inside source. Musharraf was unfazed. He simply said the Pakistani government was uninvolved, that they knew nothing about it. Continued pressure from the United States compelled Musharraf eventually to go after Khan in modest ways, such as stripping him of his official government title in early 2001; but the Pakistani nuclear entrepreneur moved forward, undeterred—while the CIA received its regular reports.

All told, the intelligence gathering secretly revealed the conduct and character of Musharraf, the Iranians, Kim Jong Il of North Korea, and, to be sure, Gadhafi. The Libyan leader had been consorting with Khan and his associates since 1997. By October 2001—when Ben Bonk was meeting with Musa Kousa in London—Libya had received some early-stage centrifuge equipment and even a package from Khan's operation in Pakistan containing a small amount of enriched uranium.

And so, we watched. Knowing everything, but frozen in inaction.

Musa Kousa's thesis for his master's degree in sociology was submitted late, a full five years after he left the East Lansing campus short of his degree to return to Libya to work for Gadhafi.

It was unfinished business. The fact that he expended significant effort—the thesis is 209 pages, with bibliography—to complete his course of study and get his master's degree is revealing, if in no other way, of the enduring appeal of free inquiry, empiricism, and other Age of Reason virtues that still define the West.

The thesis, written when Kousa was already acting as a henchman to Gadhafi, putatively examines the question of "how social-cultural-economic conditions affect political outcomes." It is, more specifically, an attempt to place Gadhafi in some broader historical context by weaving the dictator's comments—from several long interviews Kousa was granted—among quotes from thinkers on politics and leadership from Erik Erikson to Seymour Martin Lipset.

The text is naturally laudatory of the Libyan leader, but, at times, it is also incisive—in some cases, inadvertently—about how, in Kousa's words, "the personalities of individual actors are important determinants of political phenomena."

He says that Gadhafi's "legitimacy" is largely "derived from his charisma," and then quotes Max Weber's famous passage about how "the leader" has "a certain quality of individual personality by virtue of which he is set apart from ordinary men and treated as endowed with supernatural, superhuman, or at least, specifically, exceptional powers or qualities."

That age-old tautology of exceptionalism—"I rule as I rule, because I am who I am"—faced its only real challenge from the growth of republican ideals, crafted by the Greeks and carried forward, fitfully, to the pointed assertions by eighteenth-century neoclassicists like Jefferson, who helped forge that era's democratic explosion. Their disruptive thesis—that *the people* are the sovereign, and leaders serve at the public's pleasure—sought to reverse history's traditional equation of power preserving and justifying itself. Though democracy has spread—now accounting for about half the world's regimes—the conflict between the democratic and the authoritarian models has been, in fact, more of an ongoing, unfinished debate, rather than simply a case of newfound right canceling old wrongs. Both are about governance, after all, and the use of power, and each side recognizes in the other certain shared, discomfiting features. Dictators, though not elected, can indeed be ousted if a people's displeasure becomes acute; and duly elected leaders, though not granted dictatorial authority, have been known to go to great lengths to preserve and justify and, in some cases, expand their power.

All of this becomes especially pertinent for America's post-9/11 foreign policy, which, despite the high-flown rhetoric, relies to an astonishing degree on conversations with dictators. How do you get a dictator to do what you want? Publicly or privately; taking the high ground of shared goals, or the low road of coercion; treating them like legitimate paterfamilias, or secretly knee-capping their economy? Once, U.S. support for a single, comparatively presentable dictator, Ferdinand Marcos of the Philippines—whose sins were largely of the pillage variety—was a cause for controversy. Now, we were in regular, transactional dialogue with a dozen dictators, handling each on a case-by-case basis. We have a policy against terrorists, but not what might be called a dictator policy.

Save for a single unifying issue: by the fall of 2003, George W. Bush had assumed extraordinary powers to try to force various dictators to give up theirs. There seemed, however, to be surprisingly little in the way of strategies shaped by the way dictators tend to function. "Legitimacy"—for Gadhafi or Musharraf or Saudi Arabia's Abdullah—is, as Kousa and others have written, largely "derived from his charisma," and a suggestion that each ruler is using his power in a way that advances his country's interests and sense of self-worth. This is a judgment call that every subject—every militant cleric or impatient, ambitious colonel—can make on his own, especially in a time when state-controlled media is vanishing and real news, through broadcast and Internet, travels fast, with attached commentary. These changes make a dictator's traditional challenge of never "losing face" even thornier. Because their power grows from personality, duly enforced, "face" is everything. They must never be irrefutably bested by another country's champion—and, especially, of late, not bested by the "crusader" George W. Bush.

Meanwhile, the President—in Iraq and elsewhere abroad—was

trying to execute a global experiment in behavior modification in which he couldn't afford to lose face, either. Domestic issues notwith-standing, the President had taken on new constituencies among a world community whose impulses—in terms of WMD, nationalist movements, embrace of radicalism, or support of anti-Americanism—he was hoping to alter. Karl Rove's high-powered electoral machine, so potent at energizing the base and controlling messages in the United States, had no ready application overseas. Two years after 9/11, the global community was thinking constantly, almost obsessively, about the dictates of U.S. power; that's what was real to them, no mat-ter what their orientation. Fine, said many neoconservatives—that's as it should be. But, with the U.S. administration now speaking the *never give up, never give in, never admit error* language of will and clout—talking to many of the world's people, using White House parlance, "in a way they can understand"—the problem of "losing face" was suddenly every bit as acute for Bush as it was for a Gadhafi, Abdullah, or Musharraf. For Bush to "lose face" would mean a host of authoritari-ans, smelling blood, would rise to challenge him.

America's dictator-focused foreign policy was thus locked into a se-ries of face-offs. George W. Bush wanted unmanageable countries to knuckle under to the sole superpower—to change their behavior or, even, their form of government—and, optimally, to give up their de-structive weapons, not build any, stop challenging us, and see the good sense of democracy and free enterprise. And if others were going to model their behavior on these examples, they *must* know who was be-hind it: the new, emboldened United States. With each new example, the thinking went, our words would carry added force. More and more, words would be all we'd need. That's the way the experiment to "dissuade" is designed.

On the other hand, leaders, of all shapes, increasingly couldn't af-ford to do anything that America forced them to do, or even things that the United States seemed to want.

They'd lose face.

For a dictator, any dictator, that spells disaster.

★ ★ ★

By late September 2003, six months after Musa Kousa's initial overture to Tony Blair, Libya had still not presented the "deliverable" Bush
needed to trumpet how a humbled, acquiescent Gadhafi had suc-
cumbed to the new world order.

Reading Musa Kousa's thesis might have helped things along. The
choice for Gadhafi was not whether he was willing to disarm—he
knew he'd have to in order to win the sanction-free international
acceptance he craved. It was how to do it in a way that wouldn't make
him seem diminished among the Libyan people, as well as other Arab
nations, and wouldn't make his previous decisions—which had created more than a decade of sanctions and isolation for his country—
seem misguided.

Gadhafi came to power in a bloodless military coup in 1969 and always saw himself as a visionary leader, espousing his own political system, the "Third Universal Theory," which combined socialism and a
brand of Islam drawn from the country's tribal practices that he expected to be implemented by Libyan people in a form of direct
democracy. He used oil money in the seventies and eighties to pro-
mote this vision abroad, funding terrorism that he felt, with messianic
grandeur, would bring the end to capitalism and communism.

What occurred, instead, was international censure and sanctions.
In 1986, even before Lockerbie, the United States imposed bans on
business transactions with Libya and travel to the country. Starting in
1992, the United Nations imposed an arms and air embargo and
banned the export of equipment for oil refining to the country. This
seemed to trap Libya in a sandy box while its neighbors grew fast on
nineties oil money. The country's per capita GDP in 2003 of around
$6,400 was lower than many of the region's OPEC nations and un-
evenly distributed in a poorly diversified economy. The country—
slightly larger than Alaska, with a population of 6 million, 97 percent
of them Sunni, and with 54 percent of its gross domestic product
coming from oil exports—is more a Bedouin desert kingdom than

some of its Arab brethren. Under the sanctions, the oil business was flagging, as Libya was having trouble getting engineers and spare parts to keep the wells flowing at top capacity. That caused economic hardship, and the slow growth of clandestine opposition groups.

As a result of the Lockerbie settlements in the spring, the UN sanctions were due to be lifted in September 2003. But the United States wanted more concessions before lifting its own, unilateral economic sanctions against the country—namely, for Libya to give up its weapons, cut ties with terrorist groups, and make a forceful public statement of its changed intentions and character. Without that, the United States would not budge. As for Gadhafi, unless the United States joined the United Nations in lifting sanctions, he would not fully pay the Lockerbie settlement.

And so it stood. Throughout the summer, Steve Kappes and his British counterpart, MI6 counterterrorism chief Mark Allen, whistle-stopped the globe, meeting with Kousa and other Libyan fixers.

It was, in some measure, a dance of shared interests: Kousa, like Kappes, seemed to want to get the headstrong Libyan leader to the table to construct an agreement. The men talked about different proffers, different tactics, things that might sweeten the deal, and, most often, the mind of Gadhafi.

When Kappes and Allen met in Tripoli with Gadhafi for the first time in the summer, they had pressed him for specifics—what weapons the Libyans had to give up. That Gadhafi had chemical agents, especially mustard gas, was commonly known. Whether he had a delivery system that was effective, and in sound working order, was another matter. Through Urs Tinner, however, we knew that he had collected a warehouse or two of centrifuge parts. Yet the Libyan leader was coy about the full extent of his weaponry, both chemical and nuclear. The team asked the weapons question countless times. And Gadhafi answered in countless ways, while tapping his substantial charisma—his "legitimacy," as Kousa would say. There were not only the issues of what Libya *might* do, Gadhafi said at one point, but issues of what it *should* do as a sovereign state. Who, also, would ensure the country's security if neighbors did not subscribe to Gadhafi's newly enlightened stance of disarmament? What is the nature of binding agreements between independent states, and what are the limits of such agreements? And around the talks went.

With any dictator or authoritarian, there is the primacy of personality . . . writ large by power. Whatever the material points of dispute, Gadhafi, in a way, seemed to relish the encounters, turning to Kappes and Allen as proxies for the type of high-level, first-world engagements he was starved for. It was that need, as much as any, that initially brought him to the table.

One morning in the late summer, Kappes returned to Langley, snappily attired and clear-eyed, even after a high-stress visit to Tripoli and an all-night flight. He met John Moseman in the hallway.

"You're looking amazingly fresh," Moseman said, "after days of combat with Gadhafi."

"Call me crazy, John," Kappes replied, "but I think I'm beginning to like this guy."

Trusting him—an encompassing issue for both Bush and Blair—was another matter. The United States knew, of course, that Gadhafi had a budding nuclear program under way, but—in a situation that mirrored our hesitancy to tell Musharraf about our vast knowledge of Khan, or tell Saudi Arabia's Abdullah about how we knew of the U.S. mubtakkar cell—the U.S.-British team couldn't confront Gadhafi with what we knew about his centrifuges and how we knew it. It might compromise Tinner.

Gadhafi, on the other hand, wouldn't admit to a nuclear program, despite many opportunities. In governments without transparency or internal checks, leaders only admit what they're forced to admit. Even the United States of late had had some experience with that.

The consensus in the small group—Kappes, Tenet, Bush, Cheney—was that Gadhafi's hand needed to be forced.

★ ★ ★

And so did someone else's, the hand of an even more important player.

The situation in Pakistan grew more absurd month by month through late 2002 and 2003, as America built up more evidence about Khan's activities that it could not share with Musharraf, while growing ever more solicitous, often desperately so, of the Pakistani dictator and his role as combatant against al Qaeda. There was a passive-aggressive quality to the proceedings: praising Musharraf for his cooperation, the United States grew increasingly aggressive about another nuclear-enabled dictator, North Korea's Kim Jong Il, who happened to be the prime customer of Musharraf's close adviser and friend, A. Q. Khan.

Several teams huddled inside the DO, the CIA's operational side. Operatives and analysts handling Tinner met with Kappes and the Libyan team. There had already been three shipments of centrifuge equipment from Khan's operation to Libya in 2003.

A fourth, Tinner told his handlers, was due in early October. Tenet and Kappes briefed Bush and Cheney on the upcoming shipment—and recommended a plan: the double play. Finally, after all the years peering out from inside Khan's network, intelligence would result in action. The interdiction moment had arrived.

Timmer informed his CIA handlers that a ship called the *BBC China* had left Dubai for the Suez Canal carrying centrifuge equipment earmarked for Libya. The vessel's owner, a German shipping company, was asked by the U.S. government to divert the ship to Taranto, an Italian port. That's where inspectors found five large crates of nuclear equipment manufactured at Khan's Malaysian production facility, Scomi Precision Engineering, and seized by authorities. Back in Malaysia, Urs Tinner removed his personnel file from the company's records, and the hard disk carrying the company's key technical drawings from his computer, and slipped out of the country.

Several men were arrested in the coming days, including A. Q. Khan's junior partner, Buhary Sayed Abu Tahir, arrested by Malaysian police. Khan was placed under house arrest in Pakistan, while

Musharraf thought through the various ways he might handle the delicate situation of dealing with his close friend and adviser.

The ship's seizure gave the United States the chance to express outrage and public surprise about what it had secretly known for years, and demand action from both Musharraf and Gadhafi. Because U.S. knowledge seemed, then, to emerge from a single, clarifying event, it gave the dictators a chance to follow suit, to move past their many secret, disingenuous conversations with U.S. officials, and use the *BBC China* as a starting point of sorts.

Almost from the first, CIA analysts and NSC policy specialists began to look at the incident as a model, with features that included a slow, steady building of intelligence and waiting for the right moment to act. Or, as one CIA official with an affinity for basketball metaphors termed it, "waiting for the good shot."

The *BBC China* seizure would also, week by week, display the subtle, often unsettling interplay between the secret and the visible, between darkest night and rosy dawn in a so-called "war" largely fought in shadows. None of the varied players, of course, learned anything consequential from the takedown of the ship. All participants—the United States, Britain, Pakistan, Libya, probably Malaysia, Iran, and surely North Korea—had been for years *in the know.* They were most likely aware, or strongly suspected, what each of the others probably knew, even if they weren't all aware of *how* each party knew what it knew. That meant that the various populations atop which those leaders sit, especially in the putatively transparent democracies, had been studiously kept in the dark.

In the interplay between decisions made by the intelligence professionals and a small circle of policy makers—and the competing claims made by other branches of government or by the public, with its recognized right to understand what truly guides U.S. foreign policy—almost all the options reside with the parties of the first part.

That meant, for instance, long-held intelligence about North Korea's prized place in Khan's customer base got conveniently leaked a few weeks after Congress had voted in October 2002 to give Bush authorization to use force against Saddam Hussein—a dictator who, even the most suspicion-driven policy makers knew, could not be nearly as far along in the building of nuclear weapons as Kim Jong Il. It was decided, alternatively, that neither the full Congress nor the American public—debating for nearly a year whether or not Hussein was the world's most imminent threat—should know that the CIA had issued an internal briefing as early at October 2001—at the time of Ben Bonk's meeting with Kousa—that Libya had developed the first stages of a nuclear program. Or that Iran was also moving apace as a Khan customer. As the drumbeat for war against Iraq built, all of this would be considered, to borrow the legalism, immaterial.

Instead, after the *BBC China* seizure, Musharraf could express shock, just as the United States had. He fumed publicly that "we've been betrayed by our Muslim brethren," an artfully ambiguous statement that could be applied either to Khan, who'd profited mightily from his sale of Pakistan's nuclear technology, or to Gadhafi, who, it was implied, had turned in a Pakistani hero to the United States.

Khan, under house arrest, was not interrogated, and the Americans were not given access to him. They never would be. A few months later, he would go on Pakistani television and, speaking in English with a message tailored to an international audience more than a domestic one, apologize for his perfidy, and, most important, say that "there was never any authorization for these activities by the government." In all, Musharraf's shock and Khan's statement meant the Pakistani leader lost face, but only in a very small and manageable way.

The same went for Gadhafi. Takedown of the ship created the cover for a circumstance that was demonstrably beyond his control— this sort of thing will sometimes happen, after all—which left the revelation of his nuclear program simply a matter of common sense. It was, after all, already out.

At the negotiating table in Tripoli, the Libyan leader offered Kappes and Allen a Cheshire cat's smile and progress picked up. Using the seizure as a starting point, as others were doing publicly, he laid out what the United States and Britain secretly knew, for the most part, about his nuclear program. In November, some of the particulars of his disarmament protocol were decided. By December, the United States and Britain would be touring Libyan facilities, along with representatives from the International Atomic Energy Agency. They looked at centrifuge parts and components, many of them still crated. In exchange, Gadhafi got what he wanted: the sanctions were lifted. Among the country's ruling elite, the whole matter was viewed as being artfully handled, with no discernible loss of face by the leader of the revolution.

As for George W. Bush, he got to say, countless times, the thing he desperately wanted to say to help offset the crumbling Iraq experiment, a measurable "saving face" aria: that Gadhafi had given up his weapons because of how the U.S. invasion of Iraq had changed the landscape.

That was false, as were, in essence, almost all the public statements by all the involved parties in this so-called "double play." It wasn't a matter of misstatement: whether it was Musharraf or Bush, everyone knew they were lying. With almost no transparency, even with regard to the U.S. government, it is very difficult for pronouncements to be challenged by any underlying evidence, at least in the near term. That also is understood by all participants. The key—all but written into the fine print of the agreements at hand—is that all parties in power will get to "save face," or at least not lose too much. That crafted messages, coming from Islamabad, or Tripoli, or Washington, will be augmented or, at least, stay intact. That's the pact, the "shared interest"—a place where the democratic and the authoritarian are seen, these days, to have so much in common.

Through a long lens, Iraq was the failure of a conversation with a dictator, a bad instance in the case-by-case method, that ended with the traditional model of an invading, and now occupying, army. Yet, as compared to the *find them, stop them* "war on terror," Iraq was fought in daylight, with cameras whirring. And that was why, by the fall of 2003, the administration, and countless observers plastered to television sets in developed nations across the globe, were experiencing anger, puzzlement, or—to borrow from Sherwood Anderson—a "sadness of sophistication" about the U.S. invasion.

There were already demonstrable mistakes, clear from any point of view, such as not securing the country's weapons depots and disbanding the Iraqi army, a sort of professional class of soldiers who might have been bought relatively cheaply. More cheaply, that is, than the billions spent at that point to quell the riots, bombings, and insurrections that were rising through a hot summer where water and electricity were scarce and frustration plentiful.

What was the President thinking this summer, as preliminary doubts about Iraq, and its complications, from the naysayers at State and CIA were shown to be wise predictions? Glimpses of the mind of George W. Bush, rare in any period, came from two somewhat digressive remarks. The first was made at a White House press conference in July, when he said, "There are some who feel like that if they attack us [in Iraq] that we may decide to leave prematurely. They don't understand what they're talking about, if that's the case. . . . There are some who feel like, that the conditions are such that they can attack us there. My answer is, 'bring them on.' "

This, of course, is a time-honored play. When a sound blow has been landed against a champion, or he is not behaving in a confrontation as forcefully as was predicted, he'll often up the rhetoric, to show that there is no fear, or doubt . . . at least not in his mind. This sort of bravado has its place in the affairs of men. But, as Mahatma Gandhi once said, "Manliness consists not in bluff, bravado or lordliness. It consists in daring to do the right and facing consequences whether it is in matters social, political or other. It consists in deeds, not in words." While a government is represented by a leader, it is an entity of a thousand hands and faces. In this case, in the matter of Gandhi's "deeds," the government was attempting to control a nation of 27 million with a force of only 150,000, about half—or even a third—of what most military commanders with experience in such matters recommended. That lent the President's words a hollowness, just the thing you don't want when attempting bravado. Hollow posturing encourages a countering response.

The gap was enough that even Brit Hume, anchor of the supportive Fox News, asked Bush about the "bring them on" quote in an exclusive interview the President granted the network in September. Bush said the quip was mostly intended to encourage U.S. troops that they were "plenty tough" to take on disgruntled Baathists, religious extremists, and foreign terrorists—including al Qaeda—who had been flowing steadily across the country's porous borders over the past few months. "From a military point of view," Hume then asked, "do you regard that as a welcome or unwelcome development?" Bush's response, specifically, was the second revealing remark of this period: "That's an interesting question, because you know I'm a man of peace. And obviously I would hope that we wouldn't have combat. I also live in a real world of being the president during a 'war on terror.' So I guess I would rather fight them there than here. I know I would rather fight them there than here, and I know I would rather fight them there than in other remote parts of the world, where it may be more difficult to find them."

The idea of fighting "them" in Iraq so we don't have to fight them here rested on something the President would never publicly discuss: a recognition that the "homeland" was indefensible. This hard, dispiriting realization was fueled—as it had been so often—by the secret disclosures in August of an enemy casing New York City, an enemy possibly carrying massively destructive chemical weapons. This was the anxiety beneath actions and words coming from Bush and his White House.

In the long line of default analysis, a new thinking took root in the Oval Office, growing from the ashes of several failed attempts at strategy and thinning public attempts to integrate Iraq into a broader "war on terror." It was simply the gut response of *draw them to Iraq, all of them.* Make that the place of our choosing, where America's powerful military—our strength, no doubt—might finally face an assembled opponent, lured, one terrorist group after another, from a global diaspora of hideouts. It made a kind of improvisational good sense, which is why Bush felt an urge to offer it to Hume. The concept—widely understood from centuries of clashing armies and decades of cinematic westerns—is one of a showdown.

The ever attentive Donald Rumsfeld watched these public proceedings with quiet concern. He knew that this sort of tactical thrashing was not the stuff of strategy. The President's public comments reflected the gap: they lacked the borders of a coherent thought process about what the original battle against far-flung terrorists had to do with the enveloping challenge of Iraq.

Rumsfeld, according to a score of people who have served with him, is not a man who often shows his hand in the councils of state. His lexicon, even in the highest-level meetings, often rests on the pronoun "one"—as in, one would wonder, one would suppose, one might consider—as a way to tiptoe onto terra infirma without ever planting a foot. Whereas Cheney speaks of global doctrines, of the way "we must now think," Rumsfeld is anything but a tiger at the conference table.

By mid-October, though, he felt an urgency to wade into the definitive verbs and declarative statements of genuine strategy. It had, after all, been a very bad week in Iraq.

The secretary met with "combatant commanders" and posed questions. And then he wrote this memo to his highest-level quartet: his two top uniformed deputies, General Dick Myers, Chairman of the Joint Chiefs, and Marine general Peter Pace, the Vice Chairman; and his longtime brain trust of Wolfowitz and Feith.

October 16, 2003

Gen. Dick Myers
Paul Wolfowitz
Gen. Pete Pace
Doug Feith

FROM: *Donald Rumsfeld*
SUBJECT: *Global War on Terrorism*

The questions I posed to combatant commanders this week were: Are we winning or losing the Global "War on Terror?" Is DoD changing fast enough to deal with the new 21st century security environment? Can a big institution change fast enough? Is the USG [U.S. government] changing fast enough?

DoD has been organized, trained and equipped to fight big armies, navies and air forces. It is not possible to change DoD fast enough to successfully fight the global "war on terror;" an alternative might be to try to fashion a new institution, either within DoD or elsewhere—one that seamlessly focuses the capabilities of several departments and agencies on this key problem.

With respect to global terrorism, the record since September 11th seems to be:

We are having mixed results with Al Qaida, although we have put considerable pressure on them—nonetheless, a great many remain at large.

USG has made reasonable progress in capturing or killing the top 55 Iraqis.

USG has made somewhat slower progress tracking down the Taliban—Omar, Hekmatyar, etc.

With respect to the Ansar Al-Islam, we are just getting started.

Have we fashioned the right mix of rewards, amnesty, protection and confidence in the US?

Does DoD need to think through new ways to organize, train, equip and focus to deal with the global "war on terror?"

Are the changes we have and are making too modest and incremental? My impression is that we have not yet made truly bold moves, although we have made many sensible, logical moves in the right direction, but are they enough?

Today, we lack metrics to know if we are winning or losing the global "war on terror." Are we capturing, killing or deterring and dissuading more terrorists every day than the madrassas and the radical clerics are recruiting, training and deploying against us?

Does the US need to fashion a broad, integrated plan to stop the next generation of terrorists? The US is putting relatively little effort into a long-range plan, but we are putting a great deal of effort into trying to stop terrorists. The cost-benefit ratio is against us! Our cost is billions against the terrorists' costs of millions.

Do we need a new organization?

How do we stop those who are financing the radical madrassa schools?

Is our current situation such that "the harder we work, the behinder we get"?

It is pretty clear that the coalition can win in Afghanistan and Iraq in one way or another, but it will be a long, hard slog.

Does CIA need a new finding?

Should we create a private foundation to entice radical madrassas to a more moderate course?

What else should we be considering?

Please be prepared to discuss this at our meeting on Saturday or Monday. Thanks.

Despite the fact that Rumsfeld's hedging impulse, still intact, placed question marks where there could as easily have been periods, his missive was nonetheless striking in its effort to herd the many and varied cats of U.S. policy. Some of the issues he cited, DoD had control over, but most of the areas mentioned—including the catching of terrorists, an effort indisputably led by CIA—were within the purview of other departments. Yet the most stirring passage—*to know if we are winning or losing the global "war on terror." Are we capturing, killing or deterring and dissuading more terrorists every day than the madrassas and the radical clerics are recruiting, training and deploying against us?*—is a wily Rumsfeldian response to the President's "bring them on" and "rather fight them there than here."

Those statements *assumed* a kind of quantitative yardstick, much like the one Lyndon Johnson embraced in the early days of the Vietnam conflict, that the enemy is static, measurable, readily identifiable. Kill them off, and you're done.

Rumsfeld's use of "dissuading"—a favorite term in his memos from the earliest days of the administration—turns "progress," appropriately, into an active term, a moving target.

And, by the fall of 2003, there had clearly been movement in an unintended, and undesirable, direction. One hundred fifty thousand

U.S. troops in the center of the Arab world was a jihadist recruiting tool of almost unfathomable magnetism. Terrorist recruitment was on the rise, visibly and markedly, across the Arab world. CIA reports indicated that the madrassas in Yemen, Saudi Arabia, and Iran were overflowing, as were contributions to radical clerics and their operations. Images flashed to millions each day by Al Jazeera of U.S. tanks in Baghdad and Tikrit, and the carnage that was now Iraq, were dissuading young Arab men—in Iraq and across the Gulf—from standing on the sidelines. They were joining the global fight against the "crusader" Bush and his infidel army as the cause of their generation. Was our situation, in fact, one, as Rumsfeld queried, in which "the harder we work, the behinder we get?" No question mark needed there, either.

An historical irony may be that after all the search and straddle to find common purpose between two grand initiatives—the *find them, stop them* struggle and the overthrow of Hussein—there was, finally, a connection between Iraq and the broader "war on terror." It was a catalytic relationship, like gasoline on a fire.

What the American public didn't know, then or since, was that this was a particularly bad time to be facing a new wave of terrorists. Not because we didn't have a better idea of their various profiles and methods. We did. There had been progress in capturing some al Qaeda leaders, and an array of middle-rung operatives and supporters. We had learned a great deal in two-plus years about the shape and intentions of the enemy.

It's just that, in the closing months of 2003, we started to go blind.

The U.S. government, that is.

The carefully constructed global network of sigint and what can be called finint, or financial intelligence, started to go quiet.

In short, al Qaeda, and its affiliates and imitators, stopped leaving electronic footprints. It started slowly, but then became distinct and clear, a definable trend. They were going underground.

On their part, it seemed to be a matter of operational policy. Bin Laden, especially, had been careful over the years about his communications, while others, including Zawahiri, had not been quite so wary. Operations needed to be executed—a job to be done, with all deliberate speed. Thinking they couldn't be identified in the globe's welter of electronic activity, al Qaeda's operatives moved forward with some caution, but not enough. When electronically traceable activities—from satellite phone calls to bank account withdrawals—started to light up the global matrix in the basement of CIA, the agency exhibited a crucial trait, rare within the government at this point: patience. Everything was handled with care, including keeping political appointees—agents of impatience—at arm's length from the program. Principals of the NSC, one after another, were brought to the basement in Langley where Nervous Phil, agitated fellow though he was, conducted sober and elegant presentations. He flashed up Power-Points. He showed how the vast global web was lit up by tiny dots of data. Then he wished the Bigfoot well on his or her travels.

There was, in this procedure, an understanding from CIA of the value of arm's-length relationships: impatience was coming from people at the uppermost policy levels with direct and regular contact with Bush and Cheney. The duo, of course, was in a state of constant impatience—the core of their management model—and those around them were rewarded by bearing "deliverables." A hot lead. A real name matched with an alias. A capture.

What Nervous Phil knew was that the web had to extrude slowly from CIA's spinnerets, entrapping suspects gradually, so there was no causal sensation that a particular action had led to an arrest. The goal, after all, was often not immediate capture, but a "tag the beast" protocol, where the prey could then run through the jungles of Karachi or Riyadh and light up paths—paths that might connect to other beasts, maybe big ones.

And that's largely how we managed, from early 2002 to late 2003, to know a great deal about al Qaeda, get a sense of who was connected to whom, and capture quite a few suspects, most of whom have vanished into overseas U.S. prisons or similar, maybe worse destinations inside Yemen, Pakistan, Saudi Arabia, Jordan, or Egypt. Are most guilty of what they've been accused of? Some certainly are. They are all guilty of drawing suspicion—and suspicion, for the United States, is action's threshold.

Eventually, and not surprisingly, our opponents figured it out. It was a matter, really, of deduction. Enough people get caught and a view of which activities they had in common provides clues as to how they may have been identified and apprehended.

"We were surprised it took them so long," said one senior intelligence official. "But the lesson here is that with an adaptable, patient enemy, a victory sometimes creates the next set of challenges. In this case, we did some things that worked very well, and they started to evolve."

Or devolve. The al Qaeda playbook, employed by what was left of the network, its affiliates and imitators, started to stress the necessity of using couriers to carry cash and hand-delivered letters. This slowed the pace of operations, if not necessarily their scale, and that was, indeed, a victory.

"The financial area," says Buzzy Krongard, the CIA's executive director until 2004, "was the most successful, coordinated area in the entire government in the "war on terror." From what this group did, we got enormous benefits from it. It was the best example of real coordination of any, I think. They worked quietly, under the radar. Everyone benefited."

Incarnations of terror cells, meanwhile, were taking shape. Stealthy, diffuse, and largely unconnected to a centralized network, these were self-activated, often self-funded, and ready to download key operational guidance from an explosion of jihadist Web sites. There was no money to trace; no calls up and down the chain of command they needed to make. Some were franchisees of sorts, using the al Qaeda playbook and asking for clearance for large operations, just as the Saudi mubtakkar cell had. Others were more autonomous, it seemed, listening adoringly to bin Laden speeches, or Zawahiri rants, then running their own little show, an Amway model.

All of which left the matrix—an extraordinary and expensive design—in a state of increasing obsolescence. As it started to go cold, people started to drift away from their ninety-hour weeks.

Treasury's David Aufhauser handed in his resignation letter to Bush on September 2, and was gone a few months later, leaving law firm life, where he'd spent the past several decades, for a high-compensation job as general counsel for UBS, the global financial firm.

Others followed from the various financial working groups—as good a perch as any in the government from which to leap to a high parapet in the corporate realm. Of course, the revolving door was swinging freely at this point across the government. Terrorism prevention was also the business of large corporations with global reach—each, now, wanting a security chief who knew what real danger looked like. Top CIA officials, at this point, tended to hold firm with their modest salaries and government benefits, kept in place by the engaging, though exhausting struggle, and loyalty to Tenet and McLaughlin. Mueller, meanwhile, went through more partners than Dirty Harry—by now having had four different deputy directors since 9/11.

But of all those in the leadership of FBI—which still couldn't point to a single arrest and prosecution of an active, truly operational terrorist—Dennis Lormel had one of the most valuable profiles. The way terrorists moved through the planet's financial substructure, turning institutions into their hosts and operational bases, was what he knew as well as anyone. Companies started to approach him in the summer of 2003, and he rebuffed them.

What ensued is of more than passing importance. By this point, it was clear to those at the top of government that the few dozen most expert players on how the newly revealed "war on terror" might be successfully fought were leaving, one after another, week by week.

The pressures of fighting an elusive enemy from within the passive-aggressive realm of bureaucracy were particularly acute. When things didn't get done, or done right, it wasn't simply fodder for who did, or didn't, get the next promotion to a windowed office. Lives could be lost. The play of credits and debts was profound. The conventional mishaps of large organizations—a missed clue, a memo not arriving at the right office in time, a dispute between departments that ended in deadlock—could carry the weight of nightmare, and often did. Depression, anxiety disorders, and suicide attempts raced through the cubicles, and even into some upper offices. In April 2003, the head of the FBI's unit on Hezbollah and radical Shiite fundamentalists took his own life with his bureau-issue revolver.

By summer's end, Wazir's money store had closed down, with numerous arrests of midrung couriers and operatives and a trove of financial information to its credit. The credit card sweeps through First Data, now more a backup procedure due to their limited grapeshot effectiveness, ran by themselves. The FBI ran a few more wire transfer traps through Western Union for Avi Dichter—one in August, another in October—but it seemed like the prey among the Palestinian leadership was finally getting wise.

One day in early fall, Lormel sat on the edge of the bed, just like every morning. But lately, he told his wife, Molly, he'd been "having a conversation with himself." For a guy who'd leapt out of bed for twenty years, it was—even in the darkness of 4:45 a.m. so as to beat the rush hour—a somewhat unfamiliar tête-à-tête. At forty-nine, with an extra 60 pounds on the lean frame of a onetime college cornerback, a sotto voce murmur, *can I really get out of bed?* Could he walk into another long day of combat, which increasingly was one of Lormel explaining everything, again and again, to congressional oversight committees—not his forte? He had recently gotten into an argument at a meeting in the Capitol between FBI officials and Representative Frank Wolf, the Virginia Republican and member of the House Appropriations Committee. Wolf had been in a frenzy about a book he'd read—*Blood Diamonds* by Greg Campbell—asserting that al Qaeda was profiting from the diamond trade, and he was pressing the FBI for answers. Lormel, whose agents could come up with no corroboration of the allegations, said Wolf was "a pawn of the media." Wolf, veins popping from his neck, said, "Did you call me a pawn!?" Lormel said it was "respectfully—for your own good," but it was an ugly scene, ugly and disconcerting. With criminals, or even terrorists, it was a clear fight, even a fair fight. You tried to get into their heads. They tried to get into yours. Sometimes they got away. Sometimes you got them by the throat. But in office battles or hearing-room collisions, no one fought fair. They said one thing while actively doing the opposite. They smiled as they shoved in the knife. It was enough to make you prefer bona fide thugs.

So, at the end of October, walking around the kitchen on the portable phone after his usual ten o'clock dinner, he said to the head-hunter, "Yeah, tell them I'll take it."

He hung up and looked at Molly. "I can't believe you're really doing it," she said. She always figured he'd go all the way to the FBI's mandatory retirement of fifty-six. She'd remained poker-faced for months when he'd ask her what he should do. "Dennis, this has to be your decision," she'd say. "But listen to what your heart says."

"Yeah," he said, there in the kitchen. "I think it's time. Time for the next thing."

And that was it, almost.

A month and three days later, on December 1, Lormel got a check for accrued vacation pay. He'd barely taken a day off in twelve years. It ended up being "a decent chunk of change," as Dennis would say, enough for him and Molly, who does investor relations work for a financial company, to move out of their town house in the northern Virginia suburbs and build their own place. Dennis had one room of the house mapped to the inch. The basement would be a sports bar. A real one. Couple of pool tables, a shuffleboard deal, wet bar, five TVs, with cable. That's right—five. Five football games at once. He'd put his football jersey from St. Peter's College in New Jersey on the wall, and pictures of soccer games that their two sons, now grown, had played in. Dennis had been the coach. He already wasn't too crazy about the job he'd taken at AES, the large energy firm, based in Alexandria, Virginia, which said it wanted to be rigorous on compliance issues so as to guard against an Enron-like slide, or the appearance of one. But construction on the new house was due to start soon. That'd keep him busy.

They had a going-away party at FBI, a sedate affair, no alcohol, bulk-order cookies. Mueller got tied up at the last minute. John Pistole, the executive assistant director for counterterrorism and counterintelligence, came by and said a few words.

Then Dennis cleaned out his office. Not much, even after twenty-eight years. Desk stuff, family pictures, a few framed commendations, and a big poster-size montage of newspaper front pages from September 12. One of his guys made it for him. That was the day a new era had begun in America. A day when the lucky nation, with all the beaches and mountains and waves of grain, had to ask whether it was lucky anymore, and then get to work. When guys would come into his office, slump into one of the chairs—wild-eyed with anxiety and frustration—and say, "That's it!" that it was an impossible fight, that the fucking enemy could be anywhere, plotting, unseen, undetectable, and that they couldn't stop thinking about buildings burning and planes and bombs in malls, night after night, Dennis would just point at the montage. "Go look at it," he'd say. "It'll remind you why we're here."

Now he took the framed thing down, pulled the nail out of the wall with his thick fingers. Some of the intensity of 9/11 was over, dissolving among the quotidian joys of people just living their lives of bill-paying, and sitcoms, and wedding marches. And that was as it should be. But he thought about a conversation he had had a few days before with Nervous Phil, a "let's have lunch sometimes" call, and about Phil sitting there in his Langley basement, with the big board starting to go dark. The first quarter was over, and his team—he, Phil, David, and the rest—were up, no doubt. But where would the intensity come from for the next quarter, much less the next half, with 9/11 fading, no new playbook, and the opponent wising up?

He looked at "September 12" once—what a waste, what a fucking mess—and then tucked it under his arm. He knew what he'd do with it: hang it on the wall of the sports bar, next to his old jersey.

What would be left for George W. Bush, Dick Cheney, and various arms of the government once those solid NSA cables and precise financial tracking began to disappear?

The increasingly insubstantial.

The specifics, by December's end, involved *steganography*.

Don Kerr, the CIA's deputy director for science and technology, was having to explain the term, tersely and urgently, many times, starting with his briefing of the President in the Oval Office a week before Christmas. Steganography is the hiding of coded messages within transmitted formats—moving and still images, computer files containing photos, and even sound transmissions. Communicating this way is complex, and labor-intensive. Even with decoding equipment, it is difficult to decipher a numerical billboard hidden behind photos or streamed images. Even for leading experts in the practice, a group called steganalysts, it is a realm of false positives—patterns that may mean something, or may not, and usually don't.

But CIA's Office of Science and Technology was convinced that it had discovered the darkest imputations tucked within the "crawl"—the summary of headlines that runs along a TV screen's bottom edge—of the Al Jazeera daily broadcast. In the numerology, Kerr and his team asserted, were plans for an attack that would exceed 9/11.

There was, at this point, an unusual array of edgy holiday chatter. Christmastime does that in the Arab world, creating phone traffic and angry exchanges on hundreds of Islamist Web sites about the struggle through the ages of "crusaders" and Muslim holy warriors. A heart-stopping message first disseminated a few months before—calling on

Muslims to evacuate Washington, Los Angeles, and New York—was repeated on various Web sites in December. And, on the 19th—the Friday before Christmas—an audio message was broadcast on Al Jazeera from Ayman al-Zawahiri, that "two years after Tora Bora . . . we continued to pursue the Americans everywhere. . . . The forces of Islam and jihad are starting to chase the crusaders and the hypocrites of Afghanistan, Iraq, Palestine, and the Arab peninsula." Broadcast messages of this sort have often preceded attacks.

But all this was context, the setting of the table. What CIA, using the technical services of a private company, served up to the President was astonishing in its specificity and its sweep. Some numbers indicated more than two dozen flights and flight times. Other hidden compressed numbers showed the coordinates for targeting—the unfortunate places where international flights, loaded with passengers, fuel, and, possibly, chemical or biological agents, would be bound once they entered U.S. airspace from less carefully controlled foreign airports. The targets ran from ocean to ocean, Los Angeles to New York. There were coordinates for the White House, the Space Needle in Seattle, and the tiny, rural Virginia town of Tappahannock.

Some preliminary alerts were sent out on Friday, to New York and Los Angeles, and everyone edged toward panic mode. If the steganography was right, they had a few days, until early the following week, before the first flights were due to take off. So those at the very top of the administration—only NSC principals, the CIA's top brass, Homeland Security Department heads, and a few others—spent a sleepless weekend in the loop.

Finally, on Sunday, in the late morning, the President sat at the table in the Situation Room, surrounded by NSC principals and his top deputies. Everyone gave their reports, but most of the eyes were on Tenet and his briefers. It was clear to all that some of CIA's operational people—Pavitt, Kappes—were skeptical. Don Kerr and his scientists were not. Tenet seemed to be neutral. But John Brennan, head of the newly formed Terrorist Threat Integration Center—an aggregation point for all threats from all parts of the government—felt the information was sound. More broadly, it was a chance for TTIC, and Brennan, formerly Tenet's chief of staff, to flex some muscle. They did.

The discussion was nuanced, layered, with wide-ranging variables and complex proofs, like teams arguing in a math club competition.

Not the kind of discussion the President has much taste for. "All right, here's the question," he broke in. "Would anyone feel okay having their family on one of those flights?" He looked this way and that. "Do we need to go around the room?"

It was clear he didn't. Everyone looked down, nodded, pursed their lips. "Then let's do it."

Ninety minutes later, Tom Ridge held a briefing at the Department of Homeland Security's press room. The danger of an attack on the United States in the "near term," he said, was "perhaps greater now than at any point since Sept. 11, 2001."

There was more. "The U.S. intelligence community has received a substantial increase in the volume of threat-related intelligence reports," he said. "These credible sources suggest the possibility of attacks against the homeland around the holiday season and beyond."

Finally, there was the issue of scale. "Extremists abroad," Ridge concluded, "are anticipating near-term attacks that they believe will either rival or exceed" the attacks of 9/11.

The alert level was then officially raised from yellow, a state of caution, to orange, a state of alert that had been achieved five other times since 9/11, the last time the previous May, an alert attributed to the spate of bombing and gunfights in Saudi Arabia.

But this was quite different. Homeland Security was now fully up and activated and felt ready to be tested. At the top sat Ridge, a former Pennsylvania governor and close friend of the President's, and his undersecretary, Asa Hutchinson, a former Arkansas Republican congressman. They were affable men, good companions, jocular, poised, bright, and utterly overmatched.

The same could be said of virtually anyone faced with the challenge they'd accepted. It was, from the start, untenable. Integrating two agencies in the U.S. government is a daunting enterprise; three is expected to be a mess. Homeland Security now housed twenty-two agencies under its auspices.

Ridge had arrived a week after 9/11 to be the President's adviser on homeland security, and moved in a sort of loose coordination role, a man with neither staff nor budgets for nearly a year before his department was formed. That was when Hutchinson came aboard, and was briefed as to his job: to protect the "borders and transportation system of the United States from terrorists and do it in a way that is consistent with the lawful flow of commerce and protection of civil liberties." That's in the statute. The specifics start with 300 million border crossings annually, then move to airports, cargo ships, containers . . . that adds up to 1.8 billion transactions a year. After the briefing, Ridge's chief of staff, Major General Bruce Lawlor, had sent Hutchinson a note:

> Dear Asa,
> 1.8 billion transactions a year.
> How do you like your odds?
> Sincerely,
> Bruce

Hutchinson, like Ridge, knew the odds were daunting beyond calculation, or, as he later quipped—"Chances of success were minimal."

By the end of 2003, more than two years after 9/11, only 5 percent of cargo containers entering the United States were being checked. Chemical plants remained unprotected, even those next to urban areas. The same went for nuclear plants. U.S. infrastructures of all kinds were almost irresistible targets. The extent of that vulnerability was not, however, publicly known.

A few months before the Christmas alert, when New York City went dark in August, officials at Homeland Security were certain, in the first hours, that it was terrorist-related. Why? A month before, they—along with officials from DoD and the Department of Energy—had conducted a top secret cyberwarfare game in which a group of hired hackers attempted to take down a massive power grid constructed in Idaho by federal contractors. That grid, like infrastructures of all kinds throughout the United States, is controlled by SCADA: simple devices placed at key points along endless underground cables and pipes that can be remotely controlled with off-the-shelf technology. Which is precisely what the hackers in the simulation, called "Idaho Thunder," used to take down the system in minutes and even to place screens showing all was well on the grid's control panel.

In short, America was woefully unprepared for attack. Now, officials across the government would find out what it felt like to have those vulnerabilities confronted by what they thought was a genuine global alert.

Teams were dispatched to Los Angeles, where hundreds of biodetection devices were set up throughout the city and near the airport. An abandoned package caused New York's Metropolitan Museum of Art to be evacuated. Another caused New York City subways to temporarily close. The White House prepared evacuation drills. F-15s took off from bases near major target areas, just in case. Thousands of law enforcement officers around the nation went on alerts, as calls were made to British Airways and Air France: the flights had to be stopped.

Late on Sunday, Hutchinson's phone rang at Homeland Security. It was the French ambassador Jean-David Levitte. Air France had tipped him off.

"Mr. Undersecretary, what you are doing is wrong, we strongly disagree—you can't stop these flights."

"Mr. Ambassador," Hutchinson responded, after laying out some of the details of the threat. "These flights simply can't enter our airspace."

Ambassador Levitte paused. The French couldn't allow the United States to make decisions about what would, or would not, happen at Charles de Gaulle International Airport.

"Mr. Undersecretary," he said finally. "The government of France has decided, on its own, to ground the flights in question."

God bless the French. Then the debate was about whether the passengers should be notified that their flights—leaving in the next day or two, right up until Christmas Eve—were canceled. "Of course they must be notified," Levitte said. Hutchinson pushed back. "The idea is that if there's a terrorist on those flights, we want them to arrive at the airport so we can catch them."

And so, over the coming week, several dozen international flights became terrorist-catching machines. Passengers arrived at Heathrow and Charles de Gaulle, boarded flights, and then were detained, as the bags were exhaustively checked and each name on the final manifest was run through global security checks by FBI and CIA.

Arab names, of course, sparked interest. A passenger on one flight from France—a Muhammad—looked like a sure thing. He turned out to be a seven-year-old boy.

As planes sat on runways for hours, clues about possible chemical or biological attacks—emerging from the steganography—prompted more debates, including having men in hazmat suits board the aircraft.

This idea was discarded—panic would ensue—but the planes, sometimes, sat for hours as Hutchinson waited for the call that every last person on the manifest was cleared.

At 3 a.m., with a full Air France plane having sat for hours on a tarmac halfway around the world, Hutchinson waited in his office for the call from Mike Garcia, Homeland Security's liaison to the intelligence community. One name; they were waiting on one name to be cleared. Another hour passed. Finally the call came. Hutchinson thanked Garcia, as sunrise approached. He called David Colston, at FAA—the boss overseeing a battalion of Transportation Security Administration or TSA officials who had been dispatched to France.

"All's clear for takeoff, David," Hutchinson said, sighing with relief.

"Give me a minute, here, Asa," David responded. There was a pause. He got back on the phone.

"What can I tell you? The French went ahead. It's already off the ground."

By February 2004, the postmortems were already under way. There was nothing to it, to any of it.

The steganographic analysis carried little more soundness than medieval numerology.

A CIA manager involved in these deliberations struggled, a few years later, to place it all in context.

"One problem with technologists," he said, "is they always feel underappreciated. So when they're front and center, on stage, they put as much data on the table as possible."

But the problem was much broader. It had to do with the wages of fear; a situation in which right-minded people, *en masse,* all deviate downward toward a state of panic.

"No one says, 'There's no proof!'" the CIA manager exhorted, his voice rising. "We've reached the point where no one is willing to not report something because they feel it's nuts. There is no threshold. Everything is reported, everywhere. There is no judgment in the system. No one is saying, 'Based on my experience, this person is a lying dog.' No one is saying, 'These reports are completely without any foundation.'"

CHAPTER NINE

HEARTS AND MINDS

It is fitting that the election year of 2004 would be a time of disclosures.

There is, after all, so very much at stake, here and abroad, when Americans now descend on voting machines.

U.S. elections, since the fall of the Soviet Union and the arrival of a unipolar world, have taken on a note of historical distinction. There have long been empires, of course—the Greeks, the Romans, the Egyptians, the Turks—but never one where such awesome power emerges from something as delicate, as capricious and electric, as "informed consent" of the governed.

The phrase itself is a sort of road test of self-governance, posing the question of . . . by what, exactly, is consent *informed*? Informed by passion? By reason? By faith? By fear? Or, of late, by what *message* the ascent of certain leaders, or rhetoric, will send to a fractious and dangerous world?

Reason tends to demand the most effort among those choices. It is the least manageable, at least from the top down, because it relies on facts, wherever they may fall, and on an empirical model that values evidence—evidence that provides indisputable shared turf, beyond all else. The Age of Reason ideals upon which the country was founded, championed open, rigorous, fact-based debate—even reserving constitutional seats for unruly freedoms such as speech, press, and assembly—to form a sort of counterweight to faith, a titanic force, no matter how judiciously the founders attempted to circumscribe it; and to fear, so often born of ignorance, or dread of what is not known. The founders didn't use a word like "transparency" to guide their debates over checks and balances, and their attempt to empower the public will with sufficient nourishment was to make wisdom and republican virtues at least a possibility. They'd probably have used "sunlight."

Then there's "message"—something of a catchall, a calculus of perceptions, which carries none of the underlying density of the other elements but may tap several at once. It is clearly designed to persuade rather than explain, and be assessed by the receivers not only based on their personal reaction but on an appraisal of how other receivers may react. In other words, people will sometimes applaud a disagreeable, even repugnant, message if they think it will move others in a desired direction.

Message creation has a long history in the realm of self-governance: the Greek philosophers recommended strict rationality in creating "public rhetoric," and admonished those who relied on base emotions or passions; Jefferson and Franklin and Washington had messages they prized, and repeated often, displaying firmly held beliefs. But those favorite phrases were distillates of a sort, the product of lives ordered by experience, and study, fierce debate, and a search for what was known and knowable—the end of a process, not the starting point.

Nowadays, an appropriate message—shallow but wide—is often the first consideration. Yet it is the width, the reach, which, of late, has changed its character. A message can, these days, be amplified by a modern, increasingly globalized media in ways that would make the founders dizzy, and may rely for source material on vivid, fast-firing images rather than sleepy, earthbound reason or analysis. Crafted messages, in our era, have taken on an extraordinary, aerodynamic quality, and real power.

The United States, not surprisingly, has been an innovator on this score. Talk to seasoned reporters, like *The Washington Post*'s seventy-plus legend Walter Pincus, and they recall a change during the presidency of Ronald Reagan, when media manager Michael Deaver helped codify the idea that pictures matter as much as words and, maybe, *more* than policies. Knowing that the U.S. television networks had twenty-two minutes to fill each night on their news broadcasts, he made certain that Reagan had a "media event" almost every day—trumpeting a political position or a bond with a particular constituency, anything really—that the networks swiftly began to cover because they needed the picture. The major newspapers, which once wrote about presidents only when, as Pincus says, "they did something worth writing about," soon followed suit. Every day, an event and a message were launched from the White House. And then two. Then three. In the twenty years since, message management has evolved, year by year, to encase much of the process of self-governance.

Presidents, of late, are often judged as to whether they "stay on message," as though the message itself—constructed by professionals, smoothed and polished—is the master even of the duly elected leader. While public renderings of policy debates display a muddle of complex, often intractable issues about the nation's general welfare, this soft clay of message, of rhetoric with image, can be shaped into grand narratives of a man and his character.

Having gained leverage steadily in recent years, this operating model picked up surprising throw weight after 9/11. The real policy debates about the "war on terror" were, after all, conducted in secret, killing off reasoned, fact-based public discourse precisely at the time the President suddenly presided over a nation in need of clarity. The White House message machine worked overtime, without any expectation of having ever to provide underlying evidence to support what it said. The innovations at this moment were startlingly effective.

The President, who had long spoken in public about his personal faith, embraced the language of bold action and messianic faith in describing America's charge and its new, post-9/11 role. He used words like "mission" and "crusade." He spoke of a nation being guided by divine will in "defeating evil"—in this case Islamic terrorists, hatred, violence—and bringing "God's gift," the democratic form of government, to all humanity. Modern presidents, while often testifying to their personal faith, had not made this sort of Promethean maneuver, attaching the fire of fervency to their policies. When presidents from time to time invoked "God's will"—like Wilson or Lincoln—they tended to steer clear of implying they knew His will, and never claimed it in support of violence or human aggression.

Nonetheless, with fear and faith fused in a fact-starved environment, sober, reasoned debate was essentially tabled. The message of conviction and action resonated at home. And that, at the start, drew backing from abroad, attracting international support from East to West for America's opening initiatives against al Qaeda, the Taliban, and worldwide terrorism.

What was clear was that the U.S. President had, in essence, added a new constituency to his portfolio, a global community that was hyper-attentive in these redefining days after 9/11 to the words of the world's new, lone superpower, bent on action. Two constituencies—one at home, one abroad—were hanging on our every word. All this created a peculiar bind for Americans, forcing them to think globally about the calculations that underlie message—an assessment of other people's reactions. The connected, news-saturated planet no longer allowed for compartmentalization—for rhetoric à la carte, one domestic, the other foreign; one for us, the other for them. The duly elected leader clearly needed a message that spoke effectively to both constituencies, with the latter including rogue states and the terrorists themselves. One world. One message. The nation had officially entered the message business.

Firmness, fierceness, and faith became the American watchwords. It was not, of course, to everyone's liking. Muslims in America and abroad—unsure of their footing, as bin Laden and his own virulent us-versus-them view of sectarian conflict gained prominence—urged the White House to excise "crusade" from its rhetoric. They said they would, but then President Bush, instead, repeated the word again, as well as other words that carried similar connotations of holy war. This posture, meanwhile, was doing a great deal to energize his domestic core of faith-based supporters.

White House aides carefully crafted speeches to carry codes that would speak to the devout. Division—us versus them, with supporting images—works. If this elevated bin Laden in some way, so be it. He'd be dead soon anyway, administration hawks figured in 2002, as they overlooked a crucial issue: that a message that created political advantage here was creating growing opportunities for our enemies. Internally, the President dismissed concerns about how his message was playing to the nonvoting overseas "constituencies." America, through his voice, was making its intentions and feelings clear. The world's response was not a first concern. On the most pressing priorities—firing up a citizenry, nearly half of whom now identify themselves at evangelicals, and allies for the "war on terror" from kindred Western nations or newly fearful Arab ones—the righteous battle cry was tailor-made.

By the end of 2003—after conservative, generally religious Republicans showed muscle and gained seats in the midterm elections—it was becoming clear that the aria of newfound clout and faith-based certainty was, indeed, helping bin Laden. And mightily. Even after the defeats and dispersals in Afghanistan, bin Laden and Zawahiri—having managed to survive—could now claim prophetic vision: their long-predicted holy war of West and East, Christian and Muslim, had finally arrived. Bush's utterances of the word "crusade" were transmitted endlessly through the Arab world. It became his signature.

But that was still *over there*—far across the world. Americans, at this point, were still thinking about their duties during this perilous time. On balance, only a few were actually called to serve in Afghanistan, or hunt terrorists, or protect the shorelines, but everyone could do his or her part by supporting America's global message and its prime messenger. Critics, unable to access source material to make informed arguments, could offer only scattershot critiques of U.S. policy. When they did, they were criticized for giving comfort to the enemy. Even as the Iraq experiment began to turn sour in the summer of 2003, and look—even to untrained eyes—like a widening insurrection, questions of the most natural sort, like reality-based estimates drawn from long experience—such as how many troops were really needed to secure the country, or had we thought about how an Arab democracy is actually constructed—drew attacks. Pictures from Iraq, vivid and often harrowing, replaced the comforts of secrecy. But there was, through much of 2003, the added "with us or against us" leverage of young men and women in harm's way. America, for the most part, stayed *on message.*

It wasn't really until January 2004—an election year, a time when "informed consent" was all but constitutionally mandated—that *reason* seemed to catch up with *message,* as the Tortoise catches the Hare.

And the key, as always, was the arrival of discernible, indisputable facts, the oxygen—for several thousand years, really—of rational discourse.

One of the first offerings came from the former Treasury secretary, Paul O'Neill, who was quoted in my book, published that midJanuary, saying that the administration had begun planning the overthrow of Saddam Hussein at its first, postinauguration National Security Council meeting in January 2001—rather than in the more deliberative, post-9/11 evidentiary process it had advertised. He also said that, as an NSC principal, he'd read all the pertinent briefings passed from the intelligence community to the President prior to the Iraq invasion, and that none of it contained anything that would "qualify as evidence" of WMD.

While some of these charges had been rumored, the key was the arrival of a firsthand witness, someone with direct, regular access to the President, to highest-level meetings and key documents.

A tactical war of sorts had essentially begun. The administration—

freed so utterly, from 9/11 forward, from the traditional dictates of transparency—had an undiscovered country of judgments and actions to hide, from torture to illegal wiretaps to breathtaking mishaps in the so-called "war on terror," as well as certain troubling convictions that actually drove policy.

A week later, on January 20, 2004, the President held firm to message in his State of the Union address. It was at this point a familiar song to start the run for reelection, a weave of themes and punched up participles—about Godliness and resolve—drawn from rhetorical victories of the past two and a half years.

"We have faced serious challenges together, and now we face a choice," the President began, as he addressed the joint session and assorted leaders of government. "We can go forward with confidence and resolve, or we can turn back to the dangerous illusion that terrorists are not plotting and outlaw regimes are no threat to us. We've not come all this way—through tragedy, and trial and war—only to falter and leave our work unfinished."

Ascribing to the opposition positions they have not taken is a political tactic, tried and true, that marked the official start of the political season. Then, just a minute into the address, President Bush offered the central rationale for his reelection: "Twenty-eight months have passed since September 11th, 2001—over two years without an attack on American soil. And it is tempting to believe that the danger is behind us. That hope is understandable, comforting—and false . . . the terrorists continue to plot against America and the civilized world. And by our will and courage, this danger will be defeated."

The chamber erupted in applause, even the Democrats. We had not been attacked. Even if *why* was not clear—and it was the subject of fierce, secret debate inside the intelligence community—the fact stood.

This was, and would remain, the core of the reelection pitch.

Without further delay, President Bush then offered the prize "deliverable" he'd mused about when news of Gadhafi's overture was first passed along from Blair.

"Because of American leadership and resolve, the world is changing for the better. Last month, the leader of Libya voluntarily pledged to disclose and dismantle all of his regime's weapons of mass destruction programs, including a uranium enrichment project for nuclear weapons.... Nine months of intense negotiations involving the United States and Great Britain succeeded with Libya, while 12 years of diplomacy with Iraq did not. And one reason is clear: For diplomacy to be effective, words must be credible, and no one can now doubt the word of America."

Having claimed, falsely, that he knew that Libya was proof that the Iraq invasion had borne fruit, the President moved swiftly to shore up the stanchions of the burdened Iraqi experiment. "Some in this chamber, and in our country, did not support the liberation of Iraq. Objections to war often come from principled motives. But let us be candid about the consequences of leaving Saddam Hussein in power. We're seeking all the facts. Already, the Kay Report identified dozens of weapons of mass destruction—related program activities and significant amounts of equipment that Iraq concealed from the United Nations."

Three days later, on January 23, a Friday, the CIA issued a press release praising David Kay for his work as head of the Iraq Survey Group, and announced that he would resign and be replaced by Charles Duelfer, another weapons expert. That afternoon, Kay stopped by the office of George Tenet, hoping to have a last word with the DCI. Tenet was in a meeting with heads of a foreign intelligence service; Moseman, sitting in an office near Tenet's, told Kay that it wasn't going to work that day.

"But David," Moseman said, "we'd like to honor you at a luncheon for you next week sometime, bring together the people you've worked with."

Kay shuffled his feet. "I'm not sure if that's such a great idea," he said, and slipped out.

An hour later, Bill Harlow, the CIA's longtime spokesman, was on the phone to Moseman. "Kay's just talked to Reuters," Harlow fumed. "He's making statements."

Five days later, Kay slid behind a hearing table before the Senate Armed Services Committee. It was a packed house, with Virginia's ever more disgruntled Republican senator, John Warner—an ardent supporter of the President who increasingly felt he had been misled—presiding.

"Let me begin by saying, we were almost all wrong, and I certainly include myself here," said Kay grimly. "I believe that the effort that has been directed to this point has been sufficiently intense that it is highly unlikely that there were large stockpiles of deployed militarized chemical and biological weapons there."

After that, it became more personal, as various senators—Republican John McCain, Democrat Ted Kennedy—pressed Kay to opine about whether, or how, the American public had been misled.

"If I were your broker and you were investing on my advice, a course I would not advise you to do, and at the end of the day, I said, 'Enron was the greatest company in the world,' and you had lost a substantial amount of money on it . . . you would think I had abused you."

Colin Powell met a few days later with editors and reporters at *The Washington Post,* and said he was not sure he would have supported the war if he had known there were no WMD in Iraq. "The absence of a stockpile [of banned weapons in Iraq] changes the political calculus," he told them, noting that the United States went to war "with the understanding that there was a stockpile and there were [banned] weapons." In the predawn of February 3, the *Post* published this bit of frankness, and it circled the globe with impressive instantaneity.

Powell's comments caused a panic at the White House. They seemed to contradict the President and undercut the "message" of resolve Bush spoke of in his State of the Union. What to do? Counter-strategies roiled through the West Wing.

By midmorning, Powell had pulled that day's visitor, UN Secretary-General Kofi Annan, into the State Department press room for a quick, damage-control press conference.

"The bottom line is this: the President made the right decision,"

Powell now exclaimed, his voice rising. "He made the right decision based on the history of this regime, the intention that this leader, terrible despotic leader had, and the capabilities at a variety of levels, the delivery systems that were there, and there is nobody debating that. . . . It was clear that this was a regime with intent, capability, and it was a risk the President felt strongly we could not take. And it was something we all agreed to and would probably agree to it again under any other set of circumstances."

On the morning of March 11, a crowded train bustled toward Madrid, Spain. Riders on the train were early risers, up and breakfasted and aboard the rail from working-class suburbs east of town, people who, in general, couldn't quite afford the high price of desirable housing in close. Many of them were students, or young husbands and wives, or new parents, just starting out. They read *El Mundo* that morning, or listened to music on iPods, or slept, or just gazed from the warm commuter buzz, as the grassy expanses disappeared into tightened rows of homes and then other buildings, until, in the distance, the majestic Prado Museum came into view.

For many, that would be the last thing they saw. Three backpacks exploded as the train pulled into the Atocha station, hurling rubble and steel and the unwitting in every direction. Seventy people died in that first set of blasts; another 121 were killed as similar bombs detonated on nine other trains in the next few minutes. In all there were 191 dead and 1,500 people injured. Word quickly spread, and cell phones began to ring on bodies lying on train platforms; across Spain, people prayed, silently, for the loved one to pick up—please, God, pick up—just like the cell phones that rang on 9/11.

No one can be faulted for what they do at a moment like this. People wept, and panicked, and held a vigil that night and the next in the ornate, Old World squares of Madrid. The conservative government of José Maria Aznar, which, over local opposition, had sent 1,300 troops to Iraq in a show of solidarity with the Bush administration,

went down the wrong path—quickly blaming ETA, the Basque sepa-
ratist terrorist group that had been a nemesis for successive Spanish
governments. The government had its reasons. They had seized a
large stash of ETA explosives in late February, and naturally turning—
as any combatant will—toward a familiar foe, they focused on ETA,
and stopped a long-standing program of surveillance of Islamic fundamentalist cells. If analysis, all analysis, isn't hardheaded and humble,
looking for the improbable, it can be infected with the self-referential
and convenient.

That's the charitable version of what occurred, as it became clear,
three days after the explosions, that jihadists inside Spain—some of
whom seemed particularly displeased with the controversial Spanish
presence in Iraq—were almost certainly the culprits. So, Aznar's government, ahead in the polls through February, lost the national election held three days after the attacks. The winning Socialists ran on
anti-American slogans and a promise to pull Spanish troops from Iraq.
That was plenty, at this moment, to ensure victory.

In the weeks following the Madrid attacks, a large joint U.S.-
European Counter-Terrorist Intelligence Center or CTIC in France,
and intelligence offices thoughout the continent, worked furiously
piecing together what had occurred. On April 3, police closed in on
seven suspects, who cornered themselves in an apartment building in
Leganes, a Madrid suburb, and then blew themselves up. Soon, a few
accomplices were captured and the self-supporting nature of the cell
became clear: they financed operations, including the purchase of explosives, with sales of hashish and Ecstasy; they developed their own
purification rites, by drinking holy water from Mecca.

A manhunt across Europe revealed gossamer connections among a
loose confederation of similar homegrown terror groups. They were
not, clearly, linked to a tight structure and managed from on high by al
Qaeda leadership. It was more a franchisee model, with entrepreneurial groups carrying forward the goals of the larger movement—still

defined by the inspirational leadership of bin Laden and Zawahiri but self-supporting, free to settle deep *in country* and work steadily toward a destructive goal. Bin Laden had, the previous fall, issued a broadcast threat against Spain, Great Britain, and other countries supporting the United States in Iraq. And while intelligence operatives reported some linkages between a bin Laden deputy and some of the Spanish bombers, the Madrid attacks would, in essence, bring destructive force to that rhetoric.

It was firm evidence of a new al Qaeda model: an evolution driven, in part, by some of the sigint, and finint, successes of the previous two years. Communications, management, and financial support from a centralized network—which left electronic vapor that led to umpteen arrests—were shown to be unnecessary. CIA operations managers knew this might leave them in a kind of tactical cul-de-sac. It did.

Messages from bin Laden and Zawahiri created a broad strategic umbrella of goals; an umbrella beneath which disparate groups could act independently.

As one CIA analyst put it, "The relationship carried an inferential clarity, like children who, as they grow, know more and more how to please a parent." Like a wave of mid-nineties Internet start-ups, barriers to entry were low and improvisational energy was high. The goals here were not IPO millions, but no less attractive in their way: global notoriety; your picture, as a holy martyr, adorning the living rooms of countless apartments in Riyadh or Karachi; eternal bliss.

And there was more. Inside the analytical shops at CIA, and NSC, the Madrid bombings and swift follow-up investigation flowed neatly into another growing consensus—a conclusion that was the last thing anyone in the White House wanted publicized: al Qaeda might not, at this point, actually want to attack America.

A key element of that analysis was a report that had been picked up a few months before, in December 2003, by the Norwegian Defense Research Establishment—the government's intelligence arm—from a jihadist Web site with close links to Saudi al Qaeda.

The forty-two-page treatise, *Jihadi Iraq, Hopes and Dangers,* was completed in September 2003, and bears the mark of none other than Yusef al-Ayeri. It is dedicated to al-Ayeri, carries quotations from several of his books, and has the unmistakable al-Ayeri tone of analytical—as opposed to religious—fervor. It may have been written in part by al-Ayeri before his death in May 2003, some CIA analysts believe, and then expanded and burnished by his disciples.

The strategic document carries a host of pointed recommendations about how to undercut U.S. efforts in Iraq. A primary one is to isolate the United States, separate it from its allies, and specifically add to America's financial burdens by forcing the withdrawal of its few significant partners—Britain, Spain, and Poland. This line of exposition is deepened by sophisticated analyses of the domestic situation in each country and an assessment that Spain, with a large population arrayed against its Iraqi involvement, is most vulnerable to being divided from the United States. The document recommends "painful strikes" against Spanish "forces"—which may mean in Iraq or elsewhere— around the time of the upcoming Spanish election expected in spring or summer 2004. The overall strategic mission is elucidated in the report's underscored passage:

> We think that the Spanish government could not tolerate more than two, maximum three blows, after which it will have to withdraw as a result of popular pressure. If its troops still remain in Iraq after these blows, then the victory of the Socialist Party is almost secured, and the withdrawal of the Spanish forces will be on its electoral programme.
>
> Lastly, we are emphasize that a withdrawal of the Spanish or Italian forces from Iraq would put huge pressure on the British presence (in Iraq), a pressure that Toni [sic] Blair might not be able to withstand, and hence the domino tiles would fall quickly. Yet, the basic problem of making the first tile fall still remains.

That would soon happen, as Spain began withdrawing troops, as news of a "terrorist victory" circled the globe. Beneath those headlines, though, was further affirmation of what CIA analysts had first begun to see in sigint and limited humint as far back as the spring of

2002: a possible strategic shift by al Qaeda away from further attacks on the U.S. mainland. The venues for violence were Saudi Arabia; European countries, some with large Muslim populations; and certainly Spain.

The deeply classified debate over why Zawahiri had called off the chemical attacks, meanwhile, shed its old self-congratulatory thesis that this might be due to the pressure the United States was putting on al Qaeda's structure. That line of analysis gave way to growing evidence that al Qaeda might not have been trying to attack the United States in the three years since its singular triumph of 9/11.

"What we understood inside CIA is that al Qaeda just doesn't act out of bloodlust, or pathological rage. Though their tactics are horrific, they're not homicidal maniacs. They do what they do to carry forward specific strategic goals," said a senior CIA official involved in highest-level debates over bin Laden and Zawahiri during this period. "Clearly, they had the capability to attack us in about a hundred different ways. They didn't. The question was, why?"

Now, does the American public—with response to the 9/11 attacks and new global landscape indisputably the seminal issue in its national election—deserve to know that al Qaeda may not have been trying to attack America?

Without knowing it, is it possible to assess the President's central assertion that he should be reelected because he has kept us from being attacked again?

The core dilemma—can a nation fight a war in secret while preserving the values of a democracy—was becoming more acute by the hour in this, the first national election since the attacks.

In any event, myriad key facts, such as al Qaeda's status and real strategy, would remain submerged in the spring of 2004. A justification for this secrecy—and, at this point, the shadow cast over a continent of actions and rationales in the conduct of the "war on terror"—was a hard, tactical extract from the cult of message-discipline: that to let al Qaeda know certain things we knew, including that we knew that they might *not* actually have a desire to attack the U.S. mainland, would be valuable in helping them plot their strategies. And, because al Qaeda, its supporters, imitators, and adherents, are members of a vast, nonvoting global constituency that the U.S. President had now assumed, no one could know.

That meant that the dictates of "information warfare" that apply to an enemy in combat would also apply on the U.S. mainland, even though it was now democracy's quadrennial opportunity for citizens to assess the conduct of their leaders. The American public had no more right to know the government's intentions than a mid-rung al Qaeda lieutenant. If all that happened to benefit those in power, so be it.

This collision of rights and interests created an acute, subterranean stress—like tectonic plates sliding—deep beneath the American system of government and its traditions of informed consent.

What was visible on the surface, meanwhile, were internecine struggles between the forces of message discipline and those of messy, intermittently meaningful debate.

Tenet, day by day, was increasingly drawn into these battles to speak on behalf of the White House. He was, after all, a linchpin in so many of them. He knew all there was to know, of course, but was not an elected official, nor—as the DCI—was seen as someone who was driven by the electoral mandate. The CIA's long history, at least in theory, as an evidence-driven arm of government—an honest broker, without the ardent, self-protective, institutional impulses of the kingdoms of State and Defense—made Tenet particularly valuable.

So, after David Kay's disclosures, and Powell's unauthorized moment of candor, Tenet gave a speech at Georgetown broadly defending the CIA and its main consumers, the President and Vice President, on the heated issue of Iraq's WMD. He said that the inspections were not yet done. He said that everyone had acted in good faith. He said that the CIA might have not been all right, intelligence never is, but that they did the best they could. The President told Tenet he liked the speech, a real attaboy. "Nice job, George," Bush said.

But the tectonic plates continued to shift. For some in a small circle of top officials who knew what was true, the message pouring forth from the White House each day chafed, like sandpaper, on cherished, civics-class notions of the way things were meant to be.

The 9/11 Commission, which the White House had fought when it was first proposed—citing, among other things, that hearings on the Japanese attack on Pearl Harbor were delayed until after that war ended—was now more than a year along. It was arriving at key conclusions and calling witnesses from the President's innermost circle.

On March 21, three days before his scheduled appearance before the commission, Richard Clarke, Bush's counterterrorism chief, appeared on CBS's *60 Minutes.* There had, of course, been other dissenters—from the FBI whistle-blower Colleen Rowley, who detailed in 2001 how the FBI missed clues that might have helped avert 9/11; to Joe Wilson, who wrote about the thinness of the Niger claims; to Powell's chief of WMD analysts, Greg Theilmann, who said on television in February that Americans had been misled. But Clarke was different. He was the highest-ranking official, next to Paul O'Neill, to come forward, and one with duties in the area of intense interest. He described in harrowing detail how President Bush had ignored the al Qaeda threat before the 9/11 attacks because he was focused instead on Iraq—a statement that fit, like a puzzle piece, with O'Neill's disclosure in January.

At the hearings of the 9/11 Commission on March 24, Clarke apologized to the American people for not acting in time on the long-growing threat of Islamic terrorism. At the hearing table, calm before the hot lights, Clarke apologized "to the loved ones of the victims of 9/11," saying, "to them who are here in the room, to those who are watching on television, your government failed you, those entrusted with protecting you failed you and I failed you. We tried hard, but that doesn't matter because we failed. And for that failure, I would ask— once all the facts are out—for your understanding and for your forgiveness."

It was a moment. Clarke, who met infrequently with the President, directed much of his ire at Condoleezza Rice—institutionally the

President's senior designee in the formulation of foreign policy—charging that she and her boss failed to heed repeated warnings.

"George Tenet and I tried very hard to create a sense of urgency by seeing to it that intelligence reports on the al Qaeda threat were frequently given to the president and other high-level officials. And there was a process under way to address al Qaeda. But although I continued to say it was an urgent problem, I don't think it was ever treated that way."

It was among the first times that Tenet, who'd acted as something of a heat shield for Bush and Rice in numerous hearings over the past two years, was praised. Rice, meanwhile, was being bludgeoned, with Clarke claiming that, in the spring of 2001, she didn't even know the term "al Qaeda," and that she kept the most important analyses away from Bush.

What the American public lacked, at this point, was context, and a few very relevant insights. One was that Bush had been told that the National Security Council process was busted—and told repeatedly, by officials who included Secretary of State Colin Powell, the national security adviser to his father. Powell had told Bush in a meeting that the NSC process is broken and Dr. Rice is at the center of it. Without a well-functioning NSC apparatus, he told Bush, a president simply can't know what he needs to know, when he needs to know it. Bush took it under advisement. Nothing changed.

The question, beyond the NSC process and its crucial role in synthesizing issues of an ever more complex world for a presidential purview, was the matter of Rice herself. The questions for Powell and other NSC principals, fell along a single axis: was Rice not reporting key issues and differences from the principals' committee to Bush; or was she duly carrying the deliberative distillate northward, but Bush was not responsive to much of what she offered; or was Cheney acting as a screen of sorts, a filter and vetting station between Rice and the President?

All three were in some measure the case. What Tenet and Rice both understood is that a key to the mind of the President was found in the framework that Cheney provided—the one percent solution diminished the import of much of the work, the policy process, so to speak, that the NSC was designed to manage.

"It's not about our analysis," as Cheney had said, with Rice and Tenet present. "It's about our response."

The Cheney Doctrine released George W. Bush from his area of greatest weakness—the analytical abilities so prized in America's professional class—and freed his decision making to rely on impulse and improvisation to a degree that was without precedent for a modern president. Cheney essentially crafted a platform, an architecture, for Bush to be Bush, while still being President.

The problem of implementing this model comes from a steady array of inconvenient facts—the enemies of message discipline—that vast policy arms of the government churn out and then refine for presidential consumption. For a President to have so little taste for such a product was a startling occurrence for those at the level of cabinet secretaries. In the years since Bush's election, hints of it leaked out, bit by bit, through places like Treasury, EPA, and Health and Human Services. Many of the government's leading analysts and experts— best and brightest professionals—became convinced there was little point in even sending reports up the chain. Disgruntlement and concern about the irrelevance of the policy process prompted some damaging defections and public statements about the President's disengagement. But, as Washington wonks, or members of the reviled "bureaucracy," dissenters were easy marks for White House counterattack.

Yet it was crucial to the White House that this portrait of the improvisational, faith-based presidency never expand to the central, high-intensity areas like the "war on terror," or the Iraq war—realms in which young Americans were dying and the stakes were almost beyond estimation. For a President to be so divorced from the actual policy apparatus in those matters could cause a panic, and a precipitous drop in public confidence, in America certainly, and in the rationality-rooted developed world.

The job of protecting, or shielding, the President from such a downdraft fell largely to Rice—in her role as conduit for the foreign policy establishment. With the Defense Department's senior staff filled with ideologically supportive neoconservatives under Rumsfeld's tight control, and the State Department largely excluded by 2004 from the policy-making process, the pressure to support Rice and Bush came to rest squarely on Tenet. That was where the problems could potentially arise. CIA, after all, was the originator of much of the actual analysis, evidence of the world as it stood, which the President was expected to be most mindful of; in short, what, on a wide array of issues, are the real choices and consequences. When a President's words or actions seem to disregard that analysis, or ignore demonstrable evidence, it creates questions—urgent questions about the President's competence or engagement at a time of peril, or whether Cheney, or anyone, is really in charge—that race through the government like explosive gas.

Such mishaps must be immediately cast as irregular occurrences for which someone must take the blame: the President, a busy man, was simply not informed. No one would dare say that the President made it clear to his most trusted lieutenants he did not *want to be informed,* especially when the information might undercut the confidence he has in certain sweeping convictions.

Thus, it would often be Tenet, who brought analysis up the chain from CIA, who was best positioned to assume blame. And Rice was adept at laying it on Tenet. The sixteen words are simply one telling example. Rice, along with Hadley, had set up Tenet to take the fall for the sixteen words, a fall that Tenet assumed until his protective aides at CIA, outraged that their boss was constantly taking the bullet for his superiors, leaked information that forced Hadley to share culpability.

Similar battles raged on several fronts between the NSC and CIA. Rice, so close to the President that blame levied on her might splash on him, usually emerged as the victor. But now, in her hour of need— as the White House resisted giving her over to the 9/11 Commission—she called, of all people, George Tenet.

"What should I do, George?" she asked, suddenly solicitous.

"Condi, I don't think you have a choice," Tenet said. "I think you've got to do this for your own sake. You've got a reputation to protect. You are who you are and it looks like you're ducking this. If you've something to say, you better say it."

Two weeks later, on April 8, clusters formed around televisions on the seventh floor of CIA as Rice—in her creamy suit and gold necklace—raised her right hand. It was sworn testimony—something that Governor Thomas Kean of New Jersey, one of the commission's two chairmen, had pushed for. She was under oath.

But the pressure to be precise and propitious didn't seem to have much effect. Tenet watched as Rice took off after Clarke, a Tenet supporter, and even took a few shots at CIA, criticizing the agency for its lack of coordination and cooperation with FBI, and lack of specificity in relaying pre-9/11 threats. Tenet, watching the proceedings, marveled to aides about how "very clever" she was.

Rice, in fact, was leading one phase of a White House election-year counterattack against critics and inconvenient evidence.

On Sunday morning, April 18, the first of five excerpts from Woodward's book *Plan of Attack* ran in *The Washington Post*.

In the next day's excerpt was a telling scene from the December 21, 2002, meeting in the Oval Office, and the phrase "slam dunk."

Tenet read the passage and felt the knife going in. He wondered how the President could recall so clearly something Tenet himself didn't remember saying. He thought if the President remembered it, the phrase must have been a signature moment in his thinking, even though the meeting—he and McLaughlin both agreed—was about creating a polished presentation of the rationale for going to war rather than underlying evidence for doing so.

A month or so before, Tenet had wandered into Bill Harlow's office when his communications chief was on the phone with Woodward. The veteran reporter was reminding Harlow that he had described the December 2002 meeting—and Tenet's use of the phrase "slam dunk"—to Harlow and McLaughlin at a meeting the three men had in January. Harlow didn't much remember the "slam dunk" issue—Woodward, he figured, must have mentioned it in passing. But, with Tenet hovering nearby, Harlow put him on the phone with Woodward, who recounted the scene for Tenet and said—according to Tenet's recollection—that it was "no big deal."

Woodward, when questioned later, would not comment on what he did or didn't tell Tenet, but did recall that he was sure he told Harlow at some point that the scene wouldn't be played as a "big deal" in the *Post* excerpts of the book that spring.

Now, as he held the newspaper in his hand, Tenet began to wonder if the simmering concerns of Moseman and Harlow and Krongard about the White House setting him up as a "fall guy" were, in fact, justified.

The entire multiyear drama of catching Hussein with WMD, and justifying a long-sought regime change—a battle that often pitted CIA against the collected forces from DOD and the Vice President's office—was now reduced to two words, two words that Tenet didn't remember saying.

Tenet tried to shrug it off. April was a busy time. There was plenty, as always, to draw his attention and energy. There were some breakthroughs on the bioterrorism front. Some captures in Pakistan were in the offing. The same day that Woodward's first excerpt ran, in fact, Spain formally announced it would, indeed, withdraw its troops from Iraq, causing effusions of victory throughout the Arab world, many of them quite revealing, that CIA was monitoring.

"I don't think it hit immediately," McLaughlin later said about the effects of "slam dunk."

"Remember, you're on a bucking bronco, taken along to other pressing things. It's kind of like a Warner Brothers cartoon. The hammer's coming down but you don't realize it has hit until you're sitting there flat. It's only at that point, when Bugs Bunny pops up from this flattened pancake and looks at himself and says, 'Hey, someone just hit me. Someone just laid a dime on us.' "

"Then," McLaughlin said, another week or two passed, and "we said, 'Someone *really* laid a dime on us.' "

Deciding who that "someone" was left Tenet in a cul-de-sac. Many of his top aides clearly felt it was the President himself—that Rice, or Card, or Cheney wouldn't act, in this instance, like in many others, without some guidance from their boss. Tenet just couldn't bring himself to blame Bush. He and the President had a good relationship. The President didn't fire George after 9/11, and the DCI rewarded that faith mightily, doing more, he felt, than almost anyone to fight this new kind of war. He'd proven his worth. He'd earned that loyalty.

But, as April turned to May, and "slam dunk" began to take hold in the public vernacular, Tenet seemed to have the wind knocked out of him. He was tired and talking more and more to Stephanie, his wife. Her distrust of the Bush crowd now seemed to be justified. Whatever the President, or Cheney, Rumsfeld, Wolfowitz, or Feith did or didn't do; whatever CIA's analytical shop, under pressure or not, did or didn't do; whatever the real justifications for the war were, or weren't—Tenet now wore a catchphrase of culpability.

John Michael, George and Stephanie's only son, would start his senior year of high school in three months—just a year until he left for college. Tenet, exhausted, and now fulfilling the role of fall guy that he had feared Bush would tag him with after 9/11, hugged his wife.

Early on the morning of Wednesday, June 2, Tenet read over the morning papers at his desk.

The Washington Post led with the installation of Iraq's caretaker government, an event trumpeted as robustly as "Mission Accomplished" had been a year before, even though three of the five top positions went to members of the failed Iraqi Governing Council, an entity with essentially no support among Iraqis, and civil unrest was steadily growing. The more interesting story to Tenet was the front-page one in *The New York Times* about what the CIA had concluded six weeks before. Ahmed Chalabi—the Iraqi dissident and longtime neocon friend—told an Iranian official that the United States had broken the secret communications code of Iran's intelligence service. With that disclosure, a window into Iranian intelligence—with its crucial revelations about that country's activities in Shiite-dominated Iraq, as well as its nuclear ambitions—slammed shut.

It was a bad turn on the intelligence front—the Iranians were the target of so many operations—but a kind of revenge for the CIA, considering how important Chalabi had been in orchestrating the passage of tainted information on Iraq's WMD programs through the Pentagon, and into various CIA-sanctioned estimates, including the all-important NIE. The CIA's long-standing distrust of Chalabi had never been considered valid, shouted down by the neoconservatives in the Pentagon and Vice President's office who hoped he would be installed as the leader of the newly born democracy. (Chalabi for his part consistently maintained that the CIA claim that he had betrayed the U.S. was an unfounded smear.)

What had surprised Tenet and his top lieutenants over the past few months was how obstinate the Pentagon was about sticking by Chalabi. There was a meeting in March, when internal reports were indicating that Chalabi's Iraqi National Congress, INC, may have misused the funds it received from the U.S. government, pocketing some and using cash to try to bribe members of Congress. Bush had lost patience with supporting Chalabi—who had had a prized seat behind Laura at January's State of the Union—and voiced his disapproval to Rumsfeld at an NSC meeting, telling the Secretary of Defense to sever the U.S. relationship with the light-footed Iraqi. Rumsfeld said he'd get right on it. But nothing was done. The same thing happened in meetings in April and May, when Bush grilled Wolfowitz. "I keep saying we should cut it off with Chalabi, and nothing happens," the President said in frustration. He then turned to Rice, looking at her sternly. "Would you please handle this!" The Pentagon's behavior bordered on insubordination. God knows, "the man" had his hands full, with neocons on all sides, and a broken NSC process.

When Tenet thought about all that, he felt sympathy for Bush, as he often did, despite the "slam dunk" and the complications of their relationship. The President was damn well doing the best he could.

But he'd have to do it, from here on, without Tenet. Or at least that was the plan. He picked up the phone, called Moseman into his office, and told him to close the door.

"It's time," Tenet said.

Moseman, Tenet's trusted top aide, a friend from all the way back to Capitol Hill days, nodded. They'd been talking this through for weeks. It was clear Tenet had finally made up his mind.

The question, Moseman said after a bit, was "Will the President accept it?"

The last time Tenet had tried, Bush had refused him. Now the two friends ran through a kind of call-and-response—if Bush says this, I say that . . . And then Moseman called Andy Card. "George needs to see the President tonight," he told him, without elaborating. Card saw no opening, and Moseman kept it lean. In a few minutes, Card called back to say the President and DCI were set for dinner that very night.

President Bush was on a two-day sweep of Colorado, a swing state in the upcoming election. That morning, to start day two, he gave a speech about foreign policy at the graduation ceremony of the United States Air Force Academy in Denver. "We are dealing here with killers who have made the death of Americans the calling of their lives. And America has made a decision about these terrorists: Instead of waiting for them to strike again in our midst, we will take this fight to the enemy," Bush said, as the 981 graduates of the Class of 2004 rose, cheering, in a standing ovation, amid banners that read *Parati ad Bellum—Ready for War,* the class motto. "We are confident of our cause in Iraq, but the struggle we have entered will not end with success in Iraq. Overcoming terrorism, and bringing greater freedom to the nations of the Middle East, is the work of decades. To prevail, America will need the swift and able transformed military you will help to build and lead. America will need a generation of Arab linguists, and experts on Middle Eastern history and culture. America will need improved intelligence capabilities to track threats and expose the plans of unseen enemies. Above all, America will need perseverance."

After a lunch, Bush boarded Air Force One for the afternoon trip back to Washington.

Tenet, followed by his security detachment, arrived for an early dinner at the residence. The two men sat down, and Tenet began his pitch: he'd done what he set out to do, he was tired, and—after seven years, the longest-tenured CIA director in modern times—he was ready. He and Bush then hashed it out.

As the hours passed, Moseman paced the halls of Langley. That morning, he and Tenet had figured that if the meeting ran long, it meant it was not going well, that the President was trying to persuade him to stay.

And he'd have reason to try. Most observers would assume that Bush would welcome Tenet's departure; Moseman knew better. Tenet offered extraordinary strategic utility for Bush, providing cover, and lightning-rod benefits, on the WMD case—a case that, Tenet knew, was always something of a reluctant exercise for Bush and Cheney; and, at the same time, leading the administration's signature initiative, the *find them, stop them* campaign against terrorists—the prime sales pitch for reelection. A *Washington Post*–ABC News poll released the previous week showed that 58 percent of Americans disapproved of Bush's handling of Iraq, a politically perilous figure. The "war on terror"—looking, by default, more and more like electoral salvation— was the initiative Tenet essentially ran.

What Moseman also understood—like McLaughlin, Harlow, and the others—was the way Tenet's codes of loyalty operated. Anyone who did him a favor, a real favor, might well end up in a pantheon beyond judgment. The President, in sticking by Tenet after 9/11, had an honored place in that realm. The match, however, with Bush's code, a one-way, "loyalty up" model, gave great latitude to the President, a scope Bush had exercised in his many, diverse requests to Tenet—

from himself and his closest aides—over nearly three years. As it approached nine o'clock, Moseman wondered if Bush was exercising that fiat once again over his friend, forcing him to stay, even though Tenet had made up his mind that it was absolutely time finally to leave. Forcing people to do things against their will was an avocation of the President's; to do that now to Tenet would break him in two.

At 9 p.m., Moseman called the head of the security detachment. "Make sure he calls when it's over," Moseman exhorted. "I'm here. I'm waiting."

A few minutes later, the phone rang.

"It's all right, John," Tenet said, his voice heavy with relief. "It's gonna happen."

The world keeps turning, and it did that summer as the United States focused on politics and fiery rhetoric, on blame and message discipline, and on unearthing the artifacts of battles past.

Just beyond the horizon line of public combat, those who were actually fighting the "war on terror" were searching, half-blind, for the next threat.

The front was shifting on the invisible battlefield. As financial and spoken signals intelligence shrank, the Internet became ever more the focus of the minions inside U.S. intelligence—just as it was for scores of young Islamic radicals, a "base" of men and women energized by images of U.S. troops mired in Iraq and Afghanistan and, since the spring, by harrowing photographs of torture and humiliation at Abu Ghraib.

The connected planet creates all manner of loops, where knowledge spurs action, which is captured in image and word and then cycled back—the mythical perpetual motion machine come to life. There were, at this point, thousands of muscular jihadist Web sites, ideal venues for what might be called "actionable" dialogue, that created communities around ideology and supportive dispatches, constantly refreshed, but archived and searchable—each assisting in a vast equalizing phenomenon of some user's words in a blog or chatroom standing in perpetuity beside those of bin Laden and Bush, side by side, call and response.

To draw a line between acquaintance dialogue and person-to-person communication, between suggestions and instructions, would be overwhelming if it were all in English and reviewed by cities full of freshly minted PhDs. Now, put it all in Arabic or any number of linguistic strains of the Near East or South Asia, and you have your arms around the magnitude of the challenge.

McLaughlin, like NSA's longtime chief Mike Hayden, often calls it "the grind"—they use the same, unglamorous phrase—and it is a slog, all day, every day, handled largely, McLaughlin likes to point out, "by armies of very, very smart, intuitive women."

But in early June—about the time Tenet and Bush were having their late dinner—one such data-cruncher got a hit, relying on an intersection of some e-mail with a bit of sigint.

It turned out to be from Musaad Aruchi, the forty-year-old nephew of Khalid Sheikh Mohammed, and first cousin of Ramzi Ahmed Yousef, the 1993 World Trade Center bomber, now serving a life sentence in a U.S. prison. The intercepts were swiftly passed to Pakistani intelligence, who tracked Aruchi to teeming Karachi. On June 12, they arrested him and held him at an airbase for three unpleasant days before turning him over to the CIA and one of their unmarked planes, for transport to a "black site."

At this point, foreign services—whether the Pakistanis or the Saudis or the Yemenis—were skilled in the investigative protocol of their U.S. brethren: apartments were sealed for careful search, including fingerprints, computers, and cell phones, and handed to technologists for careful extractions.

Aruchi's computer had casing photos, in this case of sites in New York and landmarks of various cities. There were also phone numbers and e-mail links, one of which prompted interrogators to press

Aruchi about a man named Muhammed Naeem Noor Khan, a gifted twenty-five-year-old techie who had been to one of bin Laden's camps in 1998.

Some of the same sting operation techniques used in the Pacha Wazir storefront nearly two years before were now launched on the virtual frontier. Khan, it was soon discovered, was operating something of an Internet hub for al Qaeda out of Pakistan. In mid-June, he was placed inside a kind of digital terrarium of intense surveillance. In the basements of CIA and NSA, the grinders held their collective breath—as each e-mail, each IP number on each computer of each associate of Khan's began to light up the darkened battlefield.

Rolf Mowatt-Larssen and CIA operatives in the Gulf were picking up reports of activity among the Bahrain jihad cell—again. Bassam Bokhowa, who'd had the original mubtakkar designs on his computer, had been free, along with his compatriots, since late 2003. That was when the Bahrainis released them, claiming what the Saudis also claimed at about that time: too little concrete evidence to merit continued custody. The United States said that they'd all crop up again. And they did, in the late spring of 2004. Something was being planned, possibly an attack against the U.S. naval base in the country and the community of several thousand American citizens. The fear was that it might be a mubtakkar attack.

The CIA was confident about the intelligence—it had a strong humint source inside the community of Bahraini Islamic radicals. Yet, as was so often the case, the Bahrainis, like the Saudis or the Pakistanis, were friends, but not real friends who could be trusted—so the United States couldn't reveal the sourcing to the Bahrainis. "Just trust us," Mowatt-Larssen and the CIA station chief in Bahrain said. Of course—despite the millions we'd pumped into equipment and training for Bahrain's intelligence service, as part of our "liaison" relationship—they didn't really trust us either.

Mowatt-Larssen discussed options with his old friend Rob Richer, a top operational chief at CIA and head of the Near East division. Maybe there was something they could arrange, a few private meetings with a few key players that would convince the Bahrainis it would be "in their interest" to act. Rather than ham-handed executive orders, congressional resolutions, trade sanctions, they would cut deals in the shadows.

That, after all, had been the hallmark of Tenet's CIA in the post-9/11 period. Protecting the country was an intensely personal endeavor, where relationships took shape in dozens of countries as well-funded liaison services, or CTICs, and as frank, first-name bonds between Tenet and whoever was in charge—emir, king, crown prince, or preening general. It's the way it works in countless cultures and large organizations: if there's a perception that the top folks are friends, everyone beneath falls into line, or at least makes an effort.

Of course, this was a time of swift change at the agency. Tenet's resignation was made public on June 3; Jim Pavitt resigned the next day. The President announced that John McLaughlin would serve as interim director—and most observers assumed it would be for a while. Steve Kappes would be moving up to take Pavitt's slot as the head of the Directorate of Operations; Mike Sulick would be taking Kappes's job as number two in operations; and Rob Richer would be moving into the number three slot.

Tenet was planning a final, valedictory run through the region. It was June 15. Harlow would be coming along with Richer and Mowatt-Larssen. It was one last lap around the track . . . and they'd run it like they always had.

Mowatt-Larssen, Richer, and Tenet huddled. Calls first went to Prince Bandar. He was a close friend of Sheikh Hamad bin Isa al-Khalifa of Bahrain—and Khalifa would be the key player.

And the problem.

A House resolution had praised Khalifa when he visited the United States in February 2003: "whereas" he had supported U.S. troops with his naval base, "whereas," since assuming power in 1999, he had helped build a diversified economy, and "whereas" he had revived municipal elections in 2002 in which women could vote and be candidates. As is often the case for rulers in this region, there were a few whereases that were conveniently overlooked—such as "whereas" he spends most of his time partying in Morocco.

That's how the full-living Bandar happened to have grown close to the fifty-four-year-old king.

Bandar made the call. Khalifa had to change whatever plans he had and meet immediately with Tenet and his men. "It's a serious issue of security," Bandar pressed the king. "You have to be there."

Two days later, Tenet, Mowatt-Larssen, and Richer were sitting in a glassed-in gazebo behind Khalifa's grand house in Morocco.

Khalifa, fresh from Marrakech—a playboy's Mecca—sat between Tenet and Richer, and asked what was so very important that he had to change his schedule.

Tenet leaned in close, put his hand on the king's knee, and pressed his meaty face so close to Khalifa's that it seemed they'd butt heads.

"Your Majesty, this is scary shit.

"My guys are going to tell you about it. You know my guys. You've got to listen to this. The President knows about this. The Saudis know about this. And it's a real threat."

Richer, hard by Khalifa's left flank, hit from the other side. "Rolf will give you the specifics of the threat," he said. "And I'll tell you the ramifications if you don't move on this threat."

Mowatt-Larssen—the big man of the trio, well north of six feet—laid out the threat: the Bahrainian group had plans for an easily constructed nightmare device, a chemical bomb; their goal was to drive the United States out of the Gulf—al Qaeda's main operational focus. They would do it by creating mass casualties among Americans and Bahrainis. After a few more minutes of this, Richer turned the screw.

"The White House knows about this threat, the Saudis know about this threat, because there are links from this group to Saudi Arabia. Other Arab leaders know about this threat," Richer said. "You have to take action or we will." He paused. "Look, Your Majesty. You have the U.S. Fifth Fleet. They're your protection. They could leave."

The exit of the Fifth Fleet was a worst-case scenario for Khalifa.

"I will move on this," he fumphered. "I will get things started immediately."

That was it. Tenet rose, his men with him. It was a classic Tenet and company operation. No notes, but dead on. Tenet's relationship and forceful mien would set the stage; his deputies would press their tough points, and close the deal. Tenet told the king that he and Richer were scheduled to meet with Crown Prince Abdullah of Saudi Arabia—a country with enormous sway over Bahrain—and had to leave immediately. Mowatt-Larssen would come with them and then, tomorrow, would jet directly to Bahrain to help coordinate the country's response. Khalifa nodded, the color having drained from his face. He said he'd wrap up business swiftly in Morocco, then attend to this issue back home. "You don't have to worry."

A few hours later, the group had settled three thousand miles southeast in the Saudi Arabian port city of Jeddah.

It was an evening they'd planned in advance—a treat, an indulgence, to mark Tenet's final tour before resignation.

The trusty Bandar—always at the ready to offer gifts, some with hidden costs—had offered his estate to the team for a few days. His staff would care for them. They could make calls, even take a meeting or two—one was planned the next day with Abdullah—while kicking back.

Kicking back was certainly the order of the evening, a time to do next to nothing. Tenet, Richer, and Mowatt-Larssen were joined by Bill Harlow, Tenet's trusted director of public affairs since 1999, and another Tenet friend, a station chief—still undercover—who managed much of the region for CIA.

Soon enough, they were all in bathing suits around the pool, with cigars and brandy watching the sun set over the Red Sea.

All of this would be over soon—they would be over, as would this particular era in a grand, often desperate campaign. They'd led it, for the most part, for better or for worse. No one could take that away from them. Wars of the future would be about *finding* as much as *fighting*—about uncovering a battlefield, an ephemeral front, that would vanish and, somewhere else, reappear; about convincing potential enemies to be reluctant friends.

To manage that you need to know the *other,* the global stranger, though his life, in some distant, dusty land, could not be more different, his frame of reference, positively extraplanetary. That sentience is all but impossible to develop if your first encounter is from the turret of a tank. At this point, the traditional warriors were finding that out to the east, in Iraq, a few hundred miles from this swimming pool.

But that was far away. So, they sat, and took stock, and drank Bandar's brandy, save Harlow, who turned in early.

Tenet led the team, and, as such, there are certain things even he wouldn't say about what he felt, really felt, even with all of the blustery outbursts, and epithets, and moments of shared, crushing need.

He could say it now. "You know, I always wanted to be like you guys, to have your respect," he offered, quietly, to the smoking circle, all CIA lifers, top operatives. "That was important to me. Really was."

Mowatt-Larssen, Richer, the undercover station chief, all nodded, touched by Tenet's candor, though they understood—leading *invisibles,* that they were—that among all the public people, the *notables,* Tenet was one who truly understood where the real fight occurred. It did not happen under hot lights, or in conference rooms, where the celebrated or duly elected alit to hold forth. No, it unfurled in the shadows, beneath the line of sight, where you tracked and maybe met your opponent, your opposite number, and, that way, carried forward the sound principle of *know thy enemy.* This is solid advice, ancient really, carrying the seeds of victory and, in the end, mercy.

They all sat for a moment, with the sun vanishing, white middle-aged men, in this pleasure dome atop the seething Arab world, knowing, all of them, the perils of such work, firsthand; of knowing thy enemy, in a dusty café in Karachi, or palace in Morocco, without forgetting what you're there for, and what makes you who you are. More than any of the other *notables,* it so happened, Tenet ran, day to day, across these shadowlands, meeting and knowing reluctant friends and potential enemies, trying to close deals that might—*might*—save lives.

"We didn't grow up together, so to speak, but we always saw you as one of us," Rolf said, after a bit. "You were behind us. You looked out for us. Together, you know, I think we made a difference."

Tenet nodded. "Yeah, I think we did."

And the verbs were already past tense.

The next day, Mowatt-Larssen flew to Bahrain. The Bahraini cell was swept up a week later—six arrests were made on June 22. The homes of all the men were searched. Nothing was found. Several mullahs appealed to the government. Bokhowa, for one, had friends in high places among the country's religious Shia population. They were all released on the 23rd.

What ensued over the next month was a bout of clumsy public brinksmanship, as CIA's intelligence channel—a line that, for better or for worse, was designed to remain open no matter what atmospherics raged elsewhere—was replaced by the so-called "policy," or political, channel. The United States, outraged at the releases, threatened to withdraw its base and order all U.S. personnel and American citizens from the country.

The Bahrainis, not wanting to be publicly coerced into action by the United States—about the least advantageous move for an Arab nation of any stripe at this point—resisted.

Finally, the United States began to withdraw all personnel and close, permanently, the Department of Defense–funded school in Manama—a private school that educated the children of elites throughout the country, including children of royalty. At day's end, all politics proved to be local, even geopolitics. The six were rearrested in mid-July, though there was not quite a return to business as usual in Khalifa's kingdom. The king had been publicly bullied, never a positive outcome for a dictator—especially one who had been helpful to the United States—and radical Islamic factions in the country emerged from the incident stronger than ever.

Would the six have been released so quickly in June if Tenet were not on his way out of office? That's a matter of debate.

What is not debatable is that neither McLaughlin nor anyone else in the government had the array of personal bonds with key conditional partners in the "war on terror," from Musharraf to Abdullah to less central though important players, like Qatar's al-Thani or Bahrain's Khalifa, that could match Tenet's. Even his weakness for ready accommodation, a liability in several well-known debates in the United States, was a crucial feature in nudging foreign dictators to act. Personality can get you far in this world, and undeniably, Tenet's was a key element in much that worked in the battle against terrorists.

It was an asset, not easily replaceable, that would be missed.

Just after 10 p.m. on July 29, Senator John Kerry of Massachusetts rose to the podium at the Democratic National Convention in Boston.

The convention, up to that point, had focused ardently on Kerry's record as a Vietnam War hero, including the testimonials of men who served with him, and elegantly produced videos.

Just as the President essentially staked his claim for reelection during the State of the Union—that America was under constant threat but had not again been attacked—Kerry, a half hour into his prime-time address, made his statement of purpose: "Saying there are weapons of mass destruction in Iraq doesn't make it so. Saying we can fight a war on the cheap doesn't make it so. And proclaiming 'Mission accomplished' certainly doesn't make it so," he called out to the cheering convention hall. "In these dangerous days, there is a right way and a wrong way to be strong. Strength is more than tough words."

Five hundred miles to the south, Kerry's face, big hair, and red tie beamed from television sets in bustling rooms of CIA analysts and technical experts.

There were few places more propitious than these rooms to view the connection between the administration's fortunes and the hard-to-discuss issues of terrorism, fear, and the nation's response. In the realm of public combat, Kerry was essentially focusing on the issue of what message must be sent to the nonvoting global audience—including al Qaeda and its possible adherents—and agreeing with Bush that that message must be one of toughness, a tough leader leading a tough nation. But, he said, it would have to be more than "tough words."

No one, of course, believed Bush wasn't tough—or, God knows, that he didn't compel America to act tough, now with significant numbers of U.S. armed forces in two distant countries. Kerry's appeal, in fact, was to a rational ideal—to the gap between saying something and making it so; the belief that sound analysis should underpin words and actions. It didn't get much traction. Bush's code is that you act tough whether there's a good reason, bad reason, or no reason, and that was the posture—the message—many people preferred be sent to the most important sector of the global community, the target audience: ardent, bloodthirsty terrorists. If we couldn't reach bin Laden with a paramilitary team, at least we could reach him with our words.

People at CIA soon drifted away from Kerry's speech because they were being enveloped by a fierce battle on the field of counterterrorism—the first one in some time. Muhammed Naeem Noor Khan had been captured in Lahore two weeks before—on July 13—and forced by Pakistani interrogators, in partnership with CIA, to send urgent e-mails to a wide array of operatives, directing players from Indonesia to England to e-mail him back immediately. They did, revealing their locations, and a global manhunt was under way to sweep up as many as possible. Dozens were located—including Ahmed Khalfan Ghailani, wanted since 1998 for his role in the bombing of the U.S. Embassy in his home country, Tanzania. Ghailani was cornered, with four al Qaeda associates, at a house in the Pakistani town of Gujrat. After he, two other al Qaeda soldiers, and their families surrendered following a sixteen-hour firefight, Pakistani paramilitary units found an astonishing trove. Computers and disks, including highly detailed casing studies of five buildings: New York's Citicorp headquarters, the

New York Stock Exchange, the Prudential Tower in Newark, New Jersey, and, in Washington, the World Bank headquarters and the International Monetary Fund Building.

In a round of meetings through the weekend, the plans were pored over. Those with memories of the Christmas threat's numerology—of panic, ultimately, based on nothing—now looked at a nihilistic playbook of astonishing precision. Twenty pages of photos and specifications—upramp gradients, structural soundness, traffic flows—for each of the buildings.

They debated over the weekend whether it was an active threat. The plans had been drawn up in 2000 and 2001, though one of the five had been modestly refreshed in the past year. But now, every veiled threat from chatter or interrogations or humint—some of them pure fantasy—was viewed with rigorous application of the Cheney Doctrine. Is there even a one percent chance? Of course.

On Sunday, August 1, Homeland Security chief Tom Ridge sounded the alarm, upping the threat level to orange for the areas around the buildings. At the press conference, he failed to mention that the casing disks were from 2000 and 2001, but managed to remember to attribute the discovery of the information to the "President's leadership."

The dating on the disks was revealed the next day, even as officials ordered that the buildings in question be evacuated. "We shouldn't have found out the next day that the surveillance was done four years ago," the 9/11 Commission chairman, Tom Kean, complained. "That wasn't helpful."

Democrats were mostly in a state of shock. Howard Dean expressed a widespread suspicion, saying, "It's just impossible to know how much of this is real and how much of this is politics."

To separate the two during an election year, in which the conduct of a largely secret war was a central issue, was all but futile. What was clear from weekend polling, however, was that Kerry hadn't managed to get any postconvention bump in his ratings even before Ridge's announcement; his poll ratings actually dropped slightly. Not that the reassertion of fear didn't provide additional damage.

Meanwhile, the terrorist-catching machines churned forward.

On August 3, a dozen men were picked up in England, including Esa al-Hindi, the author of the elegantly written casing reports found in Pakistan and the head of al Qaeda in Britain. The CIA had been chasing him since KSM coughed up his name sixteen months before in one of the few products of his brutal interrogation.

Network news special reports, newspaper headlines, and long magazine narratives spilled forth during the first week of August. The enemy was out there, but armies of justice were on the march—fear and action, left hand and right, clasped.

All this—much of it care of the CIA—augured well for the President. His poll numbers were rising. He had new, fresh lines to add to his standards about the prevention of further attacks on the United States and Libya's acquiescence, for a campaign swing that week through the Midwest.

Yet all this did little to change the view of Karl Rove, his lieutenants in the President's political office, and virtually everyone around the Vice President that the CIA—like the State Department—was assembled against the President. This judgment rested largely on the succession of leaks that had emerged in recent months from both arms of government. The State Department's Office of Intelligence Analysis had produced a variety of reports before the Iraq war predicting, for the most part, the explosive mix of insurgency and inertia that had defined the first year of the U.S. occupation. The CIA had also done its share—with bleak assessments of how a U.S. invasion would stoke jihadist anger worldwide and nourish a widening base of violence-prone recruits.

CIA analysts—tagged now, as well, with Tenet's two-word assessment—felt an urge to show that policy advice in other areas had not been wrong. "It was difficult," said one former CIA manager. "We were all against the idea of Iraq, passed that analysis along, and now—because of WMD—we were being blamed for it."

The assessment that both State and CIA were partisans trying to thwart the President's reelection was subtly miscast. Their reactions weren't political; they were structural. What those in both policy shops knew—like a host of generals at Defense—was that even in the high-stakes areas of foreign policy, the basics of analytical due diligence had, in fact, been ignored, or tapped only when a "product" was needed to support policies the White House had already settled on. Their conclusion—much like that of O'Neill, a conservative Republican, or Clarke, a registered Republican who had long been fiercely loyal to codes of silence—was that this presented institutional dangers for the government and for the country.

Rather than deal with the underlying issue and offer some accommodation to the so-called "policy process"—a ready way to quell the disgruntlement—the White House's response was tactical: to intensify its search for leakers with continuous rounds of polygraph tests at CIA and among those with high-level clearances at State and elsewhere (a prime question was Have you ever spoken without authorization to a reporter?); and to conduct sweeps of executive branch communication lines, including federally issued cell phones. Such naked shows of executive power ultimately created fear, its traditional by-product of mutual distrust, and another set of lessons—like so many already roiling within the government—that few, if any, ends justify such a standard of "by any means necessary." The leaks, in any event, increased.

And CIA, the agency's remaining chiefs realized, had now lost its cover. The complex bond between Bush and Tenet—bonhomie mixed with acid, a layer cake of co-dependency—had provided unexpected protection. George could always sit with George and plead a case or take the hit. The top men had a relationship; the deputies had held their fire, a bit.

That was over. McLaughlin—thirty-two years at CIA, classically educated, tough, and earnest—would have been a traditional pick for DCI in years past. But he didn't have much of a relationship with Bush, in an administration where such things mattered.

And so did politics. Kerry had gained some ground in July by saying he would embrace all the recommendations of the 9/11 Commission. He criticized Bush—rather than Tenet and CIA—for intelligence failures, and challenged the President to fully accept, as well, the recommendations of the commission.

The response came on August 10, when the President announced that Representative Porter Goss, the Florida Republican who chaired the House Intelligence Committee—and who co-chaired, with Florida's Democratic senator Bob Graham, the Joint Intelligence Committees, or JIC, investigation of 9/11—would take over CIA. He would examine, with fresh eyes, the commission's proposals.

Goss's unique feature was that he had once been a young CIA case officer. Back in the 1960s, he had recruited spies in Western Europe and Central America, before retiring for medical reasons in 1972, starting a newspaper on Sanibel Island, and then going into politics. Goss, who was first elected to Congress in 1988 and became chairman of the intelligence committee in 1997, could be critical of the agency—he called it "dysfunctional" during the JIC hearings—but was viewed from Langley, initially, with cautious good humor. He had not been much of an agent, and senior managers assumed CIA's internal meritocracy—the one that accounted for each man's and woman's rise to a top position—would have some application. Or so they hoped.

Though McLaughlin would not be promoted, and the White House clearly wanted to display its control over intelligence matters, analysts and operators at CIA moved forward, unaffected, as though little had occurred. Paul Pillar, who coordinated intelligence analysis for the Near East and South Asia, was at this moment completing a report that Cheney had commissioned in the spring, assessing postinvasion Iraq. It was the first time the White House had asked CIA for its appraisal of the situation in Iraq. The report was particularly pointed.

It warned that the insurgency in Iraq could evolve into a full-scale guerrilla war or, worse, a civil war.

In September, it was leaked to the media. Bush, in the midst of his campaign, was irate. He was hit with a flurry of questions on the campaign trail. One day's message, then the next, was being swamped by off-message noise, with only a few dozen precious days until the election. He testily dismissed the report, which he hadn't read, saying that the assessment was "just guessing."

A few days later, Pillar was identified in a column by Robert Novak as having written the leaked report. Novak reported that Pillar gave an off-the-record speech at a private dinner in California that Condoleezza Rice attended.

This would serve as the evidence—proof of long-suspected disloyalty—the White House had been looking for.

The White House officials began to assert privately—and publicly through intermediaries—that the CIA was actively trying to undercut the administration.

John McLaughlin, still at CIA while Goss settled in, watched it all with mounting horror.

He called Andy Card's office to set up a conversation with Bush.

It happened by phone.

"Mr. President," McLaughlin said. "We at CIA are not trying to bring you down."

"I appreciate you saying that," Bush replied. The President averred that things can get tense in a political season.

The call ended. Underlying issues driving the conflict between a President and his intelligence agency at a time when intelligence is the equivalent of guns and ammunition were not discussed.

On September 24, Goss arrived as the new director and announced that four of his top appointments would be filled directly from his House staff. The quartet would act largely as a superstructure around Goss, a layer of senior staff to directly advise him on all operations of the agency. The exception would be a CIA journeyman, Kyle "Dusty" Foggo, who had been a friend and ally of Goss's during his time in Congress. Goss put Foggo in the executive director's position, the agency's number three job, replacing A. B. "Buzzy" Krongard.

The purge had officially begun.

There is no violent regime change in America.

No insurgent groups, collecting arms to attack government forces. No states of emergency, delaying elections until those in power decide it's safe. No impending civil war.

There is a process, here, where 125 million or so adults try to know what is knowable and make decisions about the nation's—*their nation's*—future.

But for those involved in the central struggle of this era—the "hearts and minds" battle with a new kind of enemy—the month leading to election day was a strange, disconnected time.

With knowledge come burdens, along with the joys and responsibilities. There are, in this hot, dry, ionized period—these years when burning buildings and a dust cloud rising are still in present memory, when the eyes still flinch at a glimpse of the Trade Center towers in some old movie—only a few perches from which you can see almost everything. Maybe too much. Not that our leaders don't have rarefied perches; they do. But they also have the worry about what people— the countless, faceless *us,* who create celebrity with our kind attentions—will think of them. They have to be mindful of presentation. This goes not just for presidents or recognizable senators, but for the George Tenets and Bob Muellers, for the Rumsfelds and Powells. For the notables, having a constituency can cloud one's vision.

Just beneath them, though, are "the invisibles"—the leading players in a global struggle; as invisible, in many ways, as their murderous opponents. They are civil servants who've had to worry only about the fight, and about winning it. Usually, this group is not so small. In most great conflicts, there is mass attentiveness. A population reads about the day's battles, and it is clear whether we won that day, or lost, and why. A reason that Iraq has drawn so much attention, beyond the harrowing specifics of Americans, and Iraqis, killed and maimed, is because it has these traditional advantages of visibility. Not in the new kind of war. A shift from angry to angry and violent in some town whose name you can't pronounce is equivalent to the assembling of armies. The day the bomb explodes, shattering a nation's psyche and sacrificing innocents, marks the end of years of to-and-fro, of small victories and silent defeats. There is no one in the battle who doubts that day will come, or that it will prompt a collective, urgent question: just what, again, are our soldiers doing in Iraq?

In October 2004, FBI agents combed the country for threats, and came up, mostly, with handfuls of sand. There were some contacts from the Pakistani cells rolled up in the summer to American e-mail addresses, but they came to nothing. That, after thousands of people were interviewed.

There had in fact been only a handful of consequential convictions, now three years since the harrowing attacks, and those were mostly for so-called "material support," a catchall charge when evidence of wrongdoing is thin. The President still asked whether there were any active cells, ready for operation, in America. The reply: none found yet.

Dan Coleman left the bureau, officially for medical reasons. As "the man who introduced bin Laden to America"—his common introduction—he had been called on in the past year for his unusually frank advice. But the angrier he got about lessons that we were having to learn over and over about the enemy, relearning each time a new manager arrived, the more his asthma kicked up. He took his pension at fifty-three, and went home with Maureen. In his attic, somewhere, is a tin box that once held Zawahiri's head. Inside of it is river mud, dried and crumbly, from across the world. He figured he'd keep it for the grandkids.

Corporate life didn't agree with Dennis Lormel. No surprise, really. He liked the money, but AES—like lots of very large companies—had a narrow transactional view of what Dennis could provide. He left after six months for a consulting firm, Corporate Risk International, that advises governments and companies about the way money—including funds earmarked for destructive purpose—moves around the world. He got his basement finished, though. A genuine sports bar, homage to battles fought and won where someone, thank God, kept score.

That's where he was sitting—the five TVs running ESPN and ESPN2, ESPN Classic, and lesser known sports cable—when he read *The Wall Street Journal* on October 20. It was a front-page story by Glenn Simpson, the *Journal*'s crack investigative reporter—one of their best—about Western Union. It laid out plenty of particulars—including Western Union's global reach, its concentration in areas, like Pakistan, where terrorists roamed free, and how hard it was for the company, or anyone else, to monitor who sent money to whom.

Lormel read the story's lead quote—there on the *Journal*'s front page, which draws about 6 million readers—from one of his old colleagues, William Fox, head of the Treasury Department's Financial Crimes Enforcement Network.

"We have come to recognize that foreign affiliates and agents of money service businesses are an issue of serious concern," Fox said in a statement. "Our concern is, do the money service businesses here really know who they are dealing with abroad, even though they are their agents? To the extent they don't, that provides a serious weakness."

Fox then told the *Journal* that he planned to "push Western Union toward closer oversight of its agents through a regulatory process known as 'industry guidance,' which is due out shortly."

Lormel smiled.

"They must be trying to drum up some new terrorist business for Western Union," he mused. "Not likely."

He knew the terrorists were moving money through untraceable hawalas and face-to-face handoffs. "If we assume they're idiots," he said a while later, "we'll be disappointed. They're not. We're in a game that's more like chess—with the whole planet as the board. But with funny rules. Our opponents seem to have a limitless supply of pieces. You knock off a pawn, or a rook, they reach into a big box and replace it. Unless you can do the same, after a while you're gonna have trouble protecting your king. Some fucking game."

Across the Potomac, at CIA headquarters, the five o'clock meetings were becoming irregular.

Goss's people, called "the Gosslings," were running loyalty tests. Goss made clear to top brass what he would later write in an all-agency memo: that CIA is there to support the policies of the administration. Period.

But with John McLaughlin at the helm, for old times' sake, they still met at 5 p.m. and felt their way, just as other combatants in this new version of "war" had done in the years since 9/11, taking the grand promises offered by the notables, and trying to figure out how the hell to make good on them.

"It was so fucking sad," said Rolf. "We still got together, but John without George—it wasn't the same. We knew our time, racing around the world, doing everything humanly possible, had ended. It made the old days seem like the Age of Pericles."

They all had their résumés ready, and were working the phones. Everyone, now, was hip-deep in the intelligence business, and confused. Departments, of all stripes, were in desperate need of "training agents" to teach them how it all worked. Rolf was getting ready to move, a few months hence, to the job of intelligence chief for the Department of Energy. The free flow of uranium and nuclear technology kept him up at night. Hank Crumpton would be moving to the State Department to head up intelligence in that realm. Charlie Allen, at seventy-two, the agency's legendary analyst and chief warning officer, would be heading up intelligence at the Department of Homeland Security—a task that Atlas might have shied away from. In fact, almost all of the dozen or so people at this meeting—even those most valuable operational bosses who'd built eyeball-to-eyeball relationships with reluctant friends around the world—would soon be gone, and the people who'd replaced them as well. The agency's role, like that of much of government, would now be to serve and support policy rather than to help create it.

As the sun began to set on Friday, October 29, they gathered on the seventh floor. The news that day was the so-called "October Surprise" broadcast by bin Laden. He hadn't shown himself in nearly a year. But now, four days before the election, his spectral presence echoed into every American home. It was a surprisingly complete statement by the al Qaeda leader about his motivations, his actions, and his view of the current American landscape. He praised Allah and, through most of the eighteen minutes, attacked Bush, tapping diverse sources from Michael Moore's movie *Fahrenheit 9/11* to statements he'd made to CNN, *Time* magazine, various outlets of the mainstream media, much reviled by the administration, and interviews with liberal journalists. He mocked Bush for being stupid, and deceptive, and corrupted by big oil and big business entanglements, like those with Halliburton. At the end, he managed to be dismissive of Kerry, but it was an afterthought in his "anyone but Bush" treatise.

Minutes after the noon broadcast, both campaigns moved on identical paths, expressing repugnance at bin Laden's attempt to sway the election: Kerry going first, with "as Americans, we are absolutely united in our determination to hunt down and destroy Osama bin Laden"; then Bush, with "Americans will not be intimidated or influenced by an enemy of our country. I'm sure Senator Kerry agrees with this." It was a hands-off issue, even for pundits who waded in during the hours after the speech to assess which campaign the statement might help. To accede that a mass murderer was tipping the American election would, in essence, be giving in to terror.

Inside of CIA, of course, the analysis moved on a different track. They had spent years, as had a similar bin Laden unit at FBI, parsing each expressed word of the al Qaeda leader and his deputy, Zawahiri.

What they'd learned over nearly a decade is that bin Laden speaks only for strategic reasons—and those reasons are debated with often startling depth inside the organization's leadership. Their assessments, at day's end, are a distillate of the kind of secret, internal conversations that the American public, and by association the wider world community, were not sanctioned to hear: strategic analysis.

Today's conclusion: bin Laden's message was clearly designed to assist the President's reelection.

At the five o'clock meeting, once various reports on latest threats were delivered, John McLaughlin opened the issue with the consensus view: "Bin Laden certainly did a nice favor today for the President."

Around the table, there were nods. Mowatt-Larssen watched the proceedings. There was some speculative talk of why—knowing that bin Laden acted out a strategic rationale—he would have done this, just as there was, Mowatt-Larssen recalled, of why the Soviets liked certain American leaders, such as Nixon: because they were consistent and predictable. Jami Miscik talked about how bin Laden—being challenged by Zarqawi's rise—clearly understands how his primacy as al Qaeda's leader was supported by the continuation of his eye-to-eye struggle with Bush. "Certainly," she offered, "he would want Bush to keep doing what he's doing for a few more years."

But an ocean of hard truths before them—such as what did it say about U.S. policies that bin Laden would want Bush reelected—remained untouched.

"It was sad," Mowatt-Larssen remembered. "We just sat there. We were dispirited. We had nothing left at that point."

For another day, maybe.

Yet there were some who'd already arrived at this shoreline among those at the very top of the government. While CIA glimpsed at the issue of bin Laden's motivations and turned away, there were those who understood just how acutely this heated, global dialogue—of ideas and message and the preservation of power, of us and them—was a mirror game, a two-way street. On that score, any number of

NSC principals could tell you something so dizzying that not even they will touch it: that Bush's ratings track with bin Laden's ratings in the Arab world.

No one doubts that George W. Bush is earnest when he thinks of the victims of 9/11 and speaks of his longing to bring the culprits to justice. Yet he is an ambitious man, atop a nation of ambitious and complex desires, who knows that when the al Qaeda leader displays his forceful presence, his own approval ratings rise, and vice versa.

No one ever said it would be simple.

And so, on we go, blindly—as so many people do, always, in their own time—through the age of terror.

AFTERWORD

The opening campaign in a war, any war, is when assumptions are challenged on the field, when the enemy's strength and character can be assessed, and the nature of the conflict slowly reveals itself.

The initial three years of the American response to the attacks by al Qaeda on 9/11 might reasonably be framed as the "first campaign" of a lasting conflict.

Already, the outlines of a core dilemma are fully formed: can America prevail in this struggle while staying true to its defining principles? The issue is not new. The country has, in the past, mobilized during wartime, engaging its resources and energies to support broad, strategic goals, some of them marked by destructive digressions of the American character. Always, though, there was the sense of a limited time of crisis with critical needs, a time that, God willing, would soon pass.

This is not so in this new battle against an invisible army of terrorists, a fact that they surely consider a strength of their tactical position.

Each moment that passes in which they survive to speak the dream of jihad, and we live with fearful regard and cramped liberties, is a moment of victory on their ledger. Those moments will add up.

What was becoming clear by late 2004 to almost all of those carrying forward "the fight"—a multitude of Mowatt-Larssens and Lormels—was that time was not on our side. The model of the modern Islamic terrorist—seasoned by violent ideology and frustration, supported by ready access to information and means of destruction, driven toward an end of martyrdom—is an elegant construct, easily replicable, difficult to counter.

Those operators and analysts, the hunters and gatherers—many of them at CIA and FBI—who'd walked in the shoes of the enemy, came away hot and sooty and wild-eyed with concern. Those responsible for many of the "first campaign's" tactical triumphs were the ones least encouraged by what those victories meant, whether their effects would last. Expressing such concerns to their counterparts on high did not always meet with the hoped-for response: added ardor, and informed clarity, about creating a strategy that made sense.

What became clear, day by day, in the opening years of the campaign is that these two groups had a shared purpose but not always shared interests. Those on high were concerned with their public standing and, at the very top, acute political needs.

There are a few postscripts on this score. One involves Jami Miscik, the CIA's analytical chief, in essence, for most of the first chapter of the battle against terrorists.

In mid-November 2004, a few weeks after the President's reelection, one of Miscik's deputies returned from briefing the Vice President. He had a request for her. Cheney wanted a portion of a particular CIA report declassified and made public. Miscik knew the report—it was about the complex, often catalytic connections between the war in Iraq and the wider war against terrorism. The item the Vice President wanted declassified was a small part that might lead one to believe that the war was helping the broader campaign against violent jihadists. The report, she knew, concluded nothing of the sort. Many of its conclusions flowed in the opposite direction. To release that small segment would be willfully misleading. She told the briefer to tell Cheney that she didn't think that was such a good idea.

The Vice President expressed his outrage to Porter Goss. A few days later, a call came from Goss's office. The call had been placed by one of Goss's executive assistants—emblematic, in that Goss did not make the call himself, of how dysfunctional relations had become at the top of CIA. The deputy expressed the DCI's displeasure. He urged Miscik to reconsider. He described Goss's position succinctly: "Saying no to the Vice President is the wrong answer."

Language is an improbably powerful thing. It's just words, after all, in a world full of noise. But certain combinations of words can move mountains and change lives. This line did that for Miscik, even after all that she, like others in embattled corners of the government, had gone through trying to preserve the basics of analysis and due diligence in the face of a one percent doctrine that could operate without them, if need be—a doctrine that prized "response" above all.

"Actually," she replied, "sometimes saying no to the Vice President is what we get paid for."

She hung up and fired off a memo to Goss, saying—she later recalled—that "this was just the sort of thing that had gotten us into trouble, time and again, over the past few years. Telling only half the story, the part that makes us look good, and keeping the rest classified. Eventually, it comes out and it looks bad, real bad, and we lose moral capital."

A few days later, Miscik got word, again from a Goss deputy, that the DCI would reluctantly support her decision. A few weeks after that, she was gone. "It was only a matter of time at that point," she recalled.

Her memo—a summation of a long-standing school of thought of which she is one of countless adherents—is, of course, classified. That means, by accepted definitions of such things, that its release would compromise the security of the nation. Indeed.

A second short postscript deals with Tenet, himself a man who had had to "mind the gap," as they say on those T-shirts, between the fast-separating continents of "our analysis" and "our reaction."

It was an untenable mission, and he'd pay dearly.

After leaving CIA, he settled into repose for a while, recovering, really, from exhaustion after leading the furious *find them, stop them* battle during this first chapter in the "war on terror." He dressed casually, often wearing jeans and a silky New York Giants jacket—a helluva nice jacket—and spending time with his handsome son and pretty wife, while unbagging a suit, here and there, for an occasional speech for good money. Tenet's pitch these days is, interestingly, an embrace of transparency, a desire to educate the public, a position he summed up nicely one day on the phone.

"This is about data, not about structure," he began, referring to some of Washington's institutional remedies to improve intelligence. "This is about the cop on the beat in Redmond, Oregon, who sees anomalous surveillance activity outside of the Microsoft headquarters, being able to plug that data into a digital communications system to find out if we've seen this in Abu Dhabi, in Ankara, in Indianapolis, or Detroit, and what did you do about it. How should I think about it, and what measures should I take. The government is moving in an overly centralized manner when what you need is decentralized pockets of data around the country, on a common communications backbone, that allow people who *own* their communities, and know them better than anybody in Washington, to figure out what they got and act against it."

Then he takes a breath, and takes it up a notch.

"It's five years after 9/11, almost, the country still doesn't have a digital communications architecture . . . to move data at the lowest levels and preferably unclassified levels, to tell everybody what we know about the strategic targeting doctrine of al Qaeda, and we know a lot. Every time you have a subway piece, it shouldn't be *de novo* . . . it's in their playbook . . . it's not about the date, time, and place of the event . . . because finding that's lucky, fortuitous, hard, and serendipitous. It's about building a system of protection based on data. . . . It's not about, it's not about this big, multilayered, fucking structure they've put together. . . . It's about speed and agility, speed and agility, and the flow of data to people who can fight. The revolution in intelligence that occurred after 1991, after the Gulf War, was substantial in terms of allowing a military commander at the farthest end of the battle to both push and pull data down to tell him what's really going on across the battlefield. That same kind of speed and agility has to be replicated inside the country. That's what I'm saying! See, they all say, well, this is a foreign threat. Well, yes, it is, except, ladies and gentlemen, it's here. The British can say it's a foreign threat, but it's living there. It's *living* inside the United States, whether you like it or not."

Later, in another conversation, he talked a bit about Iraq's weapons of mass destruction. "We were wrong," he said, almost to himself. "We weren't corrupt."

Tenet doesn't rev up on that score. He knows, smart guy that he is, that the outcome of a particularly successful White House strategy placed the sign SLAM DUNK around his neck.

It hangs right next to the Medal of Freedom Bush placed there—along with medals for L. Paul Bremer and Tommy Franks—when he stood the three of them up at a ceremony in the fall of 2004.

It's a bad combination of neckwear. One common flavor of tragedy is that strength can hold the seed of weakness—a weakness that can be exploited by someone who spots the flaw. Tenet likes Bush, trusts him, and is grateful that the Texan gave the New Yorker a chance to redeem himself after 9/11. Tenet—probably being the man most responsible, if anyone is, that America has not, again, been attacked—kept to his personal code of loyalty, never to forget a good deed done on one's behalf, and felt he had returned the favor by doing all anyone could to protect the country. Bush, though, has a more transactional view of loyalty than Tenet. It's more along the lines of people proving their loyalty by doing whatever you tell them to do. It's a bad matchup.

So, Bush hung a medal around Tenet's neck and, just days later, the White House unleashed hounds from hell—from unnamed senior officials to targeted leaks—to blame Tenet for everything, it seemed, from the Iraq war to the rise in mortgage interest rates. Tenet, most of whose acts and efforts as DCI are conveniently locked in the vault marked "Classified," was thereby propped up in the town square as the dogs tore flesh from bone, left to hold tight to evidence of his bond with the President—a medal that loses value with each passing day.

Tenet, who has remained mum, may someday speak for himself. He is working—on and off and on again—on a memoir, which may someday be published. But he is undoubtedly pained by how the White House's desire to avoid blame and instead heap it on CIA, whether for the surprise of 9/11 or the surmise of Iraq's WMD, meant that the agency would suffer and be gutted and maybe leave the country more vulnerable—a cost, it would seem, of the political mandate in a time of crisis. As to the more personal matter of loyalty's ledger, it may, in this case, be marked at day's end by the harsh reflection of Cardinal Wolsey, from Shakespeare's *Henry VIII*. Awaiting execution in Act III, he turns to his faithful servant Cromwell and says, "If I had served my God as I have served my king, He would not in mine age left me naked to mine enemies."

In the late fall of 2005, I spent a day with John McLaughlin. He'd come to Dartmouth College for a speech, planned months before, which happened to occur a few days after Dana Priest, *The Washington Post*'s crack reporter, soon to win a Pulitzer Prize, broke the story about torture occurring at CIA "black sites" hidden inside various Eastern European countries. McLaughlin shared the dais at Dartmouth with Judge Larry Silberman, a loyal Cheney ally who'd just completed the Robb-Silberman Report, blaming CIA for all the failures in prewar intelligence, though not mentioning any problematic role by the White House.

In front of a packed auditorium at Dartmouth, an edgy crowd of five hundred or so demanded explanations. Silberman was dismissive of questions about the administration's possible role in misleading the public about Iraq or encouraging torture.

McLaughlin was sober, softening the barbed comments and questions with an openness that surprised the audience. It's not about being for torture or against torture, he said several times, in artful ways. It was a difficult time, and we did some things we soon realized we might later regret.

Later that night, he and I drank Glenlivet on the rocks at the bar at the Hanover Inn.

We talked about an array of things, about how angry and dysfunctional public dialogue can be in this era, and how the gutting of the CIA—the only institution positioned, by experience and design, to protect the country against a next attack, an attack that he, like everyone else in this book, believes is a matter of when, not if—"leaves us wide open."

And then, as the hour passed, and Scotch glasses got dewy, he talked about his friend Tenet.

McLaughlin just sat for a bit, trying to get his fingers around it, the whole long saga of the two Georges. Finally, he shook his head.

"I know he wishes he could give that damn medal back."

A delusion of fierce partisanship is the view that political opponents are so utterly bankrupt of good sense, of basic human feeling, that for one to be defeated will not only mean diminution for oneself, but disaster for an unwitting country.

The strident posture of self-defense that stems from this kill-or-be-killed idea flows directly into an infallibility trap. Mistakes can't be publicly acknowledged; *certainty,* even in the face of countermanding evidence, becomes a surrogate for courage; *will* stands in for earned—and regularly tested—conviction.

The question underlying this book is whether the country's political dialogue can act nimbly enough to meet the challenges in the ensuing campaigns, the next chapters in the battle against ardent and empowered enemies, rising, perhaps, on an updraft of history. The conflicts that raged ever more intensely in the first campaign are not a strong predictor of future success.

The invisibles who tended to believe in the old-fashioned credo of the honest broker slammed into these subtle writs of infallibility. Though they had proven their mettle in battle, in the actual, round-the-clock fight, their growing concern that these efforts were more a tactical scramble than a coherent strategy—a scramble made more difficult by words and actions from on high, including the Iraq war—placed them at odds with a current version of how presidential powers are exercised.

Even by the end of 2004, that battle—between these two groups, one in the spotlight, the other in shadows—was turning to favor the former. Those who were present at 9/11, who fought the opening campaign, were leaving the government in droves. Their replacements, though as committed as their predecessors, were placed under an altered set of rules: that those involved in the thick of the fight, closer to the action and the truths that emerge from such experience, are valuable for what they do, not what they think.

Their jobs are to carry forward by whatever means necessary, even though means without clear ends have a way of becoming untethered. The traditional warning against "the ends justifying the means" carries a corollary. Without clear, attainable ends, means have a way of becoming unbound, improvised, born of dictates of the "gut" and unexamined assumptions.

The torture at Abu Ghraib and Guantánamo Bay; the construction of the great terrorist-catching machine, with its communications head and financial body; the self-interested use of classified materials to carry forward political ends; the very concealment of the true nature of what's been happening since 9/11 in favor of a sanitized, "need to know" version—are all means that, whatever their advertised value, strike at the nation's character.

And, sadly, give true comfort to our enemies, graced with more recruitment tools than they could have hoped for.

The sensation of newness about 9/11, and our response, meant—to be fair—that early on, we stumbled across this yin/yang of ends and means as though we'd never been introduced.

That period, fortunately, is now ending. We can clearly now see this age-old changeling, always at our side, two-faced, shrugging, guilt-free.

So, to end this book, which is so much about the means—about what we felt we had to do at a time of crisis and what we then tried—I make two, diverse offerings.

At a distant pole stands that singular twentieth-century thinker and practitioner of geopolitical pragmatism, George Kennan, tackling the very same conundrum. As Kennan gazed, in 1947, across a devastated Hamburg—where, during World War II, 40,000 civilians had been killed by Allied bombers—the young man wrote in his diary that

> *if the Western world really was going to make a valid pretense of a higher moral departure point—of greater sympathy and understanding for the human being as God made him, as expressed not only in himself but in the things he had wrought and cared about—then it had to learn to fight its wars morally as well as militarily, or not fight them at all; for moral principles were a part of its strength. Shorn of this strength, it was no longer itself; its victories were not real victories. . . . The military would view this as naïve; they would say that war is war, that when you're in it, you fight with everything you have or go down to defeat. But if that is the case, then there rests upon Western civilization, bitter as this may be, the obligation to be militarily stronger than its adversaries by a margin sufficient to enable it to dispense with those means which can stave off defeat only at the cost of undermining victory.*

Not long after he wrote this, Kennan thought long and hard about the opposing ideology of his day—communism—and about its flaws. At that time, many forceful, clear-eyed Americans decried this "god-less monster" and recommended a head-on assault against the Soviet Union, and China, too. Kennan, a largely invisible character of his day, though much "in the fight" as a diplomat, managed to prevail by writing a long magazine piece under an alias, "Mr. X." The article, which appeared in *Foreign Affairs,* sketched out a policy soon to be called "containment," which was adopted by the United States. Having spent time in Russia, Kennan knew the enemy, walked in his shoes, could not manage to demonize him, and predicted, rightly, that if our opponent were contained, his system of self-governance, not tied nearly so well as ours to the lights of human potential and growth, would rot eventually from within. It was a tough choice—and one that people who lived under forty years of communism may disagree with—but it was based on thinking things through with enormous, and humbling, effort before a decision about the right policy was made. The United States, in any event, did not throw its extraordinary, atom-enhanced might against its opposite number—a move that would have created a thousand Hamburgs—and, along the way, managed to preserve its "higher moral departure point" for much of the post–World War II period.

That was then.

Nowadays, in an era when so many in America and across the globe are suffused with religious certainty—exhausted, as many are, with the pace of change and the challenge of mastering Kennan-like empiricism—I offer a very old text that underlies both Christianity and Islam.

Deuteronomy 16:20 reads: "Justice, Justice, This you must pursue." Justice—an overused word these days—is not mentioned twice, however, for added emphasis. Here Hebrew scholars agree—and they don't agree on much—that it's once for the ends, and once for the means.

Fight well. And God bless.

AUTHOR'S NOTE

In October 2005, I tumbled, like a falling leaf, into a Vermont living room with William Sloane Coffin. The firebrand reverend, once of Manhattan's Riverside Church and Yale University, was in fine fettle at eighty-one, having just given a speech in a church near his hometown of Strafford and now settled into a roomful of warm tea, finger food, and admirers. I had never met him—heard about him, of course, and his particularly vociferous view of responsible public morality—and we talked, along with various New England college professors and former *New York Times* reporter Tom Wicker, about these interesting times. Sloane Coffin held forth about "power's prerogatives" and how "effectively fear has been employed to manage the political ideal." He knew what I'd been up to, grilled me on a few particulars, and then looked at me quizzically. "I never thought I'd live to see the day when old-fashioned journalism would be a form of civil disobedience."

Sloane Coffin, who would die seven months later, may have overstated it a bit—one of his gifts—but not by very much.

To report about national affairs and, especially, national security in this contentious period demands at least a spoonful of disobedience—a countermeasure to strong assurances by those in power that the obedient will be rewarded or, at the very least, have nothing to worry about.

During two years reporting and writing this book, I found myself thinking more about my sources, and protecting them, than I ever had in my twenty years as a journalist. None of them, not one, had done anything improper—legally or ethically. But they had, similarly, committed modest acts of disobedience. Those included being "off message," digging among hard lessons they'd learned for insights about how America might respond to the manifold challenges it faces, and believing that transparency and accountability are not matters of convenience in a democracy, not ever.

A few housekeeping notes are in order. One involves Yosri Fouda, al Jazeera's correspondent. Fouda and I met in Washington and London, where he went through the letter and verse of his amazing story—a story that was also ably captured in a book, *Masterminds of Terror,* that he cowrote with Nick Fielding. From our interviews, I was certain that Fouda did not know that Qatar's emir had passed details of his exclusive reporting on to the CIA. Fouda, I'm convinced, was kept in the dark.

Similarly, many of the nearly one hundred well-placed sources I relied on for this book toiled in their jobs since 9/11 on a "need to know" footing; they knew part of this initiative or that, not the whole (and if they happened to know the whole picture, they certainly wouldn't reveal it). It was for me, often, to piece it together, drawing from this wide ensemble.

What appears between the covers is, in any event, a product of their shared recollections and collected wisdom. Many are former officials with the CIA, the FBI, the White House, and also with the NSC, the State, Defense, and Treasury Departments, and assorted others. A significant number, as well, are still inside the government. This latter group includes a few officials at various departments who were granted unofficial permission to try to answer my questions. I would mention their names and offer public thanks, but—to a one—I think they'd rather I not.

For them, and all those who cooperated, participation was an act of trust—trust that this project would be an accurate and thoughtful rendering of what occurred during this bracing period of our national history. I am honored by that trust. I hope they—like the readers whom I, like every author, serve—will not be disappointed by the outcome.

ACKNOWLEDGMENTS

There are countless people who deserve thanks for ushering this book to completion.

Let me mention a few. My editor at Simon & Schuster, Alice Mayhew, was ever fierce and artful and clear-sighted about this project. She keeps her eye, always, on the prize—a book that will make a difference—and then helps make it so.

David Rosenthal, Simon & Schuster's publisher, was especially attentive to this undertaking—and its challenges—from start to finish. He and Alice, her deputy, Roger Labrie, and the whole team at Simon & Schuster pulled together all of the moving parts of a fast turnaround from manuscript to launch with the urgency of an amphibious landing.

Andrew Wylie, my agent, was a constant force of forward motion and trenchant insights. He also makes me laugh, a thing of great value when the pressure's on.

Kurt Wimmer, a partner at the Washington-based firm of Covington and Burling, signed on to provide legal assistance in 2004, when my possession of nineteen thousand internal documents from the Treasury Department and elsewhere prompted intense government scrutiny. He helped handle that matter artfully and has been an exceptional legal guide, as well, throughout this project. It troubles me that a journalist would need a lawyer to do his job; it heartens me that I have a gifted advocate from an auspicious firm.

I also had a trusty researcher on this book, Patrick Cliff, who ably dug through the vast files, countless clips, endless transcripts, and went on a few key reporting assignments. He has my gratitude, as does my old friend, Alan Wirzbicki, whom I called upon to bring to bear his fresh eyes and analytical strengths for final fact checks and updates.

My friends at the Rockefeller Center at Dartmouth College have long provided summertime refuge and the fellowship of finely-tuned minds. It is testimony to their embrace of free inquiry that they welcome me back each year, no matter what controversies I stir while away.

This was a particularly difficult book to report and write, unwieldy and slippery, and often unreasonable in its demands—which is why I'd like to offer special thanks to my family. During this project, my sons, Walter, seventeen, and Owen, fifteen, have grown through some important adolescent years. It inspires me to witness it—to play a modest role in that day-to-day miracle—and keeps me appropriately humble about the comparative import of my professional rigors. Those boys give me hope and strength.

Cornelia, my wife, has, meanwhile, made a case that with this—the third book in eight years—I should stop thanking her for her grace and wisdom and sacrifice during the always difficult process of trying to produce something that is worth reading. While respecting her position, sensible as it is, I've decided, at day's end, to opt for some extremely civil disobedience: Thanks, Corn, for everything.

INDEX

ABOUT THE AUTHOR

RON SUSKIND is the author of the number one *New York Times* best seller *The Price of Loyalty* and the best-selling and critically acclaimed *A Hope in the Unseen*. He has served as the *Wall Street Journal*'s senior national affairs reporter and lives in Washington, D.C., with his wife and their two sons.